A
THAILAND
DIARY

By

Matt Owens Rees

© Matt Owens Rees 2013 Updated © 2018

If you enjoyed this book, please encourage your friends to purchase and download their own copy and take a look at its companion volumes: *Thailand Take Two, The Thai Way of Meekness, Escape to Thailand*, and *The Death of a Thai Godfather*. A constructive Review would also be appreciated as it enables me to tailor books to what the reader wants.

Thank you for your support.

I0769912

TABLE OF CONTENTS

Acknowledgements

Introduction

Principal Characters

A Summary of the Diary Entries.

Acknowledgements

The smiling faces of the Thais can be misleading. Although noted for their friendliness and caring nature, the people of the Land of Smiles are quite shy and unassuming (*greng jai*) Together with the language barrier – the Thai language and its tones are notoriously difficult to learn – this makes it challenging for any writer of Thai lifestyle and culture to obtain reliable anthropological data on this amazing country's people.

And as was realised after publication of Margaret Mead's "Coming of Age in Samoa", an author should be very careful of the accuracy of what he or she is being told. Thais like to please and avoid conflict and argument; often they will tell you what they think you want to hear. I have been careful to avoid that by having a focus group which is comprised of Thais from varying backgrounds and with vastly different experiences.

I am therefore extremely appreciative of the opportunities which a number of Thais have given me to discuss with them, so freely and frankly, countless aspects of Thainess and Thai culture.

I thank all those who consented to be interviewed and assisted with my research. I owe them all a tremendous debt of gratitude. I acknowledge particularly Haniba, Ning, Neenee, Boon, and Lek

Introduction

How can we appreciate, understand, and enjoy the real Thailand?

The country is not like China, where it is difficult to venture off the guided tourist trails and where your movements are discreetly watched. Thailand welcomes you in discovering the ways of life and customs of the ordinary Thai. Generally Thais can be reticent and, as a proud race – patriotic to the core – a little shy of foreigners. You will often have to make the first move if you really want to understand what makes this country and its people tick. Above all, OBSERVE what is going on around you with an open and thoughtful mind.

Travel guidebooks are useful introductions to the country and provide many useful tips and ideas but they don't show you how to experience the neighbourhoods where the ordinary Thai lives.

A Thailand Diary takes you into that world. A virtual journey into an authentic Thailand from the comfort of your own armchair. In its pages, you will meet *Khun* Fon, Ratchanee, Noi, Bancha, and many others. You may be surprised as you learn about aspects of Thai life that remain undetected by the average tourist. I am sure you will find new experiences of your own, whether described here or not. Thailand will never fail to amaze.

You can of course read *A Thailand Diary* from cover to cover. But dipping into entries that may interest you is another way of reading the book. Because most readers tend to do that, you may find some repetition in the explanation of some words or concepts. I hope that does not spoil your enjoyment.

In her well-written and researched book "Mai Pen Rai Means Never Mind," Carol Hollinger captured the spirit of the Thai and the enigma of Thailand: the smiling, lay-back, and carefree lifestyle and the lack of stress and seriousness in day to day living. She mentioned the wide gap between the classes, the robust concept of never losing face or self-respect, the dislike of direct confrontation, and the firm self-belief that is linked to a xenophobic patriotism and is an integral part of Thai culture.

Little has changed since the book was written in the1960s: that in itself is testimony to the irrepressible attitudes and lifestyles of the Thai.

The Land of Smiles can also be a perplexing Land of Surprises and a Land of Secrets. Not everything is what it seems. Hollinger, Welty, and a few others understood and described the differences between eastern and western cultures but it is still not easy for a foreigner, with his or her own worldview, to fully comprehend and accept that Thai thinking can sometimes confirm Rudyard Kipling's famous comment: *East is East and West is West and Never the Twain Shall Meet.*

Let us briefly look at the essence of Thainess: the basic ethos that underpins Thai culture, and which is covered in depth in *Thailand Take Two* and in a more light hearted approach, with many examples, in *A Thailand Diary.*

I cannot do justice in a few paragraphs. The following gives a quick overview of the concepts which may appear bewildering from a western standpoint.

MAI PEN RAI

Literally mai pen rai means "never mind, it doesn't matter."

A lay-back non-serious view of life. Thais work to live and not live to work. Although they prefer to smile and avoid stressful situations and conflict, that does not always mean they are being subservient or backing-down. They have a hedonistic, pleasure seeking, outlook on life and are conciliatory in resolving arguments or problems. But Thais would rather walk away than face an argument which does not seem to be resolving a problem.

FAMILY AND COMMUNITY

Thais are more family oriented than people in the West. Communities are more closely knit. Social integration is often centred on the temple or local food market – places where people can congregate and socialise.

THE FEUDAL HIERARCHY

Almost all Thais believe that past karma will pre-determine one's position in society. The rigid class structure is respected and not questioned; not through fear but from an acceptance that everyone "knows their place." The monarchy is a force which binds the nation together: from the hi-society *amart* families with their inherited wealth and power at the top to the ordinary working Thai. There is no powerful or assertive middle class to challenge or change the Establishment. The political parties are effectively right-wing and not liberal in the western sense. No Thai believes he is equal to the next man. That's a tall order for Westerners to come to grips with. Our world view is that equality, democracy, and universal suffrage are given concepts.

FACE

This eastern concept of not losing one's reputation or good name is one of the more frustrating aspects of Thainess to understand. Although we don't like being humiliated or proved wrong in the West; in Thailand, the concept is stronger. It is simply not accepted that anyone should publicly lose face, even for the slightest of reasons. As we shall see in some of the diary entries, it is the thinking that lies behind Thais walking away from a problem and making up "white" lies. When their patience breaks, however, violence and injustice can erupt.

GRENG JAI AND NAM JAI

Thais can be hard and ruthless while also displaying kindness and caring in particular circumstances. The two concepts of *Greng jai* and *Nam Jai* are unique to Thailand and are explained by some of the events in the diary. Interestingly, both ideas have the word *jai* (heart) in their name. The relevance to Thai thinking is that they tend to be guided by their emotions (heart) rather than rational reasoning. Some Westerners have commented about this odd Thai "logic" but it is actually more of a cultural difference.

Principal Characters in A Thailand Diary

These are real people, only names are changed.

Adoon; a banker in Chiangmai
Art; a neighbour with a spirit level
Bancha; a soldier now back in the building trade
Dao; a university undergraduate
Faa; Fon's daughter foraging for insects
Fon; a neighbour lighting a candle
Geng; a drinking partner
Goong; a cashier at a photo shop
Gop; a former teacher and Louis' wife
Mana; a Thai student caught cheating
Noi; Stuart's wife, an ex-bargirl
Nok; Dao's husband with a building problem
Oh; Tong's hard-working builder husband
Ratchanee; Fon's daughter
Siriporn; a provocatively dressed visitor
Sompanya; a "hi-so" organising the opening of a toilet
Somsee; Tim's wife at their new home
Tong; an employee with a problem with her boss
Weelai; a retired Thai university lecturer
Wongpaet; the family of the murdered brother

1 January

Enjoyable Thai party last night. Everyone brought some homemade northern Thai food to share. And the karaoke really got going after a few drinks. Got up late this morning.

Had to go into Chiangmai for some garden plants. Came back and there was no sign of my dog.

Where had Talley gone this time? Cycled round for an hour or so trying to find him. Eventually found my pet playing with some of the dogs at the local *wat* (temple).

My neighbour, *Khun* Fon, had lit some candles in our spirit house and was praying for his safe return.

At what time did you actually find Talley?
Ten minutes ago.
That was precisely when I lit the candles.

Fon said we must go to the *wat* tomorrow with some gifts for the monks as a token of thanks. *It will give you merit. That's why you must go.*

Actually, I think whistling and calling out Talley's name was how I found him. But best to go along with some of the more interesting Thai traditions.

2 January

Busy day at Immigration. Not easy to find a parking spot and even more difficult to get a seat.

Rules and regulations are not standardised in Thailand. Each government official interprets them differently. Requirements for documentation at Immigration vary from office to office.

Applies to all organisations. One bank manager will open an account for you; another may say it is not possible for foreigners to have accounts in Thailand unless they have a work permit. My local immigration office has a well-deserved reputation for friendliness and trying to help you through the maze of bureaucracy. Not all offices are like that.

They have an on-line system where appointments can be made instead of queuing. My name was called right on time but no one knew which counter to go to. Once seated in front of an officer, we got though the papers quickly. I had made a checklist and there was nothing extra that she wanted. Ten minutes and I was asked to take a seat and wait for my visa extension to be signed off by the big boss.

Chatted to an American to pass away the time and we both agreed the West could learn much from the smooth administration that we were experiencing. But I had spoken too soon. My name was called and I went to the main counter.

No, there are no papers here. Please take a seat. We will get to you soon.

Ten minutes later my name was called again. The same thing happened. There was no file to be seen. I explained that my name had been called twice but they still suggested that I go back to my seat. First rule of bureaucracy: never lose your cool. It seldom gets you anywhere, and will get you nowhere in Thailand.

My new American friend and I were wondering what could be happening. It's never a good idea to challenge or complain. Thais dislike conflict and don't like losing face. My friend was all for my asking to speak to a manager. I knew that wouldn't work. The manager would lose face himself if there was some suggestion that his staff were not performing properly. I deliberated on how I was going to handle this.

I gave it a few more minutes and went up to the counter. I peered over the desks and could see my passport at the bottom of a tall heap of files.

I think that may be mine.

They retrieved it and I was soon on my way. They had been so busy that they had kept placing files on top of an ever-growing stack. When names were called, they were not able to see the hidden files. The interesting point is that, even after realising what was causing the delays for everyone in the hall, they did not feel confident enough to raise the matter with the big boss and fix the problem.

They would be challenging his authority and management ability as well as making him lose face.

3 January

Different nationalities have different senses of humour. I recall being in a UK pub one overcast day in winter. A few of us were sitting round the bar when the barman commented, *looks like rain, doesn't it?*

The fellow next to me raised his glass and sipped his beer. *Yes, tastes like it too*

We all laughed including our barman. A sarcastic joke like that, smacking of criticism of watering down the beer, may not have worked in Thailand. A blank look, walking away, or a more violent response could well follow.

Thais prefer you to join in with their own brand of humour. They will love it if you join in with their karaoke, whatever kind of voice you have. Life is about having fun, *sanuk*. When I dance, I show the world that I was born with two left feet. It matters not a jot to a Thai. Trying to dance the Thai *ramwong*, their traditional dance with a lot of symbolic hand and body movement, guarantees much laughter and smiles. That's the sort of joking and fun they enjoy. Here is a professional version.

https://www.youtube.com/watch?v=bAIUnE8Q98w

(If ctrl and click does not work, copy and paste into your browser window to watch the video)

4 January

All my family will be there including my cousin's German husband. You'll enjoy meeting him and joining in with the village festivities. It lasts all day. Plenty of food, plenty of drink. Khun Fon said I would be able to talk to a fellow foreigner.

A beer was poured before I even sat down and the food arrived whether I wanted it or not. All the houses in this small village had similar parties underway.

The official reason for the festivities was that the local temple was asking for donations to build a new toilet block. So, people kept popping in and putting a 20 baht or 100 baht note on the family's "money tree" which would be taken to the temple later. Some neighbours gave a sealed envelope with their name on and stayed for a drink and a chat. Often the envelope is an airmail envelope: much prettier.

The reality was that it was as an excuse for the whole village to get together for a day-long party, share the local gossip, and have some fun.

We visited several homes in the village and had the same Thai welcome. The lady with the German husband, Nonglak, turned out to be a close friend of the family and not a relative. That was no surprise. Close friends, family. It's not an important distinction to Thais. However, she had married an Italian and not a German. And she was now divorced and no longer married. She ran an Italian ice cream parlour in Germany for eight months of the year and holidayed with her family in Thailand in the low season.

Nonglak obviously works very hard and has been able, with funds from her former husband for sure, to build three houses in the village. One for herself, one for her parents, and one for her grandparents. I'd put the value at over 16 million baht.

5 January

Picked up my brush cutter today. Beyond repair. It's the second machine I have bought in Thailand in two years. You do have to watch quality here. You may find that essential parts of an imported product have been substituted for those of a lesser quality. Car batteries are probably the best example. Top grade cement can be delivered to a construction site. When the customer, Thai or *Farang* is no longer on site it can quickly be sent back and cheaper materials delivered.

My first brush cutter was an "own-brand" cutter purchased from a department store. It was not particularly expensive but I thought it would serve my purpose. It lasted less than a year. Professional gardeners had told me to buy only Honda models in future and I would then have no problems.

A lesson had been learned. I'll go to the largest specialist store in town. That was the best thing to do. I spent half an hour talking to the sales staff. They showed me several models and explained the advantages of each machine. Offered me a coffee. Faultless customer service.

I made it clear that I wanted only a Honda, as that manufacturer had been recommended to me.

No problem, sir. A wise choice. More expensive, but we sell lots of them and offer a twelve month full warranty.

They gave me a demonstration. It started first time. It had the Honda name and logo on the handle. I bought it and was given the warranty card and invoice, clearly marked "Honda." They didn't have a manual but said they would get me one later. *Mai mee panha*, no problem.

But I later found there was one big, big problem.

It was not a Honda. It was a copy. I took it back several times because of an oil leak and a problem with the starting mechanism. A few weeks later and the leak returned and I still had difficulties starting it. A small local dealer checked the machine and showed me that it did not have a Honda serial number on the engine.

I had the invoice and guarantee card. My initial thoughts were to take it back to the seller. But guarantees are not easily enforced in Thailand. Some large companies will just ignore you, knowing legal redress will be expensive and time consuming. Although a Thai judge will listen to both sides, there's no guarantee he will see your point or evidence.

And this company was big, very big. The word on the street was that if you had an accident involving one of their vehicles they would never be found liable. No one argued with them, whatever the trouble was. They had contacts.

This was a company not to be messed with. It would be pointless to pursue any claim. My Thai friends told me to put it down to bad luck. That is what they would do.

Living in Thailand is certainly a learning experience. Caution is better than rash courage.

6 January

Thais love most sorts of witty humour. Wordplay, clever witticisms, and humour that involves playing tricks or making a joke will fill them with amusement. They enjoy subtlety and deadpan humour. Sarcasm, however, is best avoided. It is too cutting and cruel for their taste. The word is derived from the Greek for cutting flesh!

They would appreciate listening to the following exchange at a Norfolk country fair where a peacock handler was demonstrating his skills with his collection of birds.

How old is your peacock? asks a well-heeled gent.
20 years, 6 months and 4 days
And tell me, how long do they normally live?
At least 20 years, 6 months, and 4 days.

7 January

Sunantaa rang to say that Kitaloo, her one year old puppy, had been killed in a road accident. He had escaped from their fenced garden. Unusually for a Thai, she was very tearful on the phone.

Some monks had said that a hill tribe family had accidentally ran him over and brought him to the temple for them to bury so that he could be born again. Sunantaa's husband, Surachai, was not so sure. He employs Burmese and hill tribe workers and knows they eat dog flesh. Despite not believing the monks, he was wise enough not to comment either to them or his wife. That would be a taboo in Thai culture.

His sister had said that she had seen the body in the temple. But when he went to the *wat* a second time and asked to see the grave the monks explained that he could not take the dog home for reburial. If it was indeed Kitaloo, he wanted the dog to be buried in its own garden. But Surachai could not go against the monks.

He still has his doubts about what really happened. He is too old in the tooth to think that what you are told is always factually correct.

Sunantaa is quite content to think that Kitaloo is now resting on holy ground.

8 January

Benjawan is taking a lot of time off work to look after her sick father these days. A few months ago, the bank she works for had fast-tracked her application for a transfer out of Bangkok to a branch in the province where her family lived. You will find that most companies in Thailand will be flexible and accommodating when matters of family are concerned. There is a strong concept of family in this country.

Her salary has dropped but not that significantly. In any case, she believes her family comes first and any financial loss now is not important. A girl would leave her job to look after a relative, even if there was no prospect of a family inheritance to follow. In fact, Gai, the bank's cleaner, had given her notice last month for that very reason. And her family are very poor.

Last week Benjawan worked only three days. Her deputy has now been appointed in her place. She still has her office, moving her out would have been a step too far for an employee of her length of service and experience. She concentrates now on new investment business, as that does not demand a great deal of staff supervision.

Her staff now use the word *wanna* (boss) when they speak to her ex-deputy and have dropped that title when talking to Benjawan. I thought the change would have caused more problems but it clearly has not. I suppose I should not have been surprised. Thainess always produces solutions where face is not lost and conflicts are avoided.

9 January

Murder most foul. Our *soi* (lane) is single track, so we could not get the car out when the police vehicle parked outside our neighbour's house. And you don't ask armed police officers, anywhere in the world, to move their car for you. They park where they want to park.

A crowd had started to gather outside the house. The locals wanted to know what was going on and they were waiting around to gather whatever snippets of information or gossip were available.

Ratchanee told me that one of the brothers in the house was dead. There had been some heavy drinking the night before and the men's mother had heard some shouting downstairs. She had thought nothing of it. In the morning, the mother found her son lying in a pool of blood.

The police were now investigating a murder. They will start searching for two Burmese.
The brothers drank regularly with the same group of friends from neighbouring *sois*, all Thai
nationals. Not my type, but friendly enough.

I'd never seen any Burmese, legal or illegal, in the area, and neither had anyone else.
The police didn't stay long and the family immediately started to clean the house and tidy the
garden. Monks come round quickly after a death in Thailand in order to start the funeral rites,
and it's best that everything is spotless before they arrive.

Chairs were put in the garden ready for the people who would soon be coming to pay their
last respects. A small fire was started in one corner to burn the garden debris that had just
been cleared.

We may learn more about what happened in the coming days. More likely, we will not.

Daily life in Thailand is never mundane. Nothing surprises me anymore.

10 January

Bought some short-sleeved shirts in the night market today. 250 baht each. Haggled for a
discount for buying three.

Rot dai mai kap (Can you give a small discount?)

Bargaining is expected and part of the fun. Calculators are often passed between seller and
customer, with the seller entering his price and inviting the buyer to key in his counter offer. I
agreed 700 for three.

They were good quality for a market and he had a wide variety. Decided to buy three more.
700 baht was a good price. But no, the bartering started again at 250 baht! I eventually got
them for 700. The stallholder was not going to give up his opportunity for a bit more
haggling. It's *sanuk* (fun) to a Thai.

Having sold me three shirts and knowing I wanted three more also made him realise that he
might have agreed too low a price initially.

Stalls in the less busy *sois* (lanes) in the market offer the better bargains and are anyway less
crowded. As a rule of thumb, markets such as Wararot, where there are fewer tourists than
the night market, are even better value. Shop where the Thais shop; and shop the way they
do.

11 January

National Children's day, first instigated in 1955, is now held throughout Thailand on the second Saturday in January.

It is known in Thai as *wan dek* and children look forward to a day of fun with their parents. Local authorities put on events and games especially for children, the armed services have an open day and let the kids sit in aircraft and "play at being soldiers," and the prime minister allows the youngsters to see her office and visit the parliament building. Yingluck's motto for *wan lek* for 2014 was "Be good and grateful, know your duty, have discipline, and help build the nation". Thais have a very special message to give their country's youth, unlike any advice or direction our politicians might give in the West. Thailand is fervently patriotic, as you will doubtless have noticed. Duty and discipline are well chosen words. They can be broadly interpreted as "respect the country's hierarchy, it is part of the cultural heritage."

Cinemas, elephant sanctuaries, and amusement parks give free or heavily discounted entrance fees for children. Stores hand out candy and small gifts.

12 January

Had some builders around last week to build some gates to stop the dogs wandering off. They did a good job erecting the posts firmly in position and upright. The welding on the gate frames had been carefully done.

When they tried to open the gates, though, they fouled on the ground as the gates had been hung too low. They've re-set the hinges higher now but it's taken them four visits. I have learnt never to get angry and certainly not shout when builders get things wrong. Just smile and sympathise that they have to do a bit of rectification. Pretend you would have made the same mistake if you had done the job.

There's a great deal of "suck it and see" or trial and error in Thai workmanship. They aren't bothered if something doesn't work first time. Even if they are given a plan they are unlikely to follow it too closely, preferring to rely on their own experience. Small errors in measurement are covered by *mai pen rai*, it doesn't matter. If the job looks okay when they have finished, they are content. Presentation is more important than sticking to the original plan that was specifically designed to work.

13 January

The general rule is that you *wai* (the formal Thai greeting of respect) to a person older or in a more superior position to yourself and that he or she then returns the *wai*. Like all rules, there are exceptions. Returning a *wai* is not an automatic response.

The King only makes a *wai* to a monk (as the monk is in a sense a representative of the Buddha). Monks do not return a *wai*. A superior will not always return the *wai* from a subordinate. However, if a manager met one of his staff outside the office and the staff member was with her parents, he would return the *wai*.

On my first visit to Thailand we were eating in a restaurant and there was a large party sitting opposite us. There were a dozen or so people with a very important looking guy at the head of the table. He was probably the boss and his guests were staff members. I wasn't shocked when he failed to return the *wai* from the waitress, that is not required from serving staff but I thought it was the height of bad manners when he called her over from the other end of the restaurant just to top up his glass of beer. The bottle was right next to his glass. It was not as if it was a high class restaurant with attentive sommeliers around to cater for your every whim. He did not even nod his head or thank her.

Let me say though that she showed no sign of embarrassment. Thais hide their feelings. She may well have been seething inside. As Westerners, we have to accept the customs of other nations and adapt accordingly ourselves. I would never have copied that guy's manners though. I would have filled the glass myself or, if she had come over, I would have smiled and nodded my thanks.

14 January

Talking of Thais being able to conceal their emotions reminds me of two events. The first involved an Irish priest and a parishioner; the other occurred when a visiting rugby side was returning to New Zealand after an international.

Not having been to confession or church for months, Patrick, who had a reputation for being a "tough guy," was physically shaking on being admonished by his priest for failing to attend church as often as he should. Thais would be subservient in that situation but would never have shown their emotions.

The All Blacks were given a very moving send-off at the railway station before boarding their flight home. Their tour had ended in Cardiff and there wasn't a dry eye amongst the strong burly players as the band struck up the Welsh ballad, "We'll Keep a Welcome in the Hillsides." The moving words registered with every player. Thais would have appreciated the warm farewell but no emotions would have been shown.

https://www.youtube.com/watch?v=lHVA9lME2qA

15 January

There had never been any objection by the local monks to Sengdeuan's family planting vegetables and herbs on the land between the *wat* and their property. It was technically owned by the temple it seemed but it wasn't causing any problems. The locals helped themselves to the produce occasionally, as is the custom in rural Thailand.

Then the abbot wanted to build a larger *sala*, mainly to accommodate the large numbers of mourners that came to the funeral rites. The Sengdeuan family, along with everyone else, contributed to the building costs.

The informal garden was cleared by a bulldozer early this morning. Part of that land included a short cut between two *sois*. It had never been clear whether that was municipal land or belonged to the *wat*. Nobody wanted to challenge the abbot or get the position clarified. He's allowing it to be used as a right of way. At least for the moment.

When I said that that was the Thai way, Sengdeuan replied: "It's the monks' way."

16 January

Today is National Teachers' Day in Thailand. *Wan wai kroo*, in Thai.

Pupils bring flowers to school as a thank you gesture to their teachers and as an act of merit. The day starts with the head teacher praying at the Buddha image in front of the assembled school. Other teachers read some prayers and talk about the main advantages that learning brings, and to always work hard at school.

The children then kneel before the teachers, presenting them with their bouquets and making the *wai* gesture. (the Thai form of respect and greeting.) Later, after delivering a sermon on respecting teachers and honouring the school, a monk will sprinkle holy water, *nam mon*, on the pupils as he leaves the school.

In some parts of Thailand, extra days are set aside for pupils to honour and *wai* their teachers. In the Lanna province 12 June is a popular additional choice.

If you visit a Thai school, you will not fail to be impressed by the outward politeness of the pupils. They will always *wai* you, and bend their heads as they walk past. In class, they usually stand when talking to a teacher, and ask permission if they wish to leave the room.

On returning to class, they will stand outside the door until the teacher indicates they can come in.

Looking after children is taken seriously in Thailand. Perhaps they are pampered a little too much. Some can be a little spoilt. You will make your own observations, I am sure.

Playgrounds are supervised during the day. In larger schools, teachers ensure their pupils get on the right bus when going home. Unauthorised pick-ups are forbidden. Either a police officer, a security man, or a teacher will be outside the school gates to direct traffic at the beginning and the end of the day. In one school I know, each child wears a coloured armband to indicate the correct bus for the child's destination.

17 January

No reasons given why the fruit on the Mango trees had not been protected from birds by covering each fruit with a small piece of newspaper – the traditional way to care for the fruit. The subject was changed and the other gardeners walked away to avoid losing face. After a long time, one man admitted it was merely that he had forgotten to do it.

It's not a serious crime but *farangs* get frustrated when Thais find it difficult to answer a simple question or evade an issue. It's to save face of course. It takes some getting used to. Best to try to accept it as something the Thais have always done.

By not arguing or getting into an argument, friendly atmospheres are maintained. All is forgotten by the next day. Everyone can still smile and remain friends.

18 January

Noi rang my mobile to say that Stuart, her husband, was in hospital. Visited him this evening. He was very drowsy and seemed stressed. He had been in intensive care for two days apparently. Noi should have phoned earlier.

He had slipped on a wet floor and severely injured his left knee. Given he had been admitted to the ICU, there may have been other complications. Nobody seemed to know. Thai reticence to give out information?

His private room at the hospital was like a hotel suite. Multi-channel TV, refrigerator, small microwave, coffee maker, a comfortable sofa and chairs. Plenty of wardrobe space and an en-suite bathroom. Some hospitals have VIP suites that include a small dining area for visitors, private phone line, and an internet connection.

You can ask for English speaking staff for a 25% premium, but that is not really necessary as most doctors and quite a few of the nursing staff speak good English. One hospital even offers a daily visit to your room by the hospital director. It's up to each individual patient whether that particular service is value for money. Some Westerners think it is.

Thai hospitals encourage a relative to stay overnight. It's beneficial for the patient. Nurses check patients regularly and are always on call, but having a family member present overnight is seen as a positive advantage that aids patient recovery. Noi slept over every night and spent a large part of the day at the hospital. All private rooms have a foldaway bed and I have seen relatives sleeping in quiet corridors if the family member is in a public ward. Thais don't like being too far from the family.

Thai hospitals do not have strict visiting times, and Stuart received five Thai visitors, all friends of Noi, while we were there. Most hospital visitors, anywhere in the world, try to be cheerful in front of the patient, but the Thais seem to have that concept in spades. They are ultra-cheerful and smile at every opportunity. They make it a happy shared occasion.

The Thais are like that. Funerals, too, are seen as functions when the community can get together in a social context as well as a time to pay their respects.

Thais always dress appropriately depending on the occasion and, significantly, in a way that shows their position in the Thai hierarchy. If your boss visited you in hospital, everyone present would realise his important position by his manner and the way he is dressed.

Noi had met Stuart in a bar ten years ago, but she still dresses in shorts and revealing clothes. They are still very happy together as a couple. And she is caring and looking after him well now. Nobody minds that she dresses the way she does but it is noticed and gossiped about, even by her friends. However, not in any malicious way. The hospital staff certainly noticed.

19 January

Pomelo did a really good job laying some slabs on the patio. Took his time to get them level and bedded them in well. He wasn't satisfied until it was perfect. He certainly didn't rush the work. But laying some underground pipes for a watering system did not seem to warrant the same attention to detail. The spoil from the digging was left as it lay, there were leaks from the pipe joins, and some parts of the circuit had not been completed.

Maybe it's because Thais get fed up and lose interest easily. You hear the word *nabeua* (boring) more in Thai than in other languages. Maybe it's because Thais like to impress you with their work when they first do a job for you – first impressions are important to them. *Mai pen rai* is another factor. How important is it to get things right? How much does it matter? They look for easy options when they are completing a task.

It's not laziness. Just watching the rice farmers and construction workers toiling in the heat of the Thai day will disillusion you of that perception. More, I think, of "Can I get away with it. Does it really matter?"

20 January

There's no trust law on the Thai statute books. A cautious people, the Thais believe strongly in *caveat emptor*, let the buyer beware. They distrust until they have a reason to trust, not the other way about. Guarantees are usually only for a short period. Faulty goods must usually be taken back within one week of purchase. Once you have paid for goods you are considered to have fully examined and approved them. The comment below your signature on a credit cards slip reads. "I acknowledge satisfactory receipt of relative goods/service. No Refund. Trusted transaction."

Taking a dispute to law is costly and slow and even most Thais won't bother because they know the result.

Many *farangs* here will, however, tell you that you are more likely to experience deception, cheating, and fraud from the hands of some of the foreign expat community. One tends to trust people of one's own nationality or at least any other Westerner. I was caught after buying a laptop from a smooth talking expat. It worked when it plugged into mains electricity and all seemed well. He said he'd had no problems with the machine. After paying and leaving his home, he casually remarked that the battery may need charging. In fact the computer never worked from the battery and eventually stopped functioning altogether. The repairer told me that even a Thai would never stoop that low to sell a product. In the West, *caveat emptor* is not a defense if the buyer took reasonable care and relied on a seller's recommendation. In Thailand, courts take a less sympathetic view. There is little recourse to claim you were misled.

A car dealer may sell you a vehicle that has been welded after a road accident but after painting over the weld to make it invisible. If the weld later proved to be unsafe, your action for compensation would succeed in the West because it would be shown you had not seen the weld. Not so in Thailand.

The Thai forums are full of examples of *farangs* cheating *farangs*. Expat clubs can be breeding grounds for financial advisors and others who take advantage of the lack of regulation and law enforcement in the country. Andrew Drummond gives examples.

Tourist rip-offs can occur anywhere in the world, Thailand is not excluded from that. But they are minor frauds compared with the sophisticated schemes that, for example, Drummond and others have highlighted. The website, www.andrew-drummond.com, is now blocked in Thailand, but available on virtual private networks.

21 January

Dual-pricing – having a different price for *farang* and Thai for the same goods or service – is technically illegal in Thailand. One exception is for admission to the national parks where a special provision is made to make it legal to charge more for foreigners. Sometimes, an expat can get in for the much reduced Thai price by showing a Thai driving licence.

Restaurants often have two menus: identical except for the higher price (sometimes more than double) charged to foreigners. Look carefully and you will see Thais check their restaurant bills item by item. Take a tip from them.

22 January

I just don't get it. Why do motor cyclists pull out from *sois* onto a main road without looking? This is one of the two things I still don't understand about Thailand.

Yes, some roads have cycle lanes into which they can filter reasonably safely, but most roads do not have these. As a motorist, if a car is coming towards you, you can't even swerve to avoid the rider. Is it fatalism? The Buddhist view is that life is full of suffering and is impermanent. That your life is predetermined so that you have no control over events anyway. I'm not convinced that is the reason.

The police will rarely prosecute a motor cyclist for any dangerous riding offence. Perhaps motor cyclists realise that. The motorist will usually pick up both the blame and the tab for any expenses. Particularly up-country, many riders are uninsured and may have no licence in any case.

It is common for riders to approach on the wrong side of the road. In most cases, you can clearly see them and adjust your driving accordingly. Weaving in and out of lanes is expected so there are no surprises there. Moving directly from the inside cycle track to the offside lane in order to complete a U-turn happens regularly. You'll get used to it. I have. But I still don't understand the casual and blasé way they pull out of the *sois* and the way they overtake you on the nearside when you are already signaling.

Actually, I have a theory on why they do this. More on that later.

23 January

I've got used to it. Thai driving used to scare me but I now "go with the flow." Drive defensively, assume others will make mistakes. Whichever country you drive in you will soon – or at least eventually – get accustomed to their particular way of driving.

Large trucks will always assume precedence, as if they have right of way even when they do not. Drivers of expensive looking cars will often push their way through. That's the power of hierarchy for you. All Thais know their station in life and some take full advantage of that.

In the West one car may turn at a junction in the face of oncoming traffic if it is safe to do so. Following cars usually stop. In Thailand, when one car goes all the rest will follow. I now do the same. It is understood that the cars will wait for all the vehicles to turn.

I do not miss the lack of misunderstanding that one gets in western countries when someone flashes their headlights at you. In Thailand, flashing one's lights only has one meaning: you are coming through. 99.9% of the time. I've only once seen a driver flash to let me through and his intention was clear as his vehicle was stationary. He was a tourist.

At a four-way junction some Thais will put on their hazard lights to show they are going straight on. Quite a good idea.

24 January

Paul's been here a long time but still lives the way he did in America. Sometimes it's good to keep to western standards but often entrenched habits and customs get in the way of integrating with the locals and your neighbours. When you enter a Thai home, it is customary to offer a glass of water as a refreshment. Paul never does and it does make one feel uncomfortable.

Thais notice it but don't comment. He is a very generous guy and would help anyone out I am sure. He does not think of how his failure to follow social niceties and customs gives an impression of not being polite. Some may see it as rudeness. It's a bit like not shaking hands in the West. Thais have a strong sense of what is polite and what is not.

Of course, these are the people one notices. Most expats blend in well in their communities. They are usually those who have more Thai than foreign friends and join in with local events rather than congregate with other *farangs* at expat clubs or on social media.

Seeing the real Thailand and how Thais live, particularly if here short-time as a tourist, is not easy. My advice is to observe for yourself, talk to a broad mix of Thais, and challenge the preconceptions and myths you may have heard about the country before your arrival. If you stay or circulate only with those of your own or another western nationality, I think you'll lose out on a valuable cultural experience and understanding of the people and the country.

25 January

Building regulations are not as strict in Thailand as they are in the West. Duangjai couldn't stop a vehicle-spraying factory being built right next to the new home she and her husband had bought. There are no restrictions on domestic and industrial premises being next to one another in this country. Her son became quite ill from the fumes. The factory owners helpfully responded by putting up some screening but it has never been effective. The local authorities could do nothing.

Sandra and John bought a double plot on a project in Chiangmai. It was quite a select development with reasonable space from the other houses. They put a lot of thought into the design of the house and garden, both planned to high western standards. Pride of place in the garden is their full-length swimming pool.

They were alarmed when they saw the builders erecting very tall scaffolding on a new house build right next to their home. Sandra, always the one "wearing the trousers," asked the owners if the house was going to be so high that it would overlook their swimming pool and invade their privacy.

Thais do not like blunt questions being asked of them and indeed a Thai would never ask such a question in such a forceful and rude manner. They'll gossip about it but they won't respond directly to the questioner. Someone may make a comment to her in passing and suggest she tries to find a compromise, perhaps by putting up some screening. That would be the Thai way. But Sandra is not Thai, so that may not happen. She has blotted her copy book with her neighbour now.

In the West, planning regulations may well have prevented a house being built looking straight into a neighbour's swimming pool.

26 January

There are many dogs on Thai roads in rural Thailand. Most houses have dogs roaming in the garden, though they may be caged or chained at night.

One often sees a dog asleep in the middle of the road, cars sounding their horns or swerving to avoid. Some are wild or temple dogs. Thais are not allowed to euthanise their pets and sick or unwanted dogs are left at the temple for the monks to care for.

Thailand's hot weather probably makes dogs lethargic and not want to move out of the way of approaching vehicles. They may be clever enough to realise drivers will do all they can not to hit them.

Motor cyclists have a similar view that cars will make way for them.

27 January

Laws are strict in Thailand. You cannot name and shame if the courts judge that it may harm a person's reputation. Whether your comments can be proved as truthful or not is irrelevant. Take a seat in a Thai court and watch the proceedings and note how all sides are trying to avoid conflict. Technically the system is adversarial as in our own countries but you'll not witness the cut and thrust of arguments being tested by prosecution and defence lawyers.

Investigative journalists have to take great care and the defence of public interest is not as strong in Thailand as it is elsewhere. You can Google the topic for up to date cases.

Thais will gossip about a bad builder but not take any other action. Chamnaan can only get work some distance away from our village now. "Jungle drums" are used effectively in Thailand!

When I had a problem with poor building work, I suggested what I thought was a reasonable price for what the builder had done and the cost of rectification. I agreed the figure with Chamnaan in front of the *pooyaibaan*. As usual, the builder and *pooyaibaan* were taking photos. There was no point in the builder doing so but the village will get to see the photos the headman took. That is how Thais get round the strict libel and slander laws – informal gossiping and information sharing.

28 January

Thais park where they want. It's not that they are inconsiderate of other road users. It is because they feel they have freedom to do their own thing. If the noodle shop is on a bend then that is where they will park. Other Thais don't mind. They would do the same. The police will drive past with the same *mai pen rai* attitude.

Try to merge into a main road from a side street or move into another lane to make a turn and you will in general find them very considerate drivers.

29 January

Up early this morning. Had arranged to get to Tim's new building plot by 7.30. He and his Thai wife, Somsee, have spent two months going over the plans and specifications of their new home with their builder. Tim has been sensible in checking every detail including the grade of materials being used. As is customary in Thailand, every page of the documentation was signed by Tim, Somsee, and the builder. There should be no room for a future mix-up or confusion on what had been approved.

Unlike in the West, where it is unusual for a customer to visit a new build to check how work is progressing (I suppose health and safety regulations also have something to do with that), it is common practice for Thais to make site visits once or even twice a day. The building firm respects the customer's right to make sure that everything is going according to the agreed plan. They know trust is scarce in Thailand, and people like to check up on what they are paying for.

Today was the day when the foundations were to be poured. I had suggested to Tim that we meet before the work started to make sure the holes were completely empty before being filled with concrete to the required depth. No way to verify later that the builders had not back filled with soil.

All went well and Tim took photographs of the rebar columns in their concrete footings, proudly standing to attention like soldiers in formation on the parade ground.

A village elder had come round to lead the ceremony marking the start of the build. Some coins were thrown into the foundations for luck and Tim was asked to pour some concrete into one of the holes, one of the traditions when building a house.

30 January

There have been sops to the masses (extention of the 30 baht health scheme, rice subsidies, and free computer tablets in many schools) but both main political parties in Thailand are right wing or right of centre. The party that appeared to be the more liberal introduced populist measures just before elections. There have been benefits to communities and the nation but it would be wrong to claim that any party is so left wing to consider giving real power to people through democratic elections at the ballot box. Lobbying, nepotism, and corruption are not good bedfellows with liberal policies.

Improvements in infrastructure in the North have always been associated with the Thairakthai and Peuathai parties as their leaders hail from that region. (These parties produced two prime ministers, Taksin Shiniwatra and Yingluck Shiniwatra). In the same way that London tended to get more preference in job creation, infrastructure, quality services, and so on, Bangkok traditionally was the centre of attention for projects initiated by most governments.

31 January

Today is Friday, so many Thais will wear a blue shirt or blouse, Queen Sirikit was born on a Friday so the colour is associated with Her Majesty.

The late monarch, King Bhumibol, was born on a Monday, which is why you saw a lot of people wearing yellow on that day of the week. Tuesday's colour is pink; Wednesday's, green; Thursday's, orange; Saturday's, purple; and Sunday's, red.

It was never obligatory of course but, when the king was alive, many Thais wore yellow on a Monday as a show of respect. Government officers wore their formal dress uniform on that day.

Most banks these days have their own dress code which might include the bank logo. Other businesses have their distinctive uniforms. Where that does not apply you will notice that the colours mentioned above are frequently worn. Officials dress in white with a black armband when in mourning, others in somber clothing.

1 February

The first day of February is the start of the Chinese New Year. Today is the year of the Rooster. A little over 40% of the Thai population of 70 million can claim some Chinese ancestry, 15% are ethnic Chinese with That citizenship. No wonder then that there is a high proportion of Thai-Chinese in government and big business. Youngsters today with this Chinese background tend to think of themselves as Thai whereas a few decades ago it would have been quite normal to describe oneself openly as Thai-Chinese.

The streets in the Chinese quarters of the major cities are alive with dragon dancers (to scare away the mythical beast called Nien) and acrobats. Shops do a roaring trade and everyone is happy and having fun. It is noisy, crowded, and colourful. Fireworks ward off the evil spirits.

The celebrations are a time to re-unite with family from other parts of Thailand and to pay respects to one's ancestors. Multi-course banquets with the whole family seemingly go on for hours. The children are given money in red envelopes; the adults, by tradition, an orange.

The Thai-Chinese are more superstitious by far than the Thai. You should not wash your hair on New Year's Day and shun the idea of using scissors or nail-clippers.

The actual date of the New Year and the celebratory period depends on the solar cycle. There are twelve animals associated with the festival. In 2029, the Rooster will be the symbolic animal again.

2017 Rooster
2018 Dog
2019 Pig
2020 Rat
2021 Ox
2022 Tiger
2023 Rabbit
2024 Dragon
2025 Snake
2026 Horse
2027 Sheep
2028 Monkey

2 February

Thais are shy and defensive in their relationships, especially with foreigners. They will smile, greet you in a friendly way, and go out of their way to help you. But they are inherently shy and you will have to make the first move if you want to integrate into their society or really get to know them. I'm not talking about bargirls or those trying to sell you fake gems in the tourist hotspots. I am commenting on the average genuine Thai. With a respectful approach, they will help you blend in and be part of their communities and society.

They love *sanuk* (fun) events. An impromptu karaoke in a neighbour's garden or at a local restaurant will see many Thais gathering. They won't mind if you join them. They will be happy if they see you're enjoying yourself as much as they are. It does not matter how good your singing is. Having two left feet or a voice like a foghorn is no bar. Thais let themselves go at local parties.

Nothing matters if there's plenty of *sanuk* around.

3 February

It is not often that you see a Thai posting on the internet forums here, but an interesting thread developed today. The poster was asking why her *farang* (foreigner) husband would not agree to lending her niece money to buy a house. The quick answer was that it was not a western custom to do that. The usual flaming started; all Thais are lazy, tell the family to work harder and save for a house, what does it have to do with me, it is not my family.

Her point was that she could not understand why her husband would not even **discuss** the issue. She genuinely wanted to appreciate why he was so unlike a Thai in his lack of caring for family.

Thais like living in the same compound or at the very least near each other; that is partly custom, partly a question of economics. In the West, teenagers fly the nest as soon as they can. There is not the same yearning to live close together and provide accommodation.

In Thailand, you marry the family rather than the girl or boy. Blood family comes before the husband in Thai culture. It is a difficult notion for Westerners to appreciate.

She put her point of view politely and well, recognising that we were talking of two very diverse cultures.

That did not stop someone writing that a Thai's motto is: *Marry a farang; get a house.*

4 February

Listen for the sounds of Thailand when you visit or stay here. Particularly in rural Thailand. The birds singing during the dawn chorus, the insects and frogs with their mating calls in the early evening. After a while you'll come to expect the loudspeaker announcements from the local *pooyaibaan*, the elected village council leader. Your neighbours will be eagerly awaiting his regular updates on what's happening in the community – a charity event to raise funds for the local school, a blessing at the *wat* when it opens a new meeting hall, or informing of a neighbour's recent death.

Evenings will bring the happy laughter, though not always melodious singing, from your neighbours' homes. You will hear the distant chanting of the monks from a nearby *wat* or the shouting of instructions to an outside fitness class or aerobics session.

During election time local politicians and their teams, canvassing in their slow-moving pick-up trucks, will be extolling their virtues and asking voters for their support in the upcoming elections. You'll see that quite regularly. Driving around yourself, one minute you'll see a singing and dancing crowd escorting a novice monk to his initiation, the next moment and further down the road you may hear the sad laments coming from the home of someone who has recently died, the garlanded coffin on full view outside the house.

Drive into a restaurant or shopping mall car park, and you will hear the attendants blowing whistles for all they're worth to help you park. Police use them a lot to draw attention to other cars and pedestrians and to beckon you forward. Teachers on duty outside a school entrance do the same. You are obliged to follow their directions even though they have no legal right to direct traffic.

Especially around *wats* you will hear dogs barking. Noisy fireworks will be let off to announce a death or to celebrate some event or a party.

Guidebooks will tell you there is much to see in Thailand. There is much to listen for too.

5 February

I do not think the Thais live in fear, as has been suggested by some foreign observers. They are brought up with a high regard for the respect of elders and "betters." That's not a word I like using but it accurately reflects that Thais do not believe all people are equal.

If you listen to a subordinate speaking to a superior in the work environment, you will immediately observe the difference in rank that is being shown. Both the gesture of the *wai* and the actual words used in speaking will clearly show who is who in the pecking order and the respect given to the elder or superior is very visible. An employee will be careful in making a suggestion if he or she disagrees with the boss. There will be no direct refusal of his instructions.

As Somsee said, the employee may use a different approach later and will no doubt gossip about the incident but there will be no disobedience. That may be misguided respect but it is not fear. Thais understand that many of their compatriots get their positions through whom they know and not always through merit. A move to fuller meritocracy is slow.

Political instability has been a common feature in Thailand from the early days of this fledgling democracy. I don't imagine Thais like the concept of coups d'état any more than any other nation but coups aren't quite the same here. It's usually business as usual and the foreign media particularly do not seem to appreciate the level of corruption and nepotism in the political party system. Reform and a more open education system is needed for democracy to become effective and to allow ballot boxes to determine governments that act for the benefit of all Thailand's citizens.

In the West we do not have military coups but do the big banks, oil companies, and powerful lobbyists influence the running of elected governments? Are they behaving as if they are coup leaders bent on thwarting the views of the majority electorate?

(I accept there is some fear involved. Not following the law (lèse majesté can have serious consequences for example) and Thais are aware of that. They can't always use money and contacts to avoid prosecution. They "fear" too being ostracised if they do not follow cultural norms of behavior and lifestyle.)

6 February

Thai houses usually have steep sloping roofs, high ceilings, and roofs with large overhangs. The overhangs give much needed shade from the hot sun and help keep temperatures down inside. The sloping roofs allow rainwater to get away efficiently, often into water storage tanks.

All houses will have fans and mosquito nets; upper class houses, air conditioners. Even in expensive *moobaans* (estates, projects) buildings are close together to give shade.

Benjawan's new house is being built to a newer design with one sloping roof. It has the usual sharp gradient to take away the rainwater but is pleasantly attractive. Her Thai neighbours prefer the more traditional style. All the bedrooms have balconies though Thais rarely sit or relax in them. You'll notice that as you're driving around.

During the day, most Thais will wear long trousers to protect from the sun, and sleeveless shirts and blouses are not popular. When they get home in the evening, they sit in the shade, either under the trees in the garden or in a patio protected from the sun and heat.

7 February

Had an enjoyable day at the Flower Festival in Chiangmai today. Every year there is a happy atmosphere of music and dance as the processions of flower-bedecked floats wend their way through the streets of this northern Thai city.

Banks, businesses, schools, universities, and other organisations compete to be awarded the prize for the most colourful and original float. Everyone involved in building the colourful floats will try and out-do the others. At the end of the day a member of the royal family or a civic dignitary will present the award.

Thai girls in traditional dress and musical bands precede the floral displays. Regularly, they will stop and give a demonstration of Thai cultural dance, onlookers joining in the fun.

Plant and flower vendors from all over the Northern Province exhibit their products on the side of the roads and their own displays try to rival those you see in the main processions.

8 February

Thais are always impressed by outward show. It creates a big impact on them. Substance is secondary. The car you drive, the designer clothes you wear; all are important to a Thai. More so than many other nationalities. It's a way of showing your position in society. Thais need to know where they stand in relation to you. Are you "better" than they are? Are you a social inferior? Partly a karmic conception, inequality is accepted by the Thai. It has no unacceptable undertones as in the West. Rewards and a higher station come in the next life.

Pictures of show houses for sale on a *moobaan* (gated housing community) are nothing like what you see or will actually get if you buy. Thais excel at marketing because they can let their creativity run riot. Truth and accuracy are not too important. While marketing is their forte, management is their Achilles heel.

Thais do not learn easily from their mistakes or from the experience of others. They learn by rote and by copying. They like to stick with what they already know. Accepting they are wrong or even learning something new can feel like losing face. That's one reason they rarely apologise directly. Thinking for oneself is secondary to doing as an elder or more senior person tells you.

A good example of that occurred this morning. I needed to renew my internet virus protection. There was a great webpage detailing all the improved features of the new version, its advantages, and its superiority over the competition. Good marketing.
It was when it came to buying the product that the trouble started. In order to buy the software, you need to enter a code that is obtained from an email the supplier sends you. I tried several times to explain that I could not order because I had not been sent the code. Two hours later and still no code. I tried to purchase without the code, ignoring the website instructions, and I eventually downloaded the product.

The website instructions were wrong. No code was needed. However, the Thais will not correct the webpage. That would mean someone would have to be blamed, and that is not a choice that Thais like to take. It is a "correct" cultural response as no one will lose face, but it is poor management.

The impressive marketing hype will remain. Management won't get involved or change the instructions.

Conflict and blame will be avoided.

9 February

SAD FART; but not in Thailand, it would seem. Most countries have reasonable consumer protection laws. In the UK, for example, the Sale of Goods Act 1979 protects against shoddy quality. Buy on a credit card or online and you have even more rights. Remember to complain promptly and know your legal position. The product must be of merchantable quality, the same as described at the point of sale, and you must act within a reasonable time.

Shops everywhere in the world will still try to fob you off.

Remember the mnemonic: **SAD FART**

Satisfactory quality
As
Described
Fit for purpose
And
Reasonable length of
Time.

Thailand is different. Regulations are difficult to enforce, court processes are slow, and your supplier may be a company with power and contacts. Thais anyway do not like confrontations. You may have to smile and walk away.

Sorry, no sad farts in Thailand.

10 February

Watch out for parades in Thailand when you visit. Flower festivals are colourful sights and well-advertised. Most displays and processions are listed on Google. Dates may vary year to year.

Ask locally when there are weddings and novice monk initiations. They can be noisy fun occasions where everyone joins in the celebrations along the street. Dancing, drinking, and singing. Nobody will mind when you join in.

More somber, but not in any way morbid, are funeral processions when the body is taken to the crematorium. It is interesting to witness one if you possibly can. What you will notice is the large number of people who turn out in respect. Thailand is a very community based society.

11 February

Latdaa does not like gossiping. In some ways she is not typically Thai. She is more independent than most. Her parents divorced when she was very young and she was brought up by her aunt, herself a divorced lady with her own daughter to look after.

Latdaa's strong character may be a result of having to fend for herself much of the time. Her aunt supported her as much as she could but Latdaa did not have as much help as others when studying in school and university. She found her first job by her own efforts and is doing well there. After just three years, she has been promoted to supervisor.

She asked the Japanese director of her company if she could visit the head office in Tokyo. That in itself was a pretty unusual request from a Thai. They will drop hints but won't ask directly. He readily agreed and she spent four days on a tour of the Tokyo offices and factory. It was a very full programme by all accounts. There was a great deal for her to learn and understand about the way the company operated. The Japanese, it seemed, did not mind her plain-speaking approach.

On the final day, Latdaa was allowed to spend her time sightseeing and engaging in the usual tourist activities. She choose to spend her free time with a colleague she had been introduced to in the office. They spent the day together and saw a lot of the city. The two ladies did some window shopping as the prices were too high for Latdaa to contemplate any purchasing. They both enjoyed their day.

Back in Thailand, her day of seeing the sights was the subject of much gossip and jealousy. Probably much was fabricated to make a good story. It annoyed Latdaa a little but, as she said to me, it's typically Thai to engage in tittle-tattle.

12 February

The carpenters had left some papers on top of a corner cabinet they had almost finished building. They had put away their tools, cleaned where they had been working, and were making ready to go home. For some reason, I thought it odd that they had not collected up their documents.

I lifted them up and realised why they had left them there. There was a deep and very visible scratch across the top of the unit. A tool must have been accidentally pulled across it.

Their faces were expressionless but they knew the damage was not repairable. They would have to replace the top.

No apology. If I had not spotted the damage before they left, they would have insisted when they returned the next day that it was nothing to do with them, that I had ruined their handiwork.

You have to watch out for workers covering their mistakes. It happens in offices too as we shall see.

Not losing face and not owning up to a mistake is frustrating for foreigners to experience but Thais expect it to happen. It is why they do not trust but check and watch everything so carefully.

13 February

There are many good Thai teachers, born educators. Genuine Thais who have the gift, that some of their colleagues who have been brought up on rote learning do not have, of keeping a class fully engaged and attentive. They encourage questioning and try to get their students to think for themselves rather than repeat what they have read in books or heard in class.

All classes will have youngsters that may want to steal the limelight. It is all too easy for an inexperienced teacher to respond to those same students instead of ensuring the whole class participates. Involving everyone and drawing out those who may be a little shy is the hallmark of a good educator. A lively and attentive class, with respect for their teacher, is the most wanted result.

There are some really good *farang* teachers too. But a few have poor English grammar and pronunciation themselves. Often they are backpackers or retirees who are not legally allowed to teach, unqualified, and without work permits.

Having said that, I know of one regular world traveler who has been offered a renewable contract by a school. He spends six months of every year in Thailand and returns to the school each year to teach a new set of pupils. His classes are always full of attentive children who enjoy and benefit from his teaching. He has no formal teaching qualification but his English is faultless.

14 February

Today is Valentine's Day.It can also fall on Makha Bucha day, a Buddhist festival when government offices are normally closed. Because Valentine's Day is an auspicious day to get married in Thailand, some government offices open specially to allow couples to register their marriages.

There was an article in today's newspapers about six couples getting married in Prachinburi. They are celebrating the event by competing in a series of adrenalin-pumping activities which include an escape from bloodthirsty pirates, a "flight" high above the jungle, and a mad dash away from a boulder made of flowers. The photos show a lot of youngsters having the time of their lives.

In Pattaya things are a bit more relaxed as couples attempt to break the world-record for non-stop (or almost non-stop) hugging. The current record is 25 hours, 22 minutes and 36 seconds.

Condom sales are high on Valentine's Day.

Thailand has one of the highest rates of teenage pregnancy in Southeast Asia. The Bureau of Reproductive Health says that the number of teenage mothers is second only to neighbouring Laos. After sub-Saharan Africa, Asia-Pacific is the region with the largest number of people living with HIV, and Thailand accounts for about 9 percent of that number, says HIV response outfit AVERT. About 450,000 people live with HIV among a population of 67 million, according to Thai health ministry estimates from 2013, the latest available data.

15 February

It is a nice touch that members of the Thai royal family give out degree certificates to graduates at the universities. Very few countries do that.

Dao invited us to the rehearsal. She had asked us to come to the actual ceremony but the university had the dates muddled and their email to all students gave the date of the rehearsal instead of the actual date. We were told of the error at the last minute but could not change our travel plans.

She had got up at 5am to get her hair styled and her face made up. Thais are always careful about their appearance and Dao is an attractive young lady. Today she looked like a film star. She had called the dummy run "the walking" and I could see why. All the students lined up and walked up to the stage where a stand-in handed out the certificates. This was repeated until they got it absolutely right. Yes, it was a day of much walking.

You bow or curtsy a few metres before approaching the dais just as the previous student is receiving his or her degree. Before being handed the certificate, you bow your head slightly and extend your hand as if to shake hands western style. But you do not actually complete the greeting; you flick your wrist and take the certificate, but without touching the royal hand. Walking backwards a few metres, you pause, bow or curtsy again, turn round, and walk off the stage. It takes around 30 seconds per student. All of them will be nervous on the day but honoured that a member of the royal family has made it one they will always remember.

On the day that the degree is conferred, the students' families and friends join in the celebrations, flowers and gifts are showered on the new graduates, and many photographs are taken with fellow students and teachers.

A pity that we could not see her receiving her award from a royal princess. Given the problem with her trying to find a new home to rent, I hope she enjoys her day.

Before he became ill, the late King Bhumibol presided over many degree ceremonies at the major colleges. Members of the royal family now continue that tradition.

Many families have a photograph of their son or daughter receiving their degree from His Majesty or a royal prince or princess. It always has pride of place in their homes.

16 February

I was surprised some weeks ago when I read on Suda's Facebook page, just under a picture of her son's pet.

"Some nasty man hit my dog"

Today she told me what had actually happened. Her husband had hit *Lamyai* for misbehaving. Whether it was appropriate or not is questionable. Shaking the dog immediately after the event and saying "no" in a firm voice would probably have been better.

But I now understood her comment on Facebook. She was blaming someone else and not criticising her husband.

It is the Thai way of taking out one's frustrations and anger without involving the person you are really annoyed with. You may notice it a great deal in Thailand. It is called *prachut* in Thai.

The Thai is actually directing his venom against the person who has wronged him. He is letting him know what he really wants to tell him if culture allowed such openness face to face. One's rage is projected at another person, animal or an inanimate object. The person, animal, or object is being made the scapegoat in place of the real target for anger. It is a means of staying friends with someone by not directly chastising the person who is the real object of your displeasure.

Suda was blaming the "nasty man" but not her husband. The anthropological term is projected vilification. Thais also use something similar to projected vilification when referring contemptuously to someone. Instead of using the person's name, they may say, "*farang* insists on talking to the manager" or "*kwai* (buffalo or stupid person) is late for work again.

17 February

Foreigners cannot own land in Thailand except under exceptional circumstances. You can own the house on which it stands and you can remove it brick by brick if you feel so inclined but you on no account own the land. You can own a condominium (the apartment not the land) provided that there are 50% or more Thai residents in the same apartment block. You can set up a company that owns the land and your house so long as Thais make up more than 50% of the shareholders. That is not without its problems as the Revenue department can challenge the arrangement by claiming the company was not set up to do business and make profits that could be taxed but registered only to provide the foreigner with a home.

Many expats rent or take out a lease for a certain period of time, usually 30 years. The expat becomes a lessee and not an owner, whether he funded the purchase or not. There are protections available that give him the right to live on the property during the term of the lease. One or other party can, under certain conditions, change the lease to take away the right to stay unhindered on the land. It makes it rather pointless, therefore, to have signed the lease in the first place. Some forms of lease, notably superficies, offer better protection.

Some lawyers may suggest a 30 plus 30 lease where you have the right to enter into another lease at the end of the first term. That has never been tested in a Thai court. The head of my *amphur* (local government) office said it would be illegal, that there is no reference to it in any law book. But she added that she would allow such a condition to be inserted into the document, however pointless it would be. I am sure that would not happen in the West.

Another example of avoiding open conflict between lawyer and client, just to keep the peace?

18 February

Singapore has a reputation for zero tolerance towards corruption. You would be unlikely to bribe your way out of a traffic offence.

Thailand has a more layback attitude. If a small bribe or gift can make the machinery of bureaucracy move more quickly then so be it. It is regarded more like part of one's salary or a perk of the job.

Big international corporations and politicians in Thailand are accused of giving large sums to secure lucrative contracts. Although it is not a purely Thai phenomenon, it has been present throughout Thai history and is culturally accepted in the Far East.

Corruption will not totally disappear. Singapore, with the lowest rate of corruption in South East Asia, is witness to that.

The western mindset is that corruption is wrong and unacceptable. That does of course not stop some politicians and business owners in the West indulging in the practice as they do elsewhere. Lobbyists giving "cash for questions" in parliament to sway the opinions of governments elected by the voters that put them into power? Expensive all-in holidays for the business leaders from whom favours are being sought?

The question is not whether corruption exists or should exist. The question is whether it should be seen as acceptable in a nation's culture. And if it is accepted, to what extent? Should only "minor" corruptions be allowed? And who makes that decision?

19 February

Her parents divorced when she was 10 years old and her aunt brought her up and helped her through university. It had made Duangjai very self-reliant and determined. She lacked the submissiveness that you so often see in young Thai girls. She had a mind of her own.

She and her husband worked and saved hard to afford a deposit on their new home. Duangjai has a good job and Nok works a 6-day week, doing as much overtime as he can to keep up the mortgage payments. They are not wealthy but they have enough money to live comfortably.

When they moved in, there was an empty plot of land next to them. Now, a paint-spraying unit has been built there. Even a light breeze can carry the unpleasant smell into their home. Although Nok takes a more *mai pen rai*, carefree, view of the situation, Duangjai, worried for her two year old's health, spoke to the owners and they agreed to build a small wall between the two properties to screen the spraying plant.

That has helped but it is not an effective or complete solution. There are days when you would not be able to sit outside because of the fumes. Nok will not get involved but Duangjai has spoken to them again a few times. Her next step will be to talk to the *pooyaibaan,* the village headman. Most people like him and say he is fair, so Duangjai is hoping for a sympathetic ear.

She says she will wait a week and if there is no response from the spraying company, she will go and see him. These steps cannot be rushed in Thailand. Westerners would find the slow approach quite frustrating.

Duangjai and Nok would not have bought the house if they had known the adjacent land was going to be used in this way. Unfortunately, in Thailand there is no easy way to search for planning permissions or approvals. In fact, depending on whom you know, it is possible to build without approval anyway. Some money probably helps in the decision making process.

20 February

There is no stigma in being gay in Thailand. It is not illegal and is generally accepted. A person's sexuality is his own affair. Thais will gossip but they don't concern themselves with anything that is none of their business. Families do not ostracise a son from being gay and the boyfriend would be welcome in the parents' home. They may prefer their son to be heterosexual and produce an heir but they are quite relaxed about allowing him freedom to conduct his life the way he wants.

Many foreigners are gay and live with their partners quite openly. They value Thailand's open and flexible attitude.

A lady-boy, a *katoey,* would not be ostracised in any way. Many work in restaurants as serving staff. They would use the word *ka,* the word used by females, and not *krap.*

The tell-tale sign of a *katoey* is the more pronounced presence of an Adam's apple (laryngeal prominence.) But even that is not easy to spot. Tourists, and even expats, can be misled by these very attractively dressed and made up lady-boys. There are posters on the Thai forums who comment that they've only found out their mistake when they've taken their "girlfriend" to bed!

(A caution here. Take some of what you read on Thai forums with a pinch of salt. There are some extremely useful comments. There are also some trollish responses.)

Lesbians are noticeable by their cropped hairstyles and male mannerisms. They generally still use *ka* and not *krap* though.

No one really cares about sexual orientation in Thailand.

21 February

They did not want to do it. That became clear, but it was not immediately obvious. We had agreed a fixed rate for the job of erecting posts around the perimeter fence. They had worked hard and quickly, but some of the posts were not that firmly positioned in the ground. We bought more cement and sand and they strengthened a few of the posts.

The supervisor said that he could not come back the next day as his mother was in hospital. The next day's excuse was that one of the team had a problem with his motor bike.

They had made good money from the job, but did not welcome having to do the remedial work. They never came back and they only received payment for the work they had done. One more day and they would have finished the job to everyone's satisfaction and have been fully paid.

I do not think it was a question of losing face. We had been tactful about showing where the faults were and they cheerfully went about putting some of the posts right. No, I think they had just decided that they did not want to do any more work. They were happy with what they had received and not bothered about losing the rest of the payment.

We smile and acknowledge one another when I see them in the village, so there are no hard feelings. Just have to accept that Thais can often just do what they want to do. Living in Thailand, one sees many instances that can be put down to a lack of self-discipline, responsibility, and ambition. A *mai pen rai* attitude and I suppose a somewhat stubborn streak.

Thais like to be flattered and the more you refer to their skills and abilities the better. Commenting on a worker being *geng* (clever) or his work as being *suay* (beautiful, a good job), are compliments they routinely expect.

But you need to keep a distance between yourself and the workers. They don't feel comfortable in your getting too close or friendly. They find it strange that *farangs* often treat them as equals rather than people employed to do a job. A Thai would never do that. I still like to have a joke with them though but am careful how far I go.

You need to drive a hard bargain when working out a price and always give the impression that you feel the figure agreed is not that much of a good deal. If you don't, the price will go up next time. In this case, maybe I had unknowingly made them feel I had got the better part of the transaction. They would lose face if they asked for more at the end of the job so they could not do that. But one reason for not wanting to complete the work may have been that they were embarrassed that they could have got more for the job initially but did not do so.

Face is completely non-negotiable in Thailand.

22 February

One of Ying's friends died today, he was only 42. She got a phone call at seven o'clock. News travels quickly in this country.

She had waved to him as she left the office at 4.30 after her day's work. Not realising it would be a final farewell.

Chatting on the phone about the funeral arrangements she learnt he had taken the afternoon off, gone home early, and died after playing with his children after lunch. She believes she had seen her friend's spirit and not his human self when she waved to him on leaving work.

Thais can be very superstitious and many ghost stories are probably fabrications. But some people have made plausible claims to have seen ghosts and sometimes their accounts are verified by others.

23 February

Chai's guitar, laptop, and other possessions were stacked in the corner of his home ready to be collected by the monks. It would be an act of merit, *tamboon*, to donate them to the *wat*.

We went over to the temple in the morning, lit an incense stick, and placed it with all the others beside the coffin. Then we joined the rest of his family and friends who were seated round. Chatting about anything that comes to mind, but no reference is made of the death. Buddhist belief is that death is a natural part of the lifecycle. No crying or weeping. It's always a shock to the system for us foreigners when we see how Thais react to death and funerals. I understand it now but it takes some getting used to.

If the deceased is laid to rest at home; fans, air conditioning, and jars full of scented flowers and herbs can give off a pleasant perfume. Chai's body lay in a refrigerated cabinet because it was at the temple and the building could become quite hot at times. In the summer months particularly refrigerated cabinets are used regularly.

A mini-bus will come tonight with his work colleagues so that they can pay their respects and be with the family. They will not be able to go the cremation service as it would leave the office empty. Everyone wants to go but realises it is not possible. His boss and two senior staff will attend. Ironic really, because Benjawan did not get on with his boss.

A pity that tradition could not have been changed so that two or three of his closest work mates could have taken the place of the top brass.

24 February

Duangjai had a meeting with her *pooyaibaan*. Seemed to go well, she thought. He appeared to support her concerns and will talk to the landowners. She is aware that sometimes money can change hands in order to sway an official's thinking, but she told me this would not happen in this case.

We shall see.

25 February

Car in for a service today. Did a fine job and they gave it a thorough clean inside and out. You do need to be cautious when dealing with businesses in Thailand.

Some disreputable garages will exchange a perfectly good part for one that is second hand. You will not spot the difference because they will have cleaned the engine compartment and made it look immaculate.

That certainly happened in England after the war years when small businesses were struggling to survive and were prone to cut corners in servicing. Maybe that explains why there is a tendency for this to happen today in under-developed countries.
Thai garages will always show you the empty oil container after an oil change to prove they have changed the oil. You should check the dipstick to see if the oil is in fact fresh oil. That is what the Thais themselves do.

They watch workers very carefully. It is a little mysterious and enigmatic that a country whose people are so cheerful and helpful can also display such a lack of trust between their fellow countrymen.

When I first arrived here, the truck broke down and the repair shop recommended fitting a reconditioned starter motor. They had been very helpful, typically Thai, even getting their workers to push the truck from where it had broken down to their garage. Smiles all round while I was given a few cups of coffee. Two weeks later, the truck broke down again. They had only cleaned up the starter motor and not replaced the contacts that had worn down. I am more cautious now.

26 February

Thais observe the national anthem whenever it is played in public places. At railway stations, a guard will blow a whistle to ensure everyone stands. I've seen police halt traffic in a market place. That's not usual but vendors and customers alike then stand in respect for the King.

Commercial offices do not normally stop work, diners in restaurants don't stop eating. If the public are present in a government office at 8am or 6pm, they are required to stand. (Yes, some offices are open at those hours). Most hospitals go about caring and treating patients, whether emergencies or not.

I felt a little embarrassed today though. Walking through a hospital corridor, I promptly stopped walking and stood still as the anthem began playing. It was instinctive. I would have done that for any anthem I recognised.

Everyone else stopped too even though it was clear they would not normally have been expected to do so. I could hardly start walking again just because I had made them stop. They had had no choice but to stop when they saw me, a *farang*, stand still for the anthem. They did not want to lose face.

Next time, I'll do what everyone else does. If they stand, I will. If they don't stop, I won't either. It's best to follow what the locals do but sometimes a spontaneous impulse and instinct take over.

27 February

Some comments in the Thai press today about the quality of English teachers compared to those employed in other Asean countries. Malaysia topped the list as the best in South East Asia, with Thailand coming well behind Vietnam and Indonesia. Sunantaa, who teaches in the local primary school, agrees.

Surprised that Singapore and Brunei were not mentioned. Statistics are not easy to verify on the internet and Thai newspapers sometimes put an odd spin on figures. We both thought that these two countries have higher English language skills than are being reported.

At primary and secondary level, most teachers are Thai nationals and are not particularly fluent in English, seldom having even visited an English speaking country.

Those expats that are appointed by the schools and universities must have work permits and have passed an examination acceptable to the Thai authorities showing competence in teaching a foreign language. Even then, their abilities are questionable. The standards set for testing those thinking of teaching English as a foreign language are not very high. There are some exceptionally good teachers but there are also those who should never be allowed near a classroom. The résumés of some of the candidates are full of spelling and grammatical errors.

Many expats, particularly when they first arrive, try their hand at teaching. Some volunteer their services even when they have no permit. Technically even unpaid work requires a permit, but blind eyes are turned. Backpackers wanting to earn some money as they travel around the continent often do a spell in the classroom. Many excel and make a worthwhile contribution.

The consensus though is that Thailand falls behind in the English teaching stakes overall and there needs to be a more serious review of the system compared with other countries in the Asean group.

It is not good to have a poorly educated population. Not good for democracy for one thing. The better educated a population is; the more likely the electorate will understand the policies of political parties and challenge their manifestos and actual performance.

Better training for teachers and improving fluency standards are long overdue. The people of developing countries need to rekindle a longing for education and not be fearful of voting for improved standards in their schools.

28 February

I had to make a detour today to get to the market. Reading Thai road signs when driving is not always that easy but I could make out that the road ahead was closed. I could see preparations for a wedding in the distance and there was music playing, so it was easy to guess that someone influential had had the road blocked.

I just followed the arrows for the diversion and was just sorry I had not been sent an invitation.

1 March

You will see scores of different uniforms when you are in Thailand. As elsewhere in the world, traffic police are those you notice most. To counter illegal immigration, police regularly have checkpoints on roads between major cities and near borders. Soldiers are also used to maintain and control order in Thailand.

On state occasions the military top brass, particularly the guards regiments, wear uniforms of varied colours. In the West, there is more similarity between their uniforms, with only minor differences to indicate a specific regiment.

Nurses in hospitals wear white as in most other countries. Bank employees are often dressed in accordance with the bank's own dress code or a uniform specific to that bank. Factory workers, particularly in Japanese owned companies, wear a company uniform or are fitted out in the company's colours. Unlike the Thai, the Japanese have a penchant for conformity.

Local and central government officers have uniforms, the formal dress uniform is of white and is worn with decorations appropriate to rank on special occasions and at public events. A village headman (*pooyaibaan*), who everyone would know and recognise, would only wear his white outfit at important events. These dress uniforms with their epaulettes and rows of decoration ribbons look most impressive. They are worn of course to show rank, status and to impress. The *pooyaibaan* of this village promised to get me a white uniform, though added I had to be in Thailand for a further 100 years to qualify. Thai humour.

Schoolchildren and college students adhere to a strict dress code, usually white blouse and black skirt for girls and white shirt and black trousers for boys. Most students (girls anyway) will wash and iron their uniforms each night as they may have only one set. Teachers and university staff will wear their white uniforms during special dates in the school or university calendar. Academic gowns, some of which are very colourful, are worn at degree ceremonies.

Security staff at shopping malls, car park attendants at restaurants, and also guards at banks will wear uniforms, open doors for you, and salute you. Thailand is different from the West in many ways.

2 March

Thais don't want to tell you what you don't want to hear. They will either agree with you, walk away or change the subject. They don't like saying, "No.'

They value continued friendship. Upsetting you or being in conflict is not on their agenda. I am sure you will soon detect this Thai trait. To a lesser extent it happens in other countries of the Far East.

Pomelo thought topping the trees was a good idea. Letting them grow much more and they were likely to be blown down in the next big storm. When asked if he could do the job he enthusiastically agreed. Pomelo never came round. He had not tackled a job like that before and did not have the necessary equipment.

He simply could not say "no."

3 March

Although I'd written the rest of the document required by the British consulate in English, according to their rules, I had put down my Thai address using the Thai alphabet.

I wrote it exactly the way it appears on envelopes addressed to me and how it appears on bills. There have never been problems with the post office or delivery drivers finding my house.

The consular clerk wanted the address in romanised characters. But there is no single correct way of writing a Thai word using the English alphabet. Road signs to *Sarapii* can be written *Sarapi*, *Sarapee*, or *Saarapi* depending on how the sign-writer transcribes the Thai sound. Thai has no equivalent of Chinese pinyin, which is the unique and authorised spelling of a Chinese word using the English alphabet.

I had no idea how best to write my address using English script. I wrote it phonetically, though two Thais sitting next to me could not recognise what I had written as my address. However, *rules is rules*. I gave my efforts to the clerk who promptly stamped it as approved, and charged me 2000 baht.

The next step was to get the document translated into Thai and returned to her. The translation agency was only down the road so that was no big problem. He translated most of the document but then said: *I don't understand your address. What is it in Thai?*

I gave him what I had originally written and he dutifully copied it. 500 baht and I was on my way back to the consulate. The document was stamped again. I made no comment that the address was exactly the same as I had originally written it; but I think the consular officer realised how absurd the situation was.

She'll make the same request to the next customer.

Rules is rules.

4 March

Thai humour is different. Queen Elizabeth II, when once referring to a Commonwealth visit that she undertook with her husband, famously and humourously said, *and when I say 'we' I mean my husband and I.*

She was making a joke of distinguishing between the royal 'we' (singular, meaning herself) and the plural form (meaning Prince Phillip and herself). Her remark was both funny and acceptable and drew laughter from her audience.

Although the late King Bhumibol, King Rama IX of Thailand, has made some very witty comments in his speeches, the joke quoted above would not be found amusing in Thailand.

Thai humour can be a little risqué and down to earth, but using subtlety and sarcasm does not always work in Thai jokes. Western humour often relies on making a joke against oneself or another person. It is taken as amusing comic relief. Thais dislike conflict situations.

They find word play funny. That will always get a laugh. Delicious or tasty in Thai is *aroi dee*. Say, *aree doi* (which is completely meaningless) – swapping the two words around – and you will bring the house down.

5 March

Not everything is cheap in Thailand, with imported goods carrying heavy duties. Branded drinks like whiskey, cars and high-end electronic goods can be prohibitively expensive.

Thai products can be poor value for money. Buying what appears to be a reasonably priced pair of rubber boots can lose the perception of being a bargain when they have to be replaced twice a year. The rubber content is much less than products made outside the country. Possibly corners are cut in the production process.

Thais are not keen on buying second hand clothes but, in fact, they can represent good value and good quality. They are almost always in prime00 condition and street markets are good hunting grounds. The vendors may not always admit they are second hand but that hardly matters if you inspect the goods carefully and see the quality for yourself. The previous hi-so owners, who may have bought the clothes overseas, may just have tired of them or think they have gone out of fashion.

6 March

The streetlight outside our house is no longer working and the *soi* is dark at nights. There are no rates or community charges in Thailand, no levy on an owner of the property. The electricity company won't fix it just for the benefit of two or three houses. So, we've clubbed together, bought a new bulb, and one of the lads climbed up the pole to fix it.

Everyone is happy and the utility company don't mind.

I am often surprised at how things work in Thailand. You may be taken aback too at what you see going on around you.

7 March

Saw Tim and Somsee for lunch today. Work is proceeding well on his house build. They have started making the concrete base and building up the outside walls. The men are doing the heavy work but the women are busy pulling the carts containing the made-up concrete to where most of it is needed.

The supervisor is watching and making sure the block work is being laid straight and level. One of the workers had started on the second course without cutting the first block in half. The result was that the second course was not being staggered. The join should never be above another join as that takes away the strength of the wall.

Tim saw it and quietly told the worker's boss. He was right not to get angry and make a big issue of it, and it was better that he told the boss and not the worker. The supervisor would not have liked that. He is in charge and only he gives the orders. Status is all-important in Thailand and no one must lose face. Tim emigrated from America two months ago and is learning fast that interacting with people in Thailand is not the same as in the West.

8 March

Took my tax form to the local office this afternoon. The deadline is the end of the month. The officers don't just accept it; they check it over for you. The form is in Thai, which is fair enough –UK tax forms are not in Thai!

I have difficulty accepting comments from foreigners who insist on having documentation and signage always available in English. Many think it is their right, forgetting the onus is on them to learn the language not the other way around. Thais are very accommodating when dealing with those who do not speak Thai. Westerners insisting on English is pushing it too far.

I'd made a small 28-baht mistake as I had read a Thai instruction wrongly. She corrected the whole form for me. Nothing was too much trouble. No one likes paying tax but it was a nice atmosphere in that office. The work was still being done despite the humour and laughter.

I wish I could have taken a picture of all the happy faces, taxpayers and tax collectors joking and chatting together. But it's illegal to take photos in Thai government offices.

I gave her some cherries from my garden. It's the sort of thing you do in Thailand. Everyone is forever giving and receiving small gifts. It's called *nam jai* in Thai. (literally, a heart flowing kindly with water!) It was in no way a bribe. She had already completed the form. She had gone out of her way to be helpful. For everyone, not just for me.

Can't imagine doing that in the UK or the States.

9 March

Thai prisons are not palaces or hotels. You won't see private toilet facilities or TV sets in the cells. Western jails are centrally heated with high quality medical facilities, gymnasiums, games rooms on site. Prisons in the Far East are not so comparable. Although rehabilitation and not punishment is said to be the principal aim of the penal system, the long (by western standards) sentencing imposed makes one doubt that.

Several prisoners are placed in cells with mattresses or sleeping spaces very close together. Inmates have little privacy. The daily budget for food may not be high but it is basic and healthy. There are exercise yards but life is not meant to be socially active.

However, in some prisons, at least for juveniles, prisoners are allowed free telephone access to parents and family via internet links such as Skype and Line. Mobile phones are technically banned and are regularly confiscated during spot checks. It seems difficult to control. Thailand is full of enigmas. There are rules and regulations but in Thailand enforcement is not always fully exercised. One need only look at how traffic violations are not taken seriously to realise that.

Outward appearance rather than actual substance is a feature of many aspects of Thai life. Public areas in prisons, gardens and reception centres, can be immaculate and welcoming. They are images that are very different from what one might see or experience inside. Thailand can hold surprises for observers. You may see a fine expensive-looking house with a flashy car in the driveway and then be taken aback to find mattresses and not beds in the rooms that visitors do not normally see.

It was only in 1970, after Life magazine ran a report on the Vietnamese prison in Phu Hail, that the Vietnamese closed down their "tiger cages" which housed some of their 20,000 prisoners, chained naked in rows, and beaten and dusted down with lime and water. A combination which is calculated to burn the skin. There is no evidence that Thai prisons were ever that barbaric.

In all parts of Thai society, money can make the wheels turn a little more smoothly or quickly to get things done the way you want. That may apply to well-heeled prisoners as much as to anyone else. Ordinary inmates see nothing odd or wrong in different classes of Thai being treated differently. Class and hierarchy are not only found outside prison walls.

10 March

There are very few communists in Thailand and the party and its ideas find little acceptance amongst most Thais.

Communism did not deliver any credible message that the Thai would be better off under its regime. It offered no guarantees. Its propaganda was based on rationality and not as emotionally based as the Thais would have liked and understood. Thais value the concept of fraternity (*paradorn*) where it emphasises togetherness and community. In fact, they embrace it.

But they neither understand nor accept that they should knuckle down under a system that has no appeal to them emotionally and would conflict with the present accepted hierarchical structure from the king at the top to the lowly farm worker at the bottom.

They felt communism was far too rigid and suppressed personal freedom. Loyalty to family and community were more essential than any political principles about equality for all. Thais already have a strong sense of community. Communism had no better alternative on offer.

11 March

In Thailand it is customary to invite your superior to your son's wedding at which he will be invited to speak; be the guest of honour at the opening of a new building; or ask him to sit with the family in the front row at a funeral. A great opportunity to mingle amongst the great and the good, and re-affirm your status in the community.

Khun Sompanya, desperate to re-gain some popularity, hit on the idea of inviting a senior government official to open an extension to the main office building. More specifically, to open the new toilet block. He politely declined.

It reminded me of the story of the French mayor in Gabriel Chevallier's *Clochemerle* when he planned to construct a urinal in the town square of his village in Beaujolais.

The ceremony of the loo would have attracted a lot of white uniforms and the taking of many photographs.

The younger generation, and indeed even middle-aged Thais, are beginning to shy away from such functions requiring this show of uniforms. At a recent event, it was noticeable that some key people, whom one would have expected to have turned up, were absent. Several people were not wearing their full insignia. This tradition of showing your position in public is starting to fall out of favour. But national events, especially those associated with royalty, continue to attract high numbers of participants.

Sometimes your judgment can become suspect if you try too hard to impress or show off. The Thai love of ceremonial and dressing up can, if repeated too often, become a little overbearing and boring. Showing one's rank and status in society is a Thai characteristic that the élite particularly do not always get right. It can backfire on them. *Khun* Sompanya is going to have to think of another way to be noticed in the district.

The toilet is in use but nobody was privy (sic) to any opening ceremony.

12 March

If you walk through the street markets, you will be greeted by the distinctive aromas of the variety of foods herbs and spices on offer. Apart from the smell of chili, I find it adds a certain buzz to wandering around the stalls.

There are days when you notice the smell of smoldering jock sticks as you enter a temple. You won't find incense being burned as in western churches. More usually, the Thais sprinkle odourless holy water.

In larger towns and cities, as in the rest of the world, traffic fumes give off unpleasant smells. Tuk tuks particularly give off very unpleasant exhaust gasses. In Thailand, the practice of slash and burn is a worse menace. The smoke from the burning of rice fields after harvest causes many respiratory illnesses and hospitalisations. Every year the government of the day employ campaigns to discourage the practice of slash and burn. Every year they fail. Winds carry the smog even from other neighbouring countries which adopt the same practice.

13 March

National Elephant Day attracts more Thais than tourists and is popular with adults and children alike. Entry to the parks is generally free and there is much to watch and enjoy.

Traditionally, elephants were used by the logging companies to push and pull the timber from the teak forests to the rivers. Five or six elephants would work together to roll the logs and to un-block any logjams that occurred on the rivers. In the mid nineteenth century, there were about 100,000 working elephants. No figures are available for the wild elephants that were not used as beasts of burden.

Today deforestation is strictly controlled and, apart from around 3000 wild elephants roaming the forests, elephants are mainly found in tourist parks and zoos. They are a protected species and are generally well cared for. They have been trained to play in an elephant football team, kicking around a very large football. Some have taken a brush in their mouths and tried their skills in painting on canvas. Opinion is divided on whether training elephants in this way is demeaning or whether they enjoy exercising their brains.

Visitors can take short rides or can go on treks that cover greater distances. These treks can be an enjoyable day out. One sees much of the countryside that is not visible from the tourist coaches. Some parks allow you to get very close to the elephants and encourage you to help bathe and care for them, under the supervision of the mahout. There are elephant hospitals that you can visit.

A mahout stays with his charge throughout the elephant's life and a bond develops between them. Despite that, some mahouts do get killed, particularly when the bull elephant is "in must," and experiences a surge in hormones. They can get extremely violent to humans and other elephants alike.

14 March

Thais use what I call "bum guns" instead of full bidets or the western system of wiping one's backside. These spray strong jets of water to complete the cleaning process.

Most new Thai middle-class homes are built with western toilets but there are still many squat toilets to be found even in cities. In these, a bowl is used to scoop water onto the nether regions. Toilet paper is not required.

Public toilets in Thailand are few and far between though some department stores and shopping malls now provide facilities. Still bring your own toilet paper.

The rule is not observed as much as it used to be but, if eating food with the hand as is the custom particularly in the North, use your right hand. The left is for the purposes described above.

15 March

As with other nationalities, Thais can be incurable snobs. Pannee was hosting a get-together for members of a local club and she took an instant dislike to an unaccompanied single lady, a fellow Thai, who was one of the invited guests. The lady was being quite civil and not making advances to other men, or anything like that. She was still cold-shouldered.

Pannee ran a small travel agency before she gave it up to marry a well-off Thai and not need to work anymore.

Later, at a meeting of the same club, she started a conversation with a fellow member. "Are you still living in that small rented house in Maerim?" "Oh yes, still there" was the reply. It was a false reply, the Thai lady in question had moved to a pleasant house in a select area out of town, more expensive by far than Pannee's. It was a clever lie, she did not rise to Pannee's bait but she undoubtedly stopped her being so haughty. Those friends who overheard the remark, and who knew where they both lived, tried to hide a faint smile. They knew she had already put Pannee in her place.

There are snobs everywhere but there is a minority in Thailand that think they are superior, often after marrying a well-off Thai or *farang*.

You know the type.

A person who thinks he is better than someone else, a person who wants to think he is better than someone else, a person who wants to think he is better than someone else but knows he is not, or a person who wants to think he is better than someone else and even thinks others believe it.

16 March

Picked five large bunches of bananas this morning and gave three to my neighbours. I have more than enough for the next few weeks. Sharing what you have is very much a Thai way. It shows *nam jai* (generous giving). Everyone in the *soi* is forever giving fruit, plants, and vegetables to one another. If there's no one at home, they'll put a bag of goodies on your gatepost.

Giving is always reciprocated later. It's a form of gratitude. Not to do so would be regarded as impolite. Thais will go out of their way to return a favour. We may not feel the same automatic obligation though we would be prepared to help or give something if asked.

We give gifts at Christmas in the West.

In Thailand, Christmas seems to come every day.

17 March

Thailand does not have as many libraries as other countries. There are some in Bangkok and all the country's universities have faculty and general libraries. They may not have the most up to date reference books.

The books that you find in Thai homes, if you find any, will be comics, light reading, religious (Buddhist) texts and old school textbooks.

A previous government started a scheme where all primary school children had a computer tablet to assist in their studies and Thai children are as computer literate as their counterparts in other countries. Western children will on average though have read more books than the Thai. Being too serious is not part of a Thai's make-up. Debating or discussing is too like conflict in their minds. They do of course chat about issues but they seldom argue a point through as we might in the West. Talking about politics is nowhere near as popular as is made out. *No need to be serious,* is how one Thai put it.

Voters in the West are getting disillusioned with the political class; Thais already knew what happens to politician's promises. As everywhere else, propaganda, what one reads in newspapers and how one's family always voted largely determine where one places one's cross on the ballot paper.

The family and community can be influential in Thailand. Sons and daughters may ask for advice on how to vote or indeed be told how to vote. Ballots are secret so how family members actually vote is never known. Post-election results often confirm, though, that they have voted according to the guidance given.

Money can change hands of course but I think Thais see that more as the possibility of obtaining a favour from a politician or party than as electoral fraud.

Indeed, we have "pork barrel" politics in the West where government funds are used to benefit a particular member's constituency after he has secured enough votes to get himself elected.

18 March

Some of the *farangs* who write on the Thai forums, Facebook, and other social media are in the main, but not exclusively, those who take no part in Thai communities. The majority of foreigners who are expats here want to blend in and do so successfully. The posters on the internet may be a vociferous crowd but they a minority vociferous crowd.

Most Thais are shy and you will usually need to make the first move. If you went into a bar in the UK or elsewhere in the West and did not know anyone you would walk up to the counter, order a drink, say hello, and perhaps crack a joke to break the ice.

Humour can be an entry into a Thai community. They become less scared and frightened of you. If they don't know many *farangs* and don't speak a great deal of English they will always be a little reticent at first. A joke can change that.

Go where Thais congregate. They think foreigners, particularly the Brits, are somewhat reserved and, indeed, they see that as politeness and respect it. Their expression is *"poo dee angkrit."* That does not mean they will not welcome you into their conversation and company. Just that you need to initiate the conversation.

Only in extreme cases where libelous inaccurate information is posted, particularly against the monarchy, are posts censored. The Daily Mail has been blocked on occasion - the only UK newspaper to be so sanctioned. Facebook gets taken down every so often but only for several minutes. More a warning shot over the bows than anything else. The Thai authorities realise that the media only use catchy headlines to sell newspapers and get noticed but dislike the tactic when they are spinning the facts inaccurately.

New Mandala is an odd case. It's a left wing anti-monarchist site which, interspersed with a few soundly written articles, encourages its members, many of whom are expats in Thailand, to post misinformed views and comment. They are fed tippets of information from people outside Thailand who in a sense load the gun that these expats then fire, without realising they are just contributing to the spread of incitement and propaganda initiated by New Mandala from outside the country (where they cannot be touched)

19 March

Many tourist guides and travel books give some notes on how the *wai* is used by Thais. It helps to understand the "rules."

Thais *wai* the senior or older person first and await the return of a *wai*. Always *wai* a monk whatever his age. As a member of the Buddhist monkhood, and in a sense a representative of the Buddha, he should not *wai* you back but may smile or give a slight nod of acknowledgment.

A store employee may *wai* you and the correct and expected response is to briefly bow your head and say thank you. Do not *wai*. It could be taken as your signifying that he or she looks older than you. That is neither polite nor flattering. The only time I have seen a young Thai lady blush, her face went quite red, was when an elderly *farang* couple seemed unable to stop themselves giving a series of *wais* to the check-out girl after purchasing some goods at the supermarket.

Try to be sensitive to Thai customs and don't make the same mistake.

Thais in high positions will not always return a *wai*, particularly to subordinate workers. Never *wai* a child but smile and say something friendly when you receive the *wai*. In temples, one *wais* a Buddha image.

At funerals one *wais* the Buddha image first and then the casket of the deceased. As well as being respectful, this is also a tradition linked to the superstition that it stops ghosts coming back to haunt you. It is not carried out in all Thai provinces.

The King always *wais* a Buddha image and a monk, but nobody else. The King's family *wai* the King. Senior members of the royal family would not return a *wai* to a commoner. However, I have seen a member of the royal family *wai* a group of people in response to their *wais*. But it is never given to an individual person.

Foreigners would not be considered impolite if they did not *wai* properly or if they did not *wai* at all. However, adopting this Thai way of greeting is always appreciated.

20 March

Khun Yai's house burnt down this morning. Heard about it at 10 o'clock when the *pooyaibaan* announced it on the speaker system and appealed for help. Went round after lunch and found about twenty people sitting around in the garden. Only the concrete base and foundations had survived the fire. The roof and teak walls had caved in and there was nothing left of them. The smell of burning was still in the air from two hundred yards away.

There was nothing much that now needed to be done. Some men had earlier on, before the *pooyaibaan's* broadcast, retrieved the refrigerator and had moved the daughter's car away from the flames, having to break a car window to get in.

I know that Thai communities gather at the home when someone dies. It surprised me that they do the same when a house burns down. Thais like to be together in times of trouble or hardship, they call it *blawp jai*. They get comfort from the contact. *Khun* Yai and her family are now living with her younger sister who lives close by. They will sleep in an already crowded house.

Her daughter and niece were in the garden chatting with all those who had come round. They'll return to their aunt's house tonight.

They explained how the fire started, how so many people rushed round to help; and thanked everyone for their gifts of household goods and money.

All the gifts received had first been taken to the *pooyaibaan* and one of his staff recorded the donation and description of the gift. No doubt the list will be read out at some stage over the speaker system. I find that a little strange as in the West donors names would not be made public. The Thais accept it. Perhaps that is because corruption is so widespread that keeping a record and making the value of donations known is seen as more transparent.

Khun Yai is 83. Everyone calls her *Khun Yai*, a respectful term for a grandmother. I don't know her actual name and neither do many others. She didn't want to leave her home even when the flames were getting close to her bedroom. She was carried out in a blanket.

She had lost money in the fire so I arranged for the bank to come round and estimate the value of the charred banknotes. Everyone lends a hand wherever they can but there are still smiles and nobody is dismal; that would not help anyway and I understood more today than ever before why the Thais smile and don't react with sorrow and sadness when things go wrong. Many of the smaller denomination notes were intact, the higher valued bills were the more charred. We would have called that bad luck in the West. I found myself smiling with the rest of the Thais at the irony of that situation.

I'll check with the family in a week's time to make sure the bank has responded.

21 March

A great many Thais go to the food market in the mornings to buy food rather than cook a breakfast at home. That way they meet people, share the local news, and have a friendly chat. Thais meet up in small groups when they have something relevant to talk about or even when they don't. No need for a reason to get together.

Fund-raisers and festivals at the *wat,* funerals, weddings, house warmings, and as we saw yesterday, when a house burns down. It's time to get together as a community.

Not so much nowadays, with the disappearance of village and small town shops, but in the past in the UK it was common to go to the local shop not just for provisions but for a good old chin-wag.

When I was very young, yes I know many years ago, the old folk used to gather in the local shop/cafe at about 5.30 to await the delivery of the evening newspapers on the 6pm bus from the local town. Half an hour chatting and putting the world to rights and two minutes to buy their newspapers and go home. I was given a few sweets for carrying the papers from the bus to the shop. Thai communities are rather like that.

It's a pleasant lifestyle in Thailand but I do miss the sweets.

22 March

Bumped into a Belgian friend of mine in the market this afternoon. Louis has never been under any illusions about his relationship.

He met his Thai wife when she visited his country over ten years ago. She made it clear that she was looking for a foreign husband because it would give her better security than marrying a Thai in her own country. The prospect of a higher standard of living too.

Louis was looking for someone to care for him as he got older and Thailand seemed a nice place to retire. He and Gop liked each other and have similar interests, so they moved to Thailand. Gop is his wife's nickname. All Thais have a nickname given to them at birth. *Gop* means frog.

Always a skilled handyman and interested in Do It Yourself, he has built a beautiful but small bungalow on land owned by Gop's family and now in her name. It is very high spec and the building cost just 20,000 euros.

Gop is a retired teacher and they spend half their time, during Thailand's hot season, in Europe. Gop now has dual nationality and can avail herself of western healthcare if needed. Everything is working out for the best. She has security and a good lifestyle; Louis has a wife who will look after him when he's older.

Louis did not fall for the "hey, handsome man" routine. He knew the pitfalls of marrying and settling in Thailand and proceeded cautiously and carefully. He understands the culture and how different attitudes prevail here.

23 March

The local authority come around a few times a year to spray against mosquitoes. It is a free service met out of central government funds. Important to keep windows closed and not breathe in the fumes oneself.

So long as water is moving, as with fountains, there is not such a problem. What needs to be avoided is keeping static water in rain storage butts. Frogs and some mosquitoe-eating fish can be useful in keeping mosquitoe numbers down in ponds. Remove excess vegetation. Wearing long sleeved clothes and long trousers, the lighter the colour the better, can help.

Mosquitoes hate wind so having a strong fan on when sitting outside at night is helpful. Spraying one's body with a repellant works for many people. Scented coils which you can light in the evening emit a smoke that mosquitoes dislike but which is pleasant to humans. Planting basil, lavender, citronella grass, and catnip have been known to have a positive effect. Sucking a garlic clove works for some. Giving your skin a coating of apple cider or lemon eucalyptus oil are old wives' remedies that may work.

24 March

"I don't have colleagues, I only have friends, Chaweewan declared. In a way, she is right. Thais use the word "friend" when they refer to a colleague. They have respect for older and more senior employees but it is interesting that they call them friends more often than we would in the West. It helps bonding and teamwork in the workplace. Quarrels and disagreements are easier to forget and overcome.

When Chaweewan got married five of the seven people she worked with in the office came to the wedding celebrations, including her manager. The two others had genuine excuses for not attending.

We saw at Seri's funeral, in *Thailand Take Two*, a group of a dozen or so of her friends from university days twenty years ago gather round the coffin and singing the university anthem. Two had taken time off work and travelled up from Bangkok.

Direct snubs are more difficult to give when there is a concept of everyone being friendly. The Thai will smile even when giving a rebuke. The "friendship" remains. As elsewhere in the world, the gossiping will start as soon as the person leaves the room.

25 March

Been round to *Khun* Yai's a few times this week. Around ten neighbours on most days, just staying for an hour or so, never the same people.

The monks have donated some blankets. They don't have money so can't buy gifts for *Khun* Yai. Instead they have given the family items they have received previously from members of the community. The money the monks get from people making merit partly goes towards the daily upkeep of the *wat*. Gifts they receive are re-circulated as described above. There have been questions raised and some action taken on *wats* such as Dhammakaya where misappropriation of donations has been uncovered.

Giving is reciprocated in Thailand. The monks will remind the lay people, at every opportunity, that they should give generously to the *wat*. They are returning the help and support that the temple gave them at funerals, weddings, ordinations, or when they were in difficulty. Good deeds from you will generate good deeds from others.

Giving is two-way. *Sam nak bun kun.* It would be rare to find oneself giving something to a neighbour and not getting something back at a later date.

The bank has reimbursed *Khun* Yai for the charred banknotes, the manager also giving her a personal donation from his own pocket.

The house was not insured; insurers are reluctant to cover teak houses and it's so expensive for most people. The bank may be able to arrange a mortgage but will insist on insurance cover I am sure. The community will continue to help.

26 March

Two hundred thousand baht has been raised so far to rebuild *Khun* Yai's house. Most has come from neighbours and other villagers who pop round during the day or early evening. There's a communal cooking pot with very spicy food on the stove in the garden all day long if people are a little hungry and a small donation box near the gate. The *pooyaibaan* had requested a donation from local government funds and the army sent some soldiers to demolish the rest of the house. The Royal Project provided house plans.

Pillars for the new house were delivered today, the construction firm giving a significant discount. A local farmer has leveled the land with his tractor. Now that the building can start, one of the elders in the village that officiates at funerals and house warmings arrived to perform a simple but moving ceremony on the land where the first pillar will be. He places a small tray of earth lined with banana leaves on the ground and sets several incense sticks in it. After lighting them, he prays for good luck in the building of the new home and those who will live there.

So many people turn up each day. They chat about everything under the sun and don't gloat on the misfortune. All will help at some stage during the build. *Khun* Yai's grand-daughter replaced the bandages over the burns on her legs while neighbours prepared some food. They were there to show support and they wanted to be together as a community rather than staying in their own homes. Strangers might have thought it was simply a garden party.

27 March

Part of the appeal of visiting foreign places is that one sees such opposite and varied lifestyles. No two countries are the same.

At a party in Sydney I was asked by the host, an Australian national who had lived and worked for many years in England, whether I felt the get-together was unlike those in the UK. I could not really put my finger on it; but yes, I had to say that it was different.

He asked me if anyone had asked what size house I had, what car I drove, what my job was. Nobody had asked me any of those questions. No one needed to know where I was in the hierarchy. It did not matter. The conversations were about when we were next going swimming in the pool, places we had visited with our hosts in Australia, and whether it was not time for yet another cold beer.

Social class has little relevance in Australia but is central to a Thai's thinking. Whether your wife has the same level job or education that you have does not matter in Australia. But she would not be accepted so easily into the Thai social circle with its rather strict class structure.

The car you drive and the clothes you wear matter to a Thai as it shows your position in society. They need signals like that in order to determine where you stand in the hierarchy and whether to *wai* you first. An Aussie could not care less.

28 March

Thais often ask your age so that they know whether you are higher in the "hierarchy" than they are. They'll ask your salary and other details about you too. They don't find that curiosity is in any way rude. As we have seen, Thais love gossiping about other people. It's fun, *sanuk*.

Westerners need some private time and space. That seems weird to a Thai. They will steal any opportunity to be with other people. In small villages and towns especially, you will find them chatting and passing the time of day together in small groups. Community is more important to them than it is to us. Walking along a street they will stop several times to stop and talk. Conversations can go on for a long time. If you are going to the market it may take some time to get there. If the market trader is a friend you'll obviously have many things to talk about, others in the queue behind you won't be shouting for you to hurry along

Few Thais live alone. Few go into a retirement home when they get old and unable to look after themselves. Family and community generally take on the responsibility.

29 March

In both the western and Thai military, it is the rank you salute, not the man.

I know a lieutenant colonel in the UK who now has command of soldiers who in the past were of higher rank than he was. The present difference in position is fully accepted. It is the uniform that defines the relative status and power. In Thailand particularly, the number of stripes on your sleeve and the amount of braid on your cap is important. It is there not only to impress but also to show rank, your position in the pecking order.

As well as in the police and the military, uniforms are worn by government workers, teachers, security guards, and the local village headman (*pooyaibaan*) on occasion. Most teachers wear scout uniform on Wednesdays.

How people dress shows and reinforces their position in society in relation to others. Every Thai knows where he and others stand. To some extent, he gets that clue from how people dress. The guy in an expensive suit will take precedence over others. You can see that in restaurants, the workplace, community functions, even at funerals and weddings.

30 March

In the West, we encourage children to be self-reliant as early as possible. We know they will eventually leave the nest and we want to prepare them for the big nasty world outside. We help and support them but we don't insist on their always being there with us. Thais support their offspring too but still need them close. After they leave home to marry or find a job some distance away, the children remember that support and help financially as much as they can. Their monthly salaries would be shared. They keep in regular contact. Strangely, there are foreigners living in closed communities here who are not aware of that and other customs.

Thai youngsters are not independent of their parents. They will seek advice from mum and dad, close family, and those in the community who are respected. At election time, they'll be guided by what they hear. If they're working on a construction site, they'll take heed of what an older worker tells them and copy how he works.

Western kids are more rebellious. They don't worry if they change their hairstyle knowing their parents may not approve. And in a sense their parents may be pleased they are beginning to think for themselves and do their own thing. Thai youngsters would be forever conscious of not hurting their parents' feelings (*greng jai.*) They would keep their thoughts to themselves; their foreign counterparts would be more open and not at all worried about being regarded as being too assertive.

Western parents foster independence in their children; for Thais, ensuring they are brought up with a strong sense of *nam jai* is more important.

31 March

Building is progressing on *Khun* Yai's house. The main columns have been erected. Some of the men are helping the local builders by fetching and carrying. The ladies are making sure nobody is going thirsty in the heat. Some are doing some light work whenever they can. All are offering advice to the builders, whether asked for or not. The builders smile.

When not helping, the neighbours are chatting amongst themselves and with the family. That is what is appreciated the most. Just being there for *Khun* Yai.

1 April

At first glance, it appears that Thai society demands subservience and conformity. A Thai will concur with and not argue with his elders and betters. He will obey and respect his parents and boss. It is not only or completely out of fear, it is a cultural response.

Even at university level, students are reluctant to challenge what a teacher says. The more confident may initiate a debate but if the lecturer indicates that he is right and the student is wrong, the matter ends there.

Thailand's class system and its strong regard for respect ensures there is compliance with these ideals and Thais will rarely vary from them. However, they have a strong sense of individual freedom that allows them to flout regulations if they consider they ate justified in doing so. If they don't think it's important, the *mai pen rai* attitude kicks in. Freedom to not do something if it does not matter. It's an enigma that a country that stresses conformity in its societal rules also allows individual freedom in certain circumstances. Although it's not easy to see how the two concepts can co-exist, it is clear by observation that they do.

It was probably a Thai who wrote the saying that rules are there to be broken.

One visible example is the non-wearing of safety helmets by motor cyclists. They don't want to do it. I've seen them pay the fine, put the helmet on, ride around the corner, and stop to put the helmet back in the front basket. I've seen them doing sharp U-turns to avoid the police check-points.

When Geng was killed in a motorcycle accident - he was not wearing a helmet - around thirty of his mates turned up to pay their respects at the funeral. Only two were wearing safety helmets. I seemed to be the only one who was surprised.

Individuals can and do ignore deadlines if a more essential need arises. The boss will sometimes tolerate minor lapses, sometimes not. Employees have ways of dealing with that without going against the usual rules of conformity.

Office staff, in one government office I know, are given a ten minute grace period on the official 8.30 start time. A red line is drawn under the last entry in the attendance book at that time. Worapawn and several others arrived at 8.25 one morning to find the red line had already been drawn. The boss's watch must have been wrong. They turned round and went home for the day. No arguments, no loss of face, no conflict with the boss. They made their point in the Thai way without breaking any of society's rules.

Political freedom is valued but "freedom to spit" as it is sometimes called (freedom to act as an individual in one's everyday life) always trumps it.

2 April

We've seen the influence of feudalism in Thailand. There is a hierarchy in parts of the body as well. The head, with a brain and thinking capacity, is at the top; the foot, being nearest the ground and in contact with the soil, is at the bottom.

Thais refrain from touching the head and ensure feet are not pointed towards monks, Buddha images, or indeed at other people. Shoes are not placed on furniture or at a high level. Thais will not walk under a washing line if it has undergarments hanging on it.

We visited a temple with Jenny, taking off our shoes before entering, and started chatting to a monk. The *bot* was the only building she could not enter. Women are not allowed in that most sacred area of the *wat* where the final part of the monks' ordination takes place. I showed her some photos of Thai *bots* later.

Jenny is a retired teacher and was chatting to a monk about education in temples. "As a fellow teacher, may I shake your hand," she asked. "As a monk, I cannot touch a woman," was the reply. Jenny made a deep and respectful *wai.* She had been careful to remember what she knew of the correct etiquette and kicked herself for forgetting that handshaking would be regarded as touching.

On leaving the temple she noticed that all the shoes had been turned round facing outwards as a convenience to those who had visited and making it easier to slip the shoes back on.

3 April

Until the middle of the twentieth century, rote learning was as commonplace in the UK as it is today in Thailand.

One advantage of rote learning in this country is that it trains the memory. Thais can recite word for word large chunks from books they have been told to study, which Westerners would have difficulty in doing.

The weakness is that it discourages thinking for oneself and having a questioning attitude of mind. Pupils rarely ask their teacher anything. Thai education is a rather passive process. Being critical or putting forward a point of view is not a common feature.

4 April

The roofers were on site at Tim's build today. Each tile was thrown up by hand to the worker on the roof. Amazingly, only two tiles were broken. These guys are experienced. The building firm that Tim is employing is unusual in that they use specialist tradesmen. Roofers work only on the roof, plumbers only on plumbing jobs, and carpenters only on their particular skill.

Most other building contractors have local labour where the workers can turn their hand to anything. That does not always result in the highest quality finish for the house.

The workers get around 300 baht a day, with the foreman earning around 500. They work six days a week and live on the plot, having made temporary accommodation in what will be the carport. Their children play on site but are kept away from any dangerous areas. Sometimes they help on some light jobs but not to any great extent.

5 April

"I've thrown it away. It has expired anyway," my father told the station ticket collector. I was a very young lad and on holiday with the rest of the family in Devon. My parents had bought a weekly rail rover ticket and we were able to visit so many places of interest over a very wide part of the county without restriction. Having the card had made our holiday. The best we ever had.

So why, I wondered, did Dad lie when he said he had thrown the ticket away at the end of the holiday. I was confused.

"It will be part of our holiday scrapbook, together with photographs and other souvenirs. It's part of our holiday experience, "he explained.

I had learnt the difference between a white lie and a deliberate harmful lie. The Thais too differentiate in this way. They lie to avoid losing face, to save you embarrassment, or to get out of doing something they do not want to do.

The workers repairing the fence posts (21 February) came up with several excuses (lies) why they couldn't come to finish the work: mum in hospital, problem with motorbike.

For them, telling the odd fib makes for a more comfortable lifestyle.

6 April

The dates of Thai holidays associated with Buddhism are partly determined by the full moon. Because the Buddha was born in India, those dates are decided by reference to the Indian calendar not the Thai.

Other annual holidays are given to observe a monarch's birth, death, or accession to the throne.

Most calendars and diaries show the dates. Current information is available on the internet or you can contact me.

7 April

Was having a drink with a friend when the dogs started barking. Looking out of the window, I saw a group of Thais sitting just inside my front gate. I walked over to them, more to satisfy my curiosity than anything else. Though I admit I could not understand what they could be doing squatting on my land (my wife's land, foreigners can't own land in Thailand.)

As I got nearer, I recognised *Khun* Faa and *Khun* Fon, my neighbours from the house opposite. They were using a torch to catch some *maleng*, insects that had made a nest in one of my trees. They had been attracted by the noise they were making and came over to gather some for their next meal!

No damage had been done, but a Westerner would think it odd that they just turned up without asking permission.

8 April

Faa brought over a small jar of fried *maleng*. They went down a treat spread on toast with my morning coffee.

9 April

Thais like having it both ways. It is linked, in my view, to their dislike of open conflict and disagreement and to their emphasis on not wanting to lose face. Lifestyle concepts that are difficult for Westerners to understand as they are at variance with typical western culture.

A story is told of a soldier asking the Buddha if it was wrong to fight and kill.
The Buddha asked if the soldier could resign. He said he could not.

"Then do your duty but do not hate your enemies."

In 1942 Japan invaded Thailand to give them access to British India. Prime Minister Phibun decided to cooperate rather than resist and declared war on the Allies. There was however a well formed resistance movement acting against the Japanese.

After the atomic bombs fell on Japan and it was realised that the fortune of war was changing, Phibun declared that the original declaration of war was unconstitutional and therefore void. A move that allowed Thailand to claim that as war had not been declared it did not need to surrender or make reparations.

Westerners find this switching of allegiances to suit present circumstances hard to follow, but it is a common Thai characteristic. Having said that, one can argue that some western nations did the same when they blocked war reparations due to the UK and other allies in respect of the deaths on the notorious Burma railroad. The quid pro quo was allowing troops to be stationed in Thailand during the Vietnam War and subsequently.

10 April

Big fuss on the internet forums today. An Aussie motor cyclist is in hospital and his girlfriend is dead following their road accident.

The incident was captured on CCTV and shows the Aussie tourist first turning to the left and then to the right before trying to ride into his hotel car park. A motorcyclist who was following tried to overtake and he hit both rider and pillion as they were making the turn. Witnesses say the Thai rider was following too closely and was speeding.

From the CCTV it appears there was fault on both sides. The Aussie, who may not have been used to the bike he had rented, was badly positioned for the turn. He had probably seen the hotel entrance only at the last moment. The following rider should have anticipated that cars and bikes in Thailand can and do make last minute manoeuvres without signaling. It happens all the time here. You need to look out for it and drive defensively.

It is claimed that the police were offered a bribe and the whole blame was transferred to the Aussie tourist, and that he was asked to sign a police report written in Thai agreeing he was at fault. He refused and the incident has hit the Australian media.

Normally, you have to take much of what you read on Thai internet forums with a pinch of salt. Posters misquote the facts or add snippets from their own imagination. Some will always see with rose tinted glasses the Thai point of view; others will be quick to blame the Thai and always be negative about Thailand. Balanced opinion goes by the board and flaming is the order of the day. However, this case is a little different. The CCTV evidence is clear and the foreign media reaction is unwelcome. There will be a damage limitation exercise put in place, a police officer has already been transferred, and an investigation promised.

The end result though will be that nothing will be done. Tomorrow it will be yesterday's news. Moreover, the pages reporting it in the tabloids will be used to wrap up your fish and chips. Same as in the West.

11 April

Seldom will Thais ask a direct question if they want something. Hints will start being made just before birthdays. If they disagree with what is being said in a discussion they will subtly suggest a solution later or obliquely mention something in passing at another time. Never direct.

They often make a joke about an issue rather than tackling the problem directly. Difficult to know sometimes whether it's a joke or whether they are trying to tell you something.

It's called *poot len, poot jing*. Telling a joke or being serious.

12 April

An article in today's papers claimed that although the richest Thai businessperson is not in the world's top 100 rich list, the wealth of the top forty people in the country is well in excess of £25 billion.

The striking feature is the gulf between the rich and the poor. The economic divide. A supervisor can earn over three times the wage of a worker. A manager, at least four times as much. Gross margin percentages are normally higher than in the West, particularly in the building and motor trade. Therefore, owner-managers can earn appreciably more as a daily rate than their counterparts in the West can.

Is this why petty cheating and corruption is regarded as socially acceptable, par for the course? A means for the ordinary guy to level the playing field of remuneration. Everyone has to live.

13 April

In 1888 the long-established date for New Year's Day in Thailand was changed from 13 April to 1 January, in line with most of the rest of the world. The Thais now celebrate both dates but the national holiday which starts on 13 April and lasts for three days is the more significant date for all Thais.

You will hear *sawatdee pee mai*, Happy New Year, more during this traditional holiday than on 1 January. If you hear it at all on that day. Thais will also greet you with the more formal *suksan wan pee mai* but usually on the first day only and to more senior people.
There are colourful, noisy, and happy processions through the streets, merit-making ceremonies at the *wats*, and especially the fun of splashing everyone with water. Look at the photos and videos that are on line. Groups of happy and excited Thais and *farangs* using hoses and buckets of water to throw over passers-by and onlookers. Trucks drive around with passengers in the back with water guns directed at anyone and everyone. Topping up the pistols is either from a barrel carried on board or at the many "filling stations" dotted around the area.

The tradition symbolises washing away everything bad that has happened in the past year. In the *wats* people will sprinkle water, fragrant from herbs, over you. The more high-spirited splashing and throwing, which is great fun, is reserved for the streets.

Most Thais go back to their birthplaces at Songkran to celebrate with their families. Such travel can contribute to the 100% increase in death rate on the roads over the Songkran period. Construction workers particularly may take an extended holiday in their home villages or indeed may not return to work.

Occasionally the fun can get a little out of hand. Motorcyclists can be subject to water from a high pressure hose which is potentially dangerous for riders, and the elderly or infants may be targeted. It does not happen a lot. The convention is that if people do not want to be splashed - they may be carrying a young child, for example - they indicate with a hand signal. It is usually respected, at least by Thais.

Generally it's a happy time, and everyone can take advantage of the cool water being splashed around in the hottest month of the Thai year.

14 April

In Thailand, keeping warm is not the problem. Keeping cool is. Fans are in every home; middle class Thais may have air conditioners. The Thais actually use fans more than anything else. Air conditioners may just be switched on in the bedrooms during the hot season. Thais have acclimatised to the weather.

William spends 7000 baht a month and has his air conditioning on 24 hours a day throughout the house whether rooms are occupied or not. His wife turns them off when he's out of the building.

Constantly using the system results in your not being able to do without it. And when it's really hot and you need it, it ceases to be a real benefit.

15 April

Never explain, never complain. Worapawn and all her friends in the office had decided to go on a coach trip to the White Temple near Chiangrai next week. Worapawn was organising the visit with the coach company.

Being Thai, she knew she would get only a vague answer from the coach operator about departure times and pick up points. Thais won't be specific because it could upset, annoy, or be inconvenient to any one individual. The conversation can go like this:

"The coach will arrive at about 7 o'clock outside the office main entrance."
    "The gate may be locked and I won't be able to park my car."
"No problem, the coach can pick you up outside your home. It can make a detour."
    "7 o'clock is a little early."
"No problem. The coach will wait for everyone."

It may take half an hour beating about the bush to answer everybody's concerns with much to-ing and fro-ing to make sure nobody feels they're being awkward by speaking up.

It can be amusing for us Westerners to watch how Thais handle various situations. But to get the full benefit of visiting or living in Thailand it is best to do as much observing as possible.

The cultures are different. Thais are usually vague about timings. And want to avoid argument.

16 April

Pistols at dawn. Well, not actually at dawn. And there were no pistols. But the three men were wielding machetes.

My neighbour, Fon, came over to tell me there were some men in my fruit orchard, the other side of the drainage canal, the *klong*.

The dogs followed me, which scared the two guys standing on the ground. The third man was crouching on the wall.

Tam arai na, I called out, (what are you doing?) I did not use the polite ending particle of *krap*. It was not appropriate and no Thai would have done so.

As I got nearer, I recognised one of the men as the foreman of the neighbouring factory. The men were cutting down some trees that were overhanging the boundary between the factory and my orchard. Presumably, they'd been asked to do so by the factory owner but nobody had told me and they had not come over to ask if they could go on my land. Fon had been right to warn me that there were people with machetes in the orchard. She had no way of knowing who they were or what they were up to.

People do go onto your property in Thailand if they see no harm in it. *Khun* Fon had done that herself some days back (7 April) when foraging for insects.

I had no problem with what they were doing and told them they could put the soft spoil on my compost heap, just taking away the hard wood debris.

The tone changed. I was using the particle *krap,* they were calling me *pee* (elder.)

It has always amused me that two of the most polite words in Thai are unfortunately pronounced *krap* and *pee*.

17 April

There are no dukes, earls, barons, knights or dames in Thailand. The King holds the only full hereditary title.

The titles of descendants of the monarch are limited by time, they expire after the fifth generation. Technically, they then revert to common rank. In practice they still retain some kudos. Surnames beginning with *na* indicate royal or high class heritage.

These are the main titles that are used and which you may come across.

His/her Royal Highness: immediate living member of the royal family
Somdej Phra Chao: child of king by royal mother
Phra Ong Chao: grandchild of king in line of succession
Mom Chao: grandchild of king not in line of succession
Mom Rajavong: great grandchild of king not in line of succession
Mom Luang: great great grandchild of king not in line of succession

18 April

Public services are generally run by central or local government. Mobile companies are mainly in the private sector.

Water companies, electricity utilities, most airports, seaports, and some petrol distribution are state-controlled.

The prices of water and electricity supplies and the level of funding of some capital projects are therefore not decided by boards of directors.

Not all banks are private. There is a government bank as well as a military bank.

Some $350 billion are tied up in state assets.

19 April

The Wongpaet family has started building their new home, having cleared the site where their old house had stood. It was 100 days ago today that her son had been murdered in the downstairs room while she had been sleeping upstairs.

Nothing had come of the police investigations. She and her remaining son had been staying with family nearby, not wanting to stay in her former home.

By tradition, the *tamboon roi wan* ceremony takes place 100 days after the community a death when holy (lustral) water is sprinkled on the floor of the house to honour the dead, but this family did not follow this custom. The house had already been abandoned and the circumstances of the death were still too vivid in the family's memory.

The new house is not being built on the existing foundations of the old house. That would be bad luck. But it will be of the same teak wood design. It should be finished in less than two months.

20 April

All Thais must, at all times, carry ID cards once they reach 15 years old. They can be examined on card readers and contain full details of a person's status: age, date of birth, whether married, place of birth, etc.

Banks, other than your own branch, will record the ID number for cash withdrawals.

Chaweewan showed me her new ID card which now has *Nang* and not *Nangsao* as her title, indicating she is now legally married under Thai law. I went to her wedding reception six months ago. She said she'd been too busy to actually register at the district office.

A great number of couples decide to have a Buddhist wedding and it seems relatively unimportant to make the wedding legal. The monks arrive at the home of the bride's parents at around seven in the morning, conduct a ceremony of blessing, and receive cash gifts in envelopes as a show of merit from the couple. The reception, which the guests attend, starts later in the afternoon and the monks are not present.

Village elders and not monks conduct some weddings. The exact date of the wedding is decided by the monks or elders and not by the family or couple. Some dates are more auspicious than others.

A *tabian baan* is a book which records one's address and is required for them to enroll at school or university, to vote in an election, to obtain a passport, to qualify for a driver's licence. Hospitals will need to see it when you are admitted, as well as an ID card.

Generally, nationality in Thailand is determined by the father's nationality. If a child has a Thai father or mother then it has Thai citizenship. This is important for children of mixed parentage, *look kreungs*. There are complex rules about changing the nationality of a *look kreung*.

21 April

There is little stigma attached to transgender women, lady-boys, in Thailand. Their parents may not like their son changing gender but he will not be cast out and the community will not ostracise him.

The *katoey*, as they are called in Thai, are employed alongside men in many industries. Many work in restaurants and fashion shops. They are accepted by banks and other businesses and hold positions in government offices. A large number work in nightclubs and bars and also directly in the sex trade. What is more, regular beauty contests are held to select the most beautiful *katoey*.

Some educational institutions will not employ them where they could come into contact with children while others are relaxed about it.

The lady-boys often have breast transplants, regular hormone therapy, and operations to reduce the size of the Adam's apple to make them look more like women than men. Cosmetic surgery is inexpensive and popular in Thailand.

A lady boy's Thai ID card will still show the gender as male and the authorities will treat her as a male. Hospitals may allow a *katoey* in a female ward, prisons will place in a male cell. When they speak lady-boys use the polite particle *ka,* men would use *kap* or *krap*.

A *katoey* was posing for photographs today at the local market. He, or she (?), was dressed as a Red Indian in full headdress and costume. Jokingly, I said, *law mark mark* (very handsome.) He accepted it in good humour as did the Thai crowd. *Law* is only used for handsome men; *suay* is the correct word for pretty or beautiful and applies only to women. I had not intended my joke to be sarcastic.

22 April

Conscription is obligatory for all Thai males when they reach 21. They serve for 2 years. It is also a popular profession for both men and women, Thailand does not rely on the draft to run the armed forces.

After a Thai answers the call to go to the enlistment office, and after the physical examination, he puts his hand in a box and draws out a card. If the card he picks is red he is allowed to go home and the enlistment is cancelled. If it is black, he is told where to report for duty.

Thais love the concept of a lottery.

23 April

I was stationary in traffic when a motorcyclist tried to squeeze past between my car and an old pick-up truck. He did not succeed. He scraped the paintwork along one side of my car, broke the wing mirror, and dented the rear end of the truck.

Where are the police when you want them?

I was in luck. An officer on point duty had seen what happened and told all three parties to go to the police station. Luckier still, or so I thought, the police station was only 50 yards away down a nearby *soi*.

The motorcyclist gave the truck driver 200 baht and he seemed happy with that. His truck was pretty ancient and battered anyway and he probably thought making a claim would be a waste of time. He drove off once he had the cash.

At the police station the motor-cyclist admitted blame. He could do little else. All the necessary documents were photocopied, reports were completed in triplicate, and we all went on our way after about an hour.

After a month, I went to the station to ask about progress.
"We'll send someone round to his house."
Another month went by. "He's waiting to be paid at the end of the week then he'll pay you."
Later. "He's left the country and is in Myanmar."

I should have got some money out of him as the truck driver did and not involve the police. It was a case of "can't pay, won't pay." Whether he paid the police to pursue no further, I know not.

24 April

The accepted and correct way to tip in Thailand in a restaurant, a hairdresser's shop, or at any other service establishment, is to round up, by a few baht, the bill. Give some loose change, say thank you, and smile. That is what the Thais do. The thanks and the smile are appreciated. Doing things the Thai way will make your stay here more comfortable.

A server can be embarrassed by over-tipping and it does not gain you any extra respect.

In front of foreigners or to impress social superiors, some Thais will make a show of giving a tip higher than they would normally give. But there are few Thais in that category.

In the more touristy areas, a gratuity is added to the bill and even then you may be encouraged to add a little extra. That is getting common in many parts of the world, even in China where tipping is discouraged almost to the point of being forbidden. They want only what they have legitimately earned

A former American president, Ronald Reagan, during a walk about in a Chinese village, bought some low cost souvenirs and paid with a high denomination note. He told the shopkeeper to keep the change. She insisted on not keeping the money, probably feeling a little insulted and patronised. She had charged a fair price and that was all she wanted. She followed him down the street and pressed the coins she owed him into his hands.

Reagan had been well aware of the local customs on tipping, but felt there was little he could do as he had had no loose change. Perhaps he could have bought further gifts to make up the full amount. But you don't think of solutions like that in the heat of the moment.

In rural Thailand, you will find similar attitudes among the locals. Best to do things their way. You may find that you will fit in more easily if you do.

25 April

Nonglak's *farang* friend took the shoes back to the shop twice. First the buckles broke then a crack appeared in the heel. The seller, smiling, agreed to change them again or he could choose another pair. But he could not have his money back.

It was the smiling that irritated him.

"It's not a smiling matter, is it?" he asked. Actually it was. Thais smile to hide embarrassment and to avoid argument and conflict. The assistant had done all she could by offering to replace, and doing so with a smile.

There is more than one Thai smile.

26 April

Ajarn Weelai has become a bit of an agony aunt for expats with relationship problems with their Thai partners. Fluent in English and French, she tries to help wherever she can. She has a knack for getting both sides to try to see each other's point of view and to seek out compromises. Unlike most Thais, she is aware of the big cultural differences that can cause difficulties between couples.

Her favourite saying is that when you marry a Thai you marry the family. A Thai husband would think nothing of regularly supporting his mother-in-law or helping out with loan payments for his wife's unemployed brother.

As *farangs*, we are more inclined to think it is their responsibility and should do more to help themselves. An occasional hand-out is one thing, regular payments are another.

Westerners value independence; Thais have a strong sense of *nam jai.* Being generous and assisting whenever possible comes first to them.

We pay high taxes in the West and rely on social services and the benefits they provide out of those very taxes. Thailand has no such comparable social security. Family, friends, and community provide any help that is needed.

27 April

I can count on the fingers of one hand the number of times I have forgotten to fasten my seatbelt. Even if it was not a legal requirement in Thailand, I would "clunk, click, every trip" as I would if I was driving in my home country.

But I had stopped to ask directions, and I only had to drive round a bend for 100 metres and I would be where I wanted to be. I should have remembered it was getting towards the end of the month and the police were working on making up their target quotas for driving infringements.

And as I rounded the corner, there they were. Ready to swoop. I quickly pulled on my seatbelt. One of the officers signaled for me to pull in. I lowered the window and, as is usual in Thailand, he saluted smartly. He politely asked to see my licence, asked what country I came from, and started talking about Arsenal football club. All very pleasant and friendly. This was obviously just a routine licence check. I was in luck. He was obviously a decent copper.

"I'm going to have to give you a ticket. I saw you put your seatbelt on after you came round the corner."

He still had my licence and the procedure would have been for me to go to the police station, pay the fine, and retrieve the licence. I would have to have found the station first and then wait for ages while the paper work was completed.

I decided on the Thai approach. "Pom jai ngern hai khun dio nee. Taorai na kap. (Can I pay you now? How much?)"

My wallet was 400 baht lighter but I was not given a ticket. I had my licence back. He halted the traffic to allow me to pull out, gave me an even smarter salute than before, and I was on my way.

Collecting minor fines in this way is common practice. The money is shared out later at the station. It's regarded as a perk of the job and really forms part of officers' salaries. It rewards individual officers while cracking down on motoring offences. A win-win solution.

I will be more careful at the end of May.

28 April

You don't get many bad meals in Thailand. Some restaurants will raise the price for *farangs*; some have two menus, one in English and one in Thai. The prices are not always the same. The food will be of the same high quality.

Roadside stalls and eateries serve fresh and tasty food and are extremely good value. Restaurants have been known to resource meals from them and serve them up to their customers. The only difference being the bone china plate and the posh cutlery.

But in catering mistakes can occur.

Thais will comment if food is off - although it rarely is - and it will be put right. They won't make a fuss or shout loudly or get angry. Like the Thais, the continentals have a passion for food and chefs and customers take serving quality meals seriously. Some foreigners are not so fussy and tend not to complain. The occasional rogue food vendor may realise this and try to pass off food that is stale or of poor quality.

Yesterday, it happened to me. The meat was okay but the rice was not fresh. It was cold and hard. I could not eat it.

The waitress smiled, as expected, but didn't suggest replacing the rice. Eventually, she showed me the rice cooking pot in the kitchen. The rice was warm and had a fresh aroma. I tasted a small spoonful. It was not at all like the rice I had been served. She said it was exactly same but that mine was cold because I was sitting under a fan!

Thais have an annoying habit of justifying mistakes with the most brazen lies. It irritates though I have got used to it. I had a meal when I was back home.

29 April

On 15 January the bulldozers had arrived at Sengdeuan's to clear away the vegetable and fruit garden that the abbot had said was on *wat* land. Whether it was or not was never clarified.

Today the builders have roped off a section around the main temple buildings which presumably they will lay to lawn. It will be much better than leaving the land covered in weed and debris. They have left the space between Sengdeuan's house and the roped off area as a right of way to an adjacent *soi*. So it appears the temple has either conceded it's not their property or have decided the locals can use it anyway.

Nobody will dare ask.

A telephone kiosk is standing in the area where the lawn will be. I wonder if the telephone company will move it or whether the monks will accept that the phone is on public land and adjust the perimeter accordingly?

30 April

It dropped out of fashion in the late 1960s but "sitting alongside Nelly" was an effective one-to-one training method used to teach both semi-skilled and office workers the rudiments of a job, particularly in the UK. Technical skills on the factory bench were learnt by watching and then copying from the person to who you were assigned. Would-be chartered accountants started their careers as articled clerks by making the tea and counting the petty cash.

On the job training gradually gave way to organised training schemes off site in technical colleges and in the practice of companies sending trainees on crash courses and seminars often specifically related to that particular organisation.

However, sitting alongside "Somchai" is still common in Thailand. There are advantages and disadvantages. The main problem with copying from another person is that you pick up that employee's mistakes. And when you yourself are training an apprentice you pass on that same inaccurate knowledge.

Take a look at electrical wiring in Thailand. Connections are seldom strong and sturdy. Much work in the construction industry is of low standard both because of the training method and the prevalence of a *mai pen rai*, that's good enough, attitude.

1 May

International Workers' Day, Labour Day, is a national holiday in Thailand and observed by most companies in the private sector. Government employees have to work.

2 May

Well-off Thais who have servants don't eat with them. That applies whether they are members of the upper classes or people who consider themselves of the "hi-so" set. It is normal practice, accords with the hierarchy rules, and is accepted by the maids, gardeners, and their families who live "below stairs," as we would say in the West.

Expat families can take a more liberal view and want to show they don't believe in segregation and differentials. "All men are created equal" is an admirable western doctrine but is not accepted by Thais. They know their place in this life, though may desire (by doing good deeds) for a better position in the next.

When their maid told John that her aunt and family were visiting from Isaan, John's wife invited them to dine with them. It embarrassed the maid and her relatives. Pamela's gesture was certainly well intended but not appropriate in Thai culture.

Making an offer of some food that they could eat together in the garden or their room would have been better and correct form. Pamela was trying to turn a cultural trait that the Thais have always accepted on its head.

Attempting to change a people's culture, irrespective of your thinking it's good or bad, is not something that should be on an expat's agenda when living in Thailand.

3 May

I learn something almost every day about Thai lifestyle. Keeping everyone informed through regular messages (as a rule daily) on the village loudspeaker system was, I thought, a commendable means of ensuring all the locals knew what was going on and were kept up to date on neighbourhood events.

Today I saw that it was not without its flaws.

Khun Lit, who used to garden and do odd-jobs in the village, died on Tuesday and was cremated two days ago. No one in our hamlet knew he had passed away, so could not attend the rites or the cremation. I had spoken with his sister last week and was told he was still poorly.

Because *Khun* Lit lived just outside the area covered by our loudspeaker system, his death would have been reported by his own *pooyaibaan* on that village's speaker network. In close communities boundaries are very rigid. His house was only ten yards outside our hamlet. But that was enough for the announcement not to be made here.

4 May

Kawp krua gawn; peuan gawn. Family first; friends first. Had to get some passport photos taken today. Took my queue ticket and sat down to wait, and wait, and wait.

Goong, one of my neighbours, was the cashier on duty and when she saw me, she called me over to her colleague on the photo booth. Four minutes later and everything was finished.

I do not like this pulling of rank that goes on so much in Thailand; but there was little I could do. Would have been insulting to refuse the fast tracking. Goong would have lost face in front of her colleagues.

The main point, however, is that no one minded; it was seen as quite normal and acceptable for family and friends not to have to wait in line.

It has not happened recently, but it took some getting used to when someone walked into the bank and got escorted straight to the next available cashier while everyone else waited in line. It does not bother me anymore. It is only a few minutes and everyone, Thais anyway, allow it to happen. It is usually better and wiser to go along with the popular culture.

Go with the flow.

5 May

Divorce in Thailand is commoner now than it was a decade or so ago but some stigma still remains. If the divorce is by mutual consent, it can take around one hour at the local district office. Thailand is a community property jurisdiction which means that all property acquired during marriage is spilt evenly. Even in non-contested cases, though, money usually changes hands before a party will agree to a divorce. Assets abroad are included in the definition of common property which can make a divorce between a Thai and a *farang* more complicated.

When the couple cannot come to an agreement, they have to go to court and the proceedings will be lengthy and costly. Grounds for divorce include a spouse having gone missing or being separated from his partner for more than 3 years.

Having a *mia noi*, a minor wife or what Westerners would call a mistress, is socially acceptable in Thailand so long as discretion is followed. For that reason, many wives accept the situation with an almost *mai pen rai* attitude. So long as the wife is looked after as before, and she and her husband still have their social circle and friends, she may see no reason to sue for divorce.

A similar attitude applied in the upper classes of Victorian England.

6 May

The famous white temple of *Wat Rongkhun* was severely damaged in today's earthquake in Chiangrai province. The quake, which measured 6.3 on the Richter scale, destroyed the top of a statue of the Buddha as well as many other parts of the *wat*. The devastation is greater than the monks first thought and the *wat*, one of Thailand's top tourist attractions, will be closed for the foreseeable future.

Many homes had their windows and walls knocked out, many were totally destroyed, and roads around the epicentre caved in. The tremors were felt as far away as Bangkok, a distance of 800 kilometers.

Sitting in a room and feeling the house shake from side to side and seemingly be lifted up in the air and put down again is a strange experience. Thankfully, away from the centre, structural damage is not so great: perhaps a few ornaments fall off shelves or some minor cracks appear on walls.

If driving a car, the sensation can be likened to being pushed from behind by another vehicle or being swayed by a heavy wind. It's quite unnerving.

7 May

There is a different language when you speak to royalty or talk or write about royalty in Thailand. It is called *parsa rachasap* or royal language.

Queen Victoria used a form of royal language when she said, "We are not amused," using the royal "we." It is no longer used in England other than in official declarations by the monarch. Contrary to popular belief, it is not a language spoken by the Thai king or the royal family, whether they are speaking to the people or amongst themselves.

Parsa rachasap is a vocabulary that the people use when speaking of the royals. Although it is taught in schools to a limited extent, most Thais are unfamiliar with it. A few royal words, such as those for hand and face are probably well known: *phra hat, phra phak,* respectively. But generally it is not well understood. Hospital announcements about a member of the royal family have to be translated into Thai for ordinary people to understand the *parsa rachasap* words.

But every Thai would know *Sawng Phra Ja Rern,* Long live the King, even though that is not the way it would be written in ordinary Thai.

If I were writing this in Thai, I would have to use the royal language when referring to the royal family.

8 May

Let's have a party. There are 100 *satang* to one baht, but there are no one *satang* coins. Small shopkeepers usually price in whole baht. Even 75 *satang* is only worth just over one British penny or a little under two American cents. As there are only 25 and 50-satang coins, it is not worth their while to price any differently.

But banks, filling stations, and utility companies calculate their charge to the nearest *satang*. If your electricity bill is 700.81 baht and you offer 701 baht, you will be given 25-satang change. The company round in your favour, losing 6 *satang* on the transaction. No big deal for you but significant for the company as change is rounded up for each customer.

When you fill your car up with fuel, you'll be let off a few *satang* in the same way.

However, banks are banks. They round to their advantage, sometimes to the nearest whole baht. Again, no big deal, until you work out how many transactions involving rounding they handle each month. Number of customers, number of bank tellers, number of bank branches. I'll let you do the maths. Their tills can never balance at the end of each day.

But I'm not complaining. My branch manager, Adoon, invited me to their monthly staff party last night. I always wondered where all the *satangs* went.

I don't know of any other country that rounds currency in two different ways like this. On the other hand, I don't know of any bank that invites a customer to a party. Amazing Thailand.

9 May

Today many Thais are watching the Royal Ploughing Ceremony in Bangkok on their TV sets. Those that are able to do so have travelled to Bangkok to witness the event and join in the happy atmosphere. Crowds have already gathered around the ritual site in Sanam Luang in the centre of Bangkok.

Until he was ill, King Bhumibol presided over the event every year and his people cheered him as he arrived at the ceremony. Seeing their king was probably as important to them as witnessing the actual event in all its colour and splendour.

The day starts with a blessing at the *wat* of the seeds to be planted and the implements to be used. Four unmarried women, the Celestial Maidens, follow ploughs drawn by a pair of bullocks in the traditional fashion. The women are actually employees of Thailand's Ministry of Agriculture and are chosen to help the Lord of the Harvest scatter the rice seed around the ceremonial site.

Some of the seed is gathered up for re-planting in the royal gardens in readiness for next year's crop, the rest is collected by the crowds who believe it will bring them a good harvest when planted in their own fields.

10 May

Having an argument can clear the air in the West but it is not a good technique in this country. Thais will think it is a character weakness if you argue and raise your voice.

They prefer to remain silent and not engage in a dispute. They may well walk away and comment later but in a calmer and less direct way. They won't refer to the argument but will probably hint at a solution. They are more concerned not to lose face than to bring things out into the open. They believe not arguing is being polite and respecting your feelings (*greng jai*). We think it shows weakness to not follow through in a quarrel.

11 May

Thais like the ceremony and superstition of religions. There is a large Japanese temple complex on the outskirts of Bangkok which, while having a statue of the Buddha to which they pay respect, attracts many devotees. Before the sermon starts, priests in white robes file in procession carrying urns containing cash gifts. The high priest places them on an altar-like structure.

Each member of the congregation, sitting in rows, then stretches out a hand towards the back of another member and, with the palm in a vertical position, transfers "power" to that individual. That person later turns round and performs the same service on the original giver.

No one I spoke to seemed to really understand the creed of that particular sect but they thought they were benefiting from the experience. They appeared drawn in by the pomp and ceremony. Buddhism is a tolerant religion and Thais see no difficult in practicing what we would consider animist rites alongside it.

Buddhists value the concept of karma, believing that your deeds in a previous life have resulted in your present circumstances. They accept, therefore, that fate plays a part in their lives. Suvanna Sata-anand put it in other words, "external powers and supernatural forces" are beyond our control.

Because the majority of Thais believe they have been reincarnated, they revere their ancestors. You will see this symbolically when they *wai* and pray in front of a spirit house (*san phra bhumi*) in their home or garden. The spirit house is modeled on a Thai temple with its ornate sloping roofs. It stands on a pedestal is usually about one foot in height. Some are much larger. Food and drink is placed in front of this structure every morning, always before eleven o'clock.

A tradition, which is rarer nowadays, is that when a guest arrives to stay in a Thai home, he first asks for permission from the spirits. He thanks them the next morning when he leaves. You may see this for yourself in remoter villages. Hotels, restaurants, and even banks, will have a spirit house in the foyer though you will not be expected to seek the spirits approval before entering the establishment!

Looking for good luck and a faith in superstitions sits comfortably alongside Buddhism.

"Coup-plotters still consult fortune-tellers for the most opportune time for their actions. The same goes for investors planning big projects, couples contemplating marriage, parents-to-be facing a Caesarian birth, wives hoping to see off mistresses, mistresses hoping to confound wives." (Sanitsuda.)

Spirits also live in trees which is why you will see saffron coloured bands around their trunks. Drivers will *wai* them as they pass in the same way they *wai* when a shrine has been erected at an accident black spot where many have died.

Old spirit houses are hardly ever destroyed. They are left with others outside the *wats*. Ceremonies take place whenever a spirit house is moved from one location to another or when it is replaced. Chamnaan moved his *san phra bhumi* to clean under it and position it nearer the wall. That necessitated a rite lasting a half hour.

12 May

In Thailand, when a foreigner is able to say hello, excuse me, and thank you in Thai, he is immediately elevated to the status of *geng* (clever) for his language proficiency.

Thais appreciate your efforts and it is a sensible and reasonable way to integrate into society. This is not just showing how you are accepted in the community but also is a good example of the Thai use of politeness and respect. And in any event, Thais love the giving and receiving of flattery.

13 May

"I must apologise for my countrymen, Matt." The site manager was genuinely sincere and apologetic that problems had occurred in the building of the new house. He did not accept the *mai pen rai* attitude of the workmen or that quality control had passed some of the work which had not been done properly.

There were no wires leading into an electric power point that had been positioned in the wall. That was not carelessness or forgetfulness, it was not an example of *mai pen rai*. It was avoiding doing the job properly and hoping to get away with it.

The plans had called for a one metre hole to be dug to provide a concrete foundation for a small water feature. I watched them go down only ten centimetres. They wouldn't follow the plan. They tried to prove they had excavated to one metre by drilling down into the hole with an electric drill. When the drill was removed they proudly showed that the drill bit was covered in concrete dust. On withdrawing the drill from the hole, it would have passed through the top ten centimetres. So of course, it was bound to be covered in flakes of concrete.

I suggested they dug down the full one metre so that it could be shown that the concrete was not 1 metre thick. Ah no, they could not do that. They might cut into an electric cable. They had had no qualms about using an electric drill earlier!

They agreed to be paid slightly less than they demanded and I cancelled the rest of the contract. Sometimes Thais can make up plausible stories which are sometimes not that easy to see through. Sometimes they are too ridiculous for words. Many expats get frustrated by this attitude of some Thai workers. It is as if they are just playing a game with a foreigner. Thai owners watch their builders very carefully and make sure they don't cut corners.

Possibly the best example of this Thai characteristic was an incident relating to Prime Minister Somchai. He was Prime Minister for just under 3 months and dismissed from his position on the technicality of hosting a cooking show while in office. In reality, as every Thai knew but were unable to comment, he had upset some political factions. Cooking was not the issue.

14 May

Apart from in the very major cities, you don't find many police on duty at night. There is an emergency number to contact them but response time is not that rapid. Rain can be heavy in Thailand. I passed an "abandoned" check-point today with the officers sheltering from the storm.

There are claims on the internet forums of police corruption particularly in Phuket and Pattaya. Small bribes are commonplace in Thailand. In some ways, these are regarded as perks of the job and additions to the very low salaries paid. Officers have to provide their own revolvers though they have access to heavier armament when required.

Tourist police, recruited from the *farang* population, work closely with regular officers in areas where there are many foreign visitors. They do not carry guns and have limited powers of arrest but they are able to sort out the minor problems that can occur when tourists are unaware of local laws and customs. Whether some volunteers join for the macho image or to serve the public is debatable.

There is talk now of making the police service responsible to parliament under a minister of state with guarantees of its independence from political power. Despite the authority's efforts to change the image, Thais tend to distrust police and keep their distance.

15 May

As Louis said today, all nationalities are different. He sees a wide variety of differences between people of other countries. He thinks the way of life here can be poles apart from those of France.

If we accept that the Brits, Germans, and Americans all have different worldviews and attitudes from the French then we should expect even greater differences when we observe the cultures and customs of Thailand and other countries of the Far East.

He made the observation that we would not bat an eyelid if we saw Martians living and thinking in ways unlike ours. We would acknowledge that people of a different planet may not be like us and we would not be surprised by what we see. Some foreigners should perhaps be a little more understanding of Thais and appreciate they live in a very different eastern culture.

His comparison with Mars was amusing but, when you consider it, he has a valid point.

16 May

Fon used the expression "American share" today. I had not heard that before. She was referring to the custom many foreigners have of paying individually for meals and other costs such as movie tickets. "Going Dutch" is how some Westerners would call this idea of paying one's own bill. Among Thais of the same age or rank of course each pays his or her way.

More usually, in Thailand, the oldest, richest, or more senior person would pay. Because of their perception of foreign wealth, that often means any *farang* present pays. Thais find it extraordinary that *farangs* don't adopt the Thai convention.

Not all Thais appreciate that we were brought up in a different society where different "rules" and traditions apply. The people of Thailand are conscious of their class structure and to allow a junior person to pay would result in both the giver and the receiver losing face and feeling uncomfortable. There would be a loss of respect too. The junior party would reciprocate later by helping or returning the kindness in a different way.

At table, the youngest would serve food to the older or more senior members and ensure water and drinks glasses are replenished. In the workplace, they would express their gratitude by assisting the boss whenever possible. They may not like their superior, they may disagree with his decisions, but that does not stop them exhibiting *nam jai* (caring) to him as he does to them.

17 May

Dressed in old jeans, John was being shown round a new house they were thinking of buying on an up-market housing project. He was with his latest Thai girlfriend who was wearing a very short skirt.

Clothes and how you present yourself are important to Thais. The salesman thought these poorly clad people were time wasters and he was only going through the motions of trying to make a sale. They had arrived in a *tuk tuk* and he was keen that, as soon as possible, they ordered another to take them back to wherever they had come from.

But it was not a *tuk tuk* that arrived, it was a top of the range brand new Mercedes. John had arranged for it to be serviced and cleaned and for the service centre driver to bring it round to the project to collect him and his girlfriend.

Not being dressed as the salesman expected had meant a lost sale. He was kicking himself. Not literally, he did what all Thais do and smile. Too much *mai pen rai* and not wanting to lose face in his make up to try to retrieve the sale.

If they have money or position, Thais will dress accordingly to show it. *Farangs* don't always parade their wealth for all to see.

18 May

Ayers Rock has always been in Australia. Been there for millions and millions of years. Surely, it does not matter who owns it. Why fight and quarrel over it? The aborigines can't see the logic of arguing. It belongs to everyone. The Thais would appreciate that sentiment. To them nature is there for everyone to enjoy.

Thais look at land ownership differently from Westerners. Spare land next to a road, railway line, or next to a *wat* is often cultivated by the locals. No harm is caused and it benefits everyone.

Earlier, we saw Faa and family coming into my garden unannounced to gather insects (7 April), and workers going on another person's land to trim the overhanging branches of a tree. Thais do not look at land ownership the way we do in the West.

With very few exceptions, all land in Thailand must be owned by, or in the name of, a Thai. Complex legal schemes to circumvent the legislation rarely work in practice – whatever the lawyers lead you to believe. Land in Thailand is for the Thais.

19 May

An interesting exchange that has been reported elsewhere. A good example of Thai humour and its limitations.

Colonel Jaran: What are you doing, soldier?

Bancha: Breaking eggs so that I can make omelettes for the men, sir.

Colonel Jaran: I realise that, soldier. Even so, you are breaking them two at a time.

Bancha: That's quicker, sir.

Colonel Jaran: What if one of them is bad?

Bancha: A bad egg, sir? In the Thai army, sir?

An amusing anecdote but an unusual one. As much as they love making jokes, Thais would not normally say anything like that to a superior. They are far too conscious of a person's position and any possible loss of face or respect.

But, as we see when we meet Bancha later, after he leaves the army and returns to the building trade, he can be a rather untypical Thai.

20 May

What I notice most about the Thais is that they smile a lot. It's the impression everyone gets when they first come here.

They don't talk loudly and detest aggressive language and behaviour. Quarrels and disagreements are anathema to the Thais. They have a laid-back hassle free lifestyle (*mai pen rai*) and come across as having a very caring and helpful attitude.

Family and community is important to them and they will seize any opportunity to be with other people.

The other side of Thailand, which is a bit of an enigma, is the corruption and violence that is endemic in the culture. Corruption is seen as normal, as part of one's salary and part of everyday commercial life. It is changing but changing slowly. Violence can stem from a distrust of biased law enforcement. Disputes are usually handled locally.

At times, Thailand is a perfect paradise on earth, at others; it can be a dangerous den of deception, dishonesty, and deviousness.

Thais dislike criticism of themselves and their country and are patriotic to the point of xenophobia. I always try to avoid saying or doing anything that makes them feel they are losing face. It is not easy to be direct, firm, fair, and tactful at the same time. Praise should be laid on with a shovel when it is necessary, as indeed the Thais do. That helps.

21 May

The licencing laws forbid the sale of alcohol at certain times of the day in Thailand. Supermarkets and some restaurants enforce the rules strictly. But smaller, family owned, *mama and papa* shops will generally oblige.

One can always stock up in advance and a little known rule allows supermarkets to sell drinks if they are in large cases.

During local and national elections, and on holidays like *Songkran*, alcohol sales are banned as these events can encourage too much drinking.

Thailand is not the only country to do this. At election time in Greece, drinking is prohibited. But a waiter in a taverna will serve you wine with your meal if you ask nicely. The wine will come in a teapot and you drink from a cup. Tastes the same.

22 May

Two days ago, martial law was declared and today General Prayuth announced a coup. He is acting prime minister and the army has taken over the government. There is a curfew from 10pm to 4am but there has been no violence. Groups of more than five people are prohibited from gathering in public. When the coup was first announced, all radio and TV programs were taken off the air and the stations were manned by the military. Regular announcements are being made to advise people to stay calm and refrain from making any critical comments.

Some politicians, journalists, and academics have been arrested and taken for questioning. The military has set up the National Committee for Peace and Order (NCPO) and promises reform of the democracy and the suppression of violent demonstrations and acts of disorder.

Some of the media have reported opposition to the moves, mainly on the detention of certain people, but generally the coup is now a *fait accompli*.

Thais are getting on with their daily lives as they have done for every other coup.

23 May

Unlike in the West, houses depreciate in value in Thailand in the same way as other assets such as cars. Because a *farang* will pay a higher price than a Thai for a house or condominium, he is particularly subject to this loss of value if he tries to sell. It can come as a bit of a shock. Getting a Thai that you know well to negotiate for you when purchasing is a good idea. Though it can backfire if the Thai is also looking for a commission from the vendor. Maybe a smarter option is to offer a small commission to the wife, partner, or friend. You then get a Thai price.

Partly because Thais hold on to land, from small parcels to large tracts, as future investments or as a place to retire, land does increase in value. Prices near shops, markets, a good road, and services are higher than in outlying districts. The thought of an attractive cottage in the country in a secluded area does not appeal to a Thai as much as it might to a Westerner.

24 May

The old chestnut that Thais will always cheat you and that it is in their blood is overplayed. The poor of under-developed nations often have to resort to cheating in order to survive. That's a generalisation though it is true that Thais are always on the lookout for *kamoeys* (thieves) loitering near their homes. It is one reason they keep dogs, particularly in rural areas. In this village every house has at least one dog. Thais routinely lock rooms they are not using when builders etc are on site.

There are scams and frauds throughout the world and Thailand is no exception. However, the fraudsters are not all of Thai nationality. Well dressed and well-spoken foreigners ply their trade in selling dodgy investments and other financial products. They'll sell you overpriced or worthless products if there is money in it for them.

They hover around tourist spots and expat clubs where their victims believe that they are among people who speak their language and whom they can trust. Their guards are down and they become ripe pickings for these charlatans.

The Thai legal process is slow and their concept of no conflict gives rise to a doctrine of not naming and shaming. Libel laws in Thailand do not allow you to damage a person's "reputation," whether your comments are truthful and provable or not.

Foreign confidence tricksters know this and take advantage of it. www.andrew-drummond.com is a source of factual reports on the subject but the address is blocked in Thailand.

25 May

Saw an amusing sign on an ATM machine today. You will see many examples of Thai words translated into English and which cause some amusement.

NO HAVE MONEY
The machine was out of cash and the bank staff had translated the Thai expression word for word (*Mai mee ngern*)

It got me thinking how useful it is to look at how Thais construct their sentences. When speaking or writing in Thai, we could copy their word order.

If you ask a Thai where he is going (*pai nai*, go where?), he may, for example, respond by saying *pai tanakarn*, (go bank). In English we would say "I am going to the bank" If we copy the Thai grammatical structure, we know we need to omit the words "I am" and "to the" just leaving the two words "go" and "bank."

Thais keep their sentence structures simple, are economical with words, and use their own names in place of personal pronouns.

I like beer would translate to "Matt likes beer". *Matt shorp bia.*

26 May

The social structure of Thailand does not assume all men are created equal. Every Thai knows and accepts his position on that ladder of hierarchy with its duties and obligations. They believe they were born before and will be born again.

It is one of the concepts of Buddhist teaching that good deeds will determine one's place in the next life. So the question of being equal does not arise. They acknowledge that, from past conduct, they cannot be equal. That does not mean they do not hold with democracy. They have welcomed free elections and the ability to register their vote to determine the government they want. They believe in one man, one vote. However, Thais do not take that to mean that they are equal.

Western commentators on democracy, born and brought up in a different culture, have a difficulty in understanding the Thai thinking on this.

We (Westerners) hold these truths to be self-evident. Thais look to their social structure and Buddhist teachings. Their democracy will develop differently from ours because of their particular take on Thai culture and Thai thinking.

Never the twain shall meet? I don't think it needs to, in the sense of being exactly the same. What needs to meet is an understanding of cultures and lifestyles. Copying good aspects; rejecting those that do not work for them.

Countries can grow into their respective democracies depending on their own way of thinking. Thais like strong beneficent leaders, preferably those they have voted into power. If they see they are corrupt and not delivering the promises of democracy they were given during election campaigns, they start to yearn for a solid hard-hitter who will have no truck with corruption and power politics. Finding and accepting such a person is the eternal difficulty. And attacking corruption can be selective. No country truly has a zero tolerance to that policy. Some people and organisations are just too important to try to control. One only has to look at the big banks and financial institutions in the West to realise that. "Too big to fail."

27 May

Mike arrived this morning a bit jet-lagged. Some travellers set their watches to the time at their destination when flying long haul because you're training your mind to accept a new time zone. Generally, it is a good idea and may help to limit the effects of jet lag. Try to get some sleep if it is currently "sleep time" at your arrival point so that your body clock can adjust.

Airlines advise exercising occasionally. Walk up and down an aisle a few times if you are awake, and practice some of the recommended in-flight exercises by keeping your limbs moving.

Certainly keep hydrated by drinking a lot. I don't think alcohol in moderation is a problem, though the crew encourage drinking only water and soft drinks.

Most passengers have their own favourite techniques.

28 May

Thais obey people not rules. Unless they think they can get away with it, the class and social structure of Thailand is so strong that children obey parents, older people, and those in authority.

Children and young adults will not openly go against their parents' wishes. They may not carry them out with goodwill but they will do as they are told. Well, sort of.

Her new boyfriend did not impress Yoopaa's mother and father. He was Thai and came from a good and reasonably well off family. He and Yoopaa were madly in love with each other and had been going steady for two years. For whatever reason, her parents just couldn't get on with Sagon. The more he tried to be friendly and to help the family; the more they seemed to dig their heels in.

Parents must be obeyed in Thai culture. Most couples will not go against their parents' wishes on choice of partners. Yoopaa eloped to another province with her fiancé and got married there. It avoided open opposition to her parents. I think they will come round eventually and fully accept their daughter's new husband. We shall see. Let's give it three or four months. Maybe in August or September.

Sagon is 33 and still lives with his 74-year-old mother. His parents divorced when he was fifteen. He respects his mother but she finds it difficult to control him. He can't hold a job down for more than a few weeks at a time and he is mixing with friends who are experimenting with drugs. Sagon has no problem ignoring the law on drugs (penalties are high in Thailand) but he will not openly go against his mother. He may sulk and he has an awkward streak but he helps on their 3-rai lamyai farm. He sees that as his filial duty.

The police and the judiciary are not held in high esteem (they represent the rules) but the elected village headman, the *pooyaibaan*, is regarded differently. He is a respected member of the community and is seen as "one of us," albeit on a higher level from other villagers. The village headman has had words with Sagon.

29 May

New microwave delivered today. In Thailand, the drivers will unpack and set the equipment up for you and make sure it's functioning properly. They'll even program your TV or satellite dish if that is what you have bought. Even if it takes some time. All part of the service.

I have only seen a few self-service fuel stations in Thailand. An attendant is always at hand to fill up the tank. Your windscreen will get washed too if you ask. In fact, the attendant, seeing a dirty screen, will more often than not take the initiative to suggest a clean. The staff do not expect a tip but most drivers give some small change.

Customer satisfaction is part of the Thai caring attitude.

30 May

Shrubs and trees can be planted in the wrong place, watering may be neglected in the hot season. The nursery may forget (?) to take off the hessian wrapping round the root ball. It doesn't matter. Plants are cheap and can be replaced, labour is cheap and plentiful.

The tiled floor is not level. The grouting between each tile is flaking in places because the mix is too watery. There is a small gap between the double doors after they've been closed. It's not that noticeable and a tiny piece of netting can be fitted later to stop mosquitoes coming in. It doesn't matter.

A neighbour has piled some hedge clippings outside an empty plot of land. It will compost eventually. It doesn't matter.

One of the hill tribe labourers working for a builder cut through an electric cable leading to three houses on the *soi*. It was repaired in two hours. Not too inconvenient and no point making a big fuss about it. It doesn't matter.

Mai pen rai. We are probably more ambitious, more perfectionist, than the Thai. But, chilling out is better than freaking out.

31 May

People are as a rule moved sideways rather than being dismissed or sacked. Moved to inactive posts until perhaps they are back in favour with a new boss or superior. They can stay despite there being no work given to them. Turning up each day and sitting at an empty desk with no in-tray, no emails, and no meetings to attend.

However, if Thais get bored with a job they may move on to a different company or department. In the construction industry they might go back to their home village in the provinces. They may or may not return to the building trade. They may try their hand at taxi driving for a while. Thais are not lazy. They have a different work ethic, they work to live and not live to work, and their compliance to concepts of *mai pen rai* and enjoying life, *sanuk*, are overriding.

The Thai economy is labour intensive and there is much over-staffing. If you walk around a department store you will see that there are often more sales staff than customers. Many companies can afford spare capacity because wage rates are low.

1 June

He was still smiling but the Smile Apologetic had turned to the Smile of Embarrassment.
I don't know whether he imagined himself to be a boy racer or a would-be grand prix
champion, but Somson jumped into the client's car and drove off at breakneck speed to park
it in the company's parking lot. He clipped the wing mirror.

Although the *farang* customer knew it would be replaced at no cost to himself, why on earth
were the manager and the young lad smiling. They didn't even apologise.

Smiles can look the same. He was seeing the smile of apology. To save face, both employees
of the company were covering the incident with a smile. The driver would be taken to task
later but he would not be told off in front of a customer or a work colleague. Somson may
have to pay something towards the cost of replacement.

Mark was annoyed and felt insulted that they were smiling at him. You would not do that in a
western country and he said so quite forcibly.

They still smiled. But now it was the smile of embarrassment that a foreigner did not
understand the Thai cultural trait of smiling when things go wrong. Shouting and getting
angry was not going to get the repair done more quickly.

The first smile was the apology, the final smile was disbelief that an issue was being blown
out of all proportion (as the Thais would see it).

(Addendum) I am currently waiting in the service reception area of Toyota while my car is
being serviced and editing this piece.

On arriving, I signaled left to turn into their car park and a motor cyclist overtook on my left
and then turned right into their staff parking lot. I could easily have hit and seriously injured
him. When at reception he calmly walks in and smiles at me. A smile of apology, not
realising he could have been on his way to hospital rather than starting work in Toyota.

2 June

Look kreung is the name given to a child of a mixed Thai and *farang* marriage. Born into a
family that is in general wealthier than one where both parents are Thai, the child can end up
spoilt and with an over-inflated view of his or her self-importance.

Naturally, Winston Whitehall wants the best for his daughter. We all want the best for our
offspring, whether we are Thai or *farang*. Soonan goes to a private international school where
there are pupils of all nationalities. Lessons are in English and Thai. Winston pays for extra

classes in martial arts, piano and dance which other Thai families with children at the school cannot afford. That is not lost on young Soonan who has become snobbish and precocious. She completely ignores the piano her father has bought her and wants nothing to do with it.

Thais don't discipline their children as firmly as we might in the West, but Winston's wife faces an uphill struggle whenever she tries to correct her daughter's rudeness. Her husband always backs Soonan.

A Thai child will invariably *wai* an adult automatically. Soonan will *wai* when told by her mother.

Older *look kreungs*, after leaving school or higher education, tend to associate with other *farangs*. There are exceptions but they are few and far between. The Whitehall family is typical of many Thai-*farang* families, particularly where there is a big difference in age between the husband and wife.

3 June

Not questioning the boss or your head office when you've spotted a mistake they've made or not wanting to offer some suggestions you think are valid is typical in Thailand. It stems from the entrenched values of hierarchy and class in Thai society.

Older staff will never challenge; younger staff are at least conscious of a need for a change in attitudes, even though they are reluctant to question.

Most large companies and organisations put a lot of resources and time into training but it tends to be a one-way communication. Pertinent ideas from trainees are not encouraged. Hierarchy rules. Benjawan told the trainer that her branch had many queries on the atm withdrawal limit. Could it not be put on the website for all customer to see together with other product information?

You can guess the response.

4 June

Anne speaks some Thai, not fluently but she gets understood. She understands that Thais have different worldviews and concepts from us Westerners. She doesn't get it right all the time though.

She knew that Thais habitually check up on builders when new houses are under construction. We don't often do it in our home countries. For health and safety reasons we may be discouraged from being on site and it is not customary to watch over people working. We can anyway fall back on guarantees if work is eventually found to be faulty.

I had suggested she be present when the foundations were being laid. Once any below-ground work is completed and covered over, there is no way of checking depth and strength. She lives in Maerim which is on an earthquake fault line, so I was surprised when she said she'd visit regularly during the build but only to check any work that was visible.

What the eye does not see..................

5 June

Saw what looked like an interesting magazine article on the London Motorexpo today. Great colour pictures on the cover. Captions in English. The photos inside were good too. All taken professionally and full of detail. However, the magazine was entirely in Thai script. Only the makes of the cars were in English.

The website of one of the largest home improvement businesses in Thailand has a page headed "*Let's get ready for party time.*" This is what gets people's attention. Thai and *farang*. The rest of the page describing their b.b.q products is in the Thai language.

Rich Thais like to have a lighter skin colour than their fellow citizens. Sales of whitening powder are high in Thailand. The model demonstrating the b.b.q on the website is an attractive Thai lady with western skin colour. It is interesting the way westernisation is being used by the Thai.

This country is one of the few I know that uses the English language in this way in their marketing. Titles in English to grab attention. The detail in Thai.

I've often picked up what promises to be an interesting magazine at a news stand, only to find it's all Thai inside.

6 June

Thais don't plan. They don't like committing themselves or making themselves responsible for anything. They don't want to be held to account.

Nothing in life is permanent. Therefore, there is no point in thinking about what you may do tomorrow, next month, or next year. That idea originates from Buddhist thinking. Tomorrow you may die and be re-born.

Planning for a rainy day is not a Thai priority. Pension plans are not popular even with wealthy Thais. They like investing in gold and land. In a strong family and community based society, you receive help from them not the state or an insurance company.

Farangs should plan wisely though. They are not as well tuned in to the communities in which they live. People will help but you need to have more of a monetary back-up than a Thai would need. There is the perception anyway that all foreigners are well off and don't need outside help.

Expats who are settled here also need to be aware that, because of the family culture, it is expected that one day your partner's aged parents will move in with you. You marry the family not the wife in Thailand.

7 June

The building of Wongpaet's new house in the *soi* has come on well. It took just one day for the men to weld the roof structure together and a further day to lay the asbestos roof panels. The walls have been built and rendered but have not yet been painted. Most of the inside electrics have been done. Apparently, the total material cost for the build so far is 90,000 baht. That seems a reasonable price for a simple 4 by 8 metre house with one main room, shower, and small kitchen.

The family is now waiting to get some more money together to complete the painting and plumbing. They are having a *tamboonbaan* (house warming) tomorrow even though the house is not completely finished.

8 June

Some confusion over the time of the *tamboonbaan*. Although younger Thais tend to use the twelve-hour clock as we do in the West; 10am and 10pm, for example; older Thais, particularly in the rural areas, tell the time using the traditional system that divides the day into four 6-hour blocks.

It is not easy to grasp when you first learn the language. 7pm is nung tum, one hour after 6pm. Nung is Thai for one.

2am   sawng moong chao
5am   ha moong chao
8am   pet moong chao
11am sipet moong chao
Noon tiang wan

3pm bai sam moong
6pm hok moong yen
7pm nung tum
10pm see tum
Midnight tiang kern

Tamboonbaans are normally held in the mornings, so when one of the youngsters gave the time as *see moong* all the Thais present assumed she really meant 10 o'clock in the morning. An older person would have made it clearer by saying *see moong chao,* if 10am was the scheduled time. In fact, the ceremony was due to start at four in the afternoon (*bai see moong.*) The young woman had used *see moong,* using the westernised language she would use with her friends. She had meant 4pm not 10am.

Everybody turned up at 10 in the morning.

Having arrived at the wrong time, we all sat and chatted anyway for an hour or so before returning home.

We came back at 4pm. Some arrived soon after. It did not matter because the monk did not come until an hour later, at 5 o'clock, anyway. The ceremony lasted about an hour and a half and ended with the monk blessing all present with holy water. Family members were given the *sai sin,* the white thread that the monk ties around your wrist after the ceremony. The owner of the home then sprinkled holy (lustral) water on the outside walls of the house. The party then really got going.

It was a good feeling that the family was able to move on from the sad event a few months ago and good that the community was part of that moving on.

Meeting and socialising with friends in Thailand tends to revolve around set events: those organised by the local *wat* (temple), weddings, funerals, *tamboonbaans* (house warmings), etc.

Popping round your friends' home for dinner together is more unusual in Thailand. Meeting at restaurants and at social functions such as Wongpaet's *tamboonbaan* is the norm.

9 June

Went to the bank today and was introduced to a manager who was on a visit from their head office in Bangkok. I think she wanted to meet an expat customer as the bank is keen to sign up more foreigners. We chatted for about a quarter of an hour.

Although she then excused herself by saying she had an appointment with an outside client, she was actually in the branch to conduct appraisal interviews with the staff and did not leave the building.

I would not have expected her to give me details of her role in the bank but she need only have said, "nice meeting you, hope to see you again." Thais like to elaborate on a story instead of giving a simple, direct, and truthful response.

The branch manager told me later that she was not that high up in the bank, only one grade higher than she was. There was an understandable jealousy in that remark.

10 June

Particularly in the early morning after dawn has broken and in the evening as the sun is going down, Thais take to the streets to jog or take a cycle ride to keep fit. Even small villages have jogging circuits and fitness parks provided free by the local authority.

As a predominantly agricultural society, a great number of Thais keep healthy by working in their gardens or in their rice fields and smallholdings.

The more well to do members of the community and many expats have exercise machines in their homes. I can't say if they are well used.

11 June

One of my neighbour's, Geng, has designed and built an ornamental water-driven rice grinding machine. It will make an eye-catching water feature.

Traditionally, water pours into the cups of a wheel which makes it turn and power a hammer-like device which repeatedly grinds the rice. They aren't used anymore and they needed a great amount of water to turn the huge wheel.

Geng came over to check where I wanted it positioned. He was petrified of one of my dogs, *Nam Som*. She has a loud bark and is wary of those she does not know well but she is not dangerous and would not bite anyone. He should have ignored her instead of showing he was scared. Once an animal senses someone is afraid, it has the upper hand and *Nam Som* would not stop barking at him. Her instinct told her that he was afraid. Apparently it's called operant conditioning. Not many people know that! (Apologies for using a Michael Caine catchphrase)

Thais keep dogs to deter burglars rather than have them as family pets. Often chained and encouraged to be fierce, the dogs scare most Thais.

Geng is a popular nickname in Thailand, and literally means clever. I know several Thais called Geng. Not all live up to their nickname but they are all decent guys who make good friends.

12 June

"Do you want me to service you?" I explained to the lady behind the post office counter that "serve" would be the better word. She has been on duty several times when I have visited the office and they were not busy so I pointed out that "service" is used when a stud animal is brought in to impregnate a female and is also slang for having sex with someone.

It is not her fault of course. She and others accept what their teachers tell them. It is commendable that, as well as qualified and certificated teachers, we have expats who volunteer to teach English to youngsters in both primary school and elsewhere. But, not all are as well versed in English grammar and vocabulary as they should be.

By coincidence, I noticed, on driving home, a sign advertising an ASEAN event.

We welcome you and wish to service you.

13 June

Reported in the UK media today. The Guardian, in a six month investigation, concluded that CP Foods, which supplies Walmart, Carrefour, Cosco, and Tesco gets its fishmeal from companies that own and operate boats in Thailand's prawn fishing industry and that they are manned by "slaves."

Escaped migrant workers from Cambodia and Burma spoke of 20-hour shifts, beatings, and killings. Reports cannot be confirmed but campaigners claim there are as many as half a million workers who are underpaid or not paid in Thailand and are therefore technically slaves. CP have accepted there is some misuse of labour in the supply chain but say only a small amount of their fish comes from uncertified suppliers. The US state department has given Thailand a low rating in its human trafficking index.

Thailand's prawn fishing industry is the largest in the world and CP's assets are around 365,000 million baht. The chairman is ranked the 58th richest man in the world by Forbes.

14 June

Coming back on the overnight bus from Bangkok, it is remarkable to see so many houses by the side of the road lit up with outside lights. Western countries don't usually keep their houses illuminated during the night.

Thais are somewhat security conscious and anxious, at times a little paranoid, when it comes to protecting their homes. There are few routine police patrols at night, certainly not in the rural areas, and response times are slow. It would be unusual for a Thai living in the countryside not to have a guard dog to ward off burglars. Many *moobaans* (housing estates) have private guards at the main gate, but they may not always be on duty for the entire night.

Although there are no formal neighbourhood watch schemes here, Thai families look out for one another. Strangers in the vicinity would be quickly noticed and everyone alerted. Jungle drums don't only operate in the jungle.

Security firms, often armed, are employed by businesses, and they might also pay for special police inspections, the officers signing a timesheet outside the premises to prove they called by.

Night watchmen used to call out the time in Victorian England as similar proof that the streets were being patrolled.

It's five o'clock and all is well, was a common cry in the larger cities.

15 June

Even a light rain shower will see Thais rush for cover. Westerners tend to welcome the cool refreshing rain.

Tropical storms, some only lasting ten minutes or so, aren't so agreeable. I saw the clouds gathering this afternoon and heard the first rumblings of thunder. Enough time to dash into a coffee shop and have a drink until it passed over. Gusts of wind frequently precede a storm. That is a good indicator too.

The rainy season in Thailand is from July to October but as elsewhere in the world the seasons are changing. This year we have had more than is usual for the months of May and June.

16 June

It is not true that I had nothing on. I had the radio on. (Marilyn Monroe) A famous and true quip from the famous star.

Thailand has been tagged the land of sun, sand, sea, and sex for scores of years. Because the economy benefits from its image as a world centre for sex tourists, the sex industry is tolerated quite openly. Lip service may be paid to changing these perceptions but the cash flow generated is good for the country's GDP and boosts the profits of other sectors of the economy.

The number of prostitutes is probably around two million. Not all of them are Thais and the greater number are not forced into the trade. Supporting one's parents and older relatives is an overriding factor in Thailand and girls regularly send a big slice of their earnings home. Soliciting is not illegal unless it occurs "openly and shamelessly or causes a nuisance to the public. That is a rather vague definition in a country where the interpretation and enforcement of laws can change depending on the political emphasis at the time.

As we noted in *Thailand Take Two*, provision of escort or massage services is not illegal. Pole dancing is considered a cultural art form by the authorities. Recruiting bargirls to drink with clients in a bar is not against the law. Scantily clad girls sitting in a row outside a karaoke club and smiling at potential punters are committing no offence. Calling out "Hey, you handsome man" is not soliciting but a mere expression of a man's physical attraction. Young women wearing numbered tags and sitting in a "goldfish bowl" waiting to be chosen by men sitting in rows gazing at their sexy bodies is nothing to do with paid prostitution.

The girls sit behind the glass screen watching TV and gossiping amongst themselves. There can be a lot of bitchiness and jealousy with the girls and mood swings can result in aggression. Their obvious boredom is only relieved when their number is called and they rush to get towel and soap.

Away from the "goldfish bowl" venues and the flashier nightclubs in the big cities, you find many smaller bars in every Thai town where the girls will congregate. A number of girls are looking for long term relationships with *farangs* to give them and their families a better standard of living. Marrying a much older man may be a small price to pay for that enhanced security.

Some women will engage with a number of men at the same time, merely ensuring that they never meet. If one of her catches is currently resident abroad, she will expect a regular money transfer into her bank account.

17 June

Thais are hesitant in giving an opinion or relaying information. They prefer a more senior person to assume accountability. A store manager may ring head office rather than make a decision or commit himself to an action. It is not so much Thai shyness or a lack of confidence as wanting someone higher in the company chain of command to take responsibility and, possibly, the blame if something goes wrong.

Thai bank managers, for example, do not have discretionary overdraft limits. They have to get approval from head office.

Ajarn Welai wanted to know if the satellite dish she was looking at could receive French language channels. The salesman told her that it could receive programmes from all over the world but he was not able to point out which channels were included in the specification. He rang his head office who confirmed what he probably already knew: that the satellite had a finite number of channels that it can connect with. An additional dish or a product with a self-seeking facility would have been required.

He was pretty vague on the terms of the guarantee and he referred that to head office too. It had many exclusions and was for one year only. He was familiar with that of course but he wanted to make a sale. Passing the question up the line would have got him off the hook.

18 June

Renewed my Thai driving licence today. Only took twenty minutes including the test; they had all my previous information on their computer screen. Still needed to provide copies of my passport and visa, a couple of photos, a doctor's note, and evidence of my address. That was fair enough.

My fitness to drive certificate from a local doctor cost just 50 baht; he just asked me if I felt okay and chatted with me for a few minutes, no need for any examination. Some places will charge 200 baht or more for a signature on a bit of paper. The disadvantage of such a visit to a doctor is that, while you save money, you don't get a decent check-up. Serious problems could be missed.

Embassies will provide a proof of address (though they never require actual evidence of where you live) for around 1000 baht or Thai immigration will provide what is needed for half that price. Having a *tabian baan* is a better alternative. This is a yellow house registration book obtained at the local government office (*amphur*) free of charge.

You will have to provide photocopies and translations of many documents but it is still cheaper and quicker than using embassy services and it is your permanent record. It can get expensive to visit your embassy every time you need to confirm where you are living.

The actual driving test took about 5 minutes. To check reflexes you are sat in front of a screen and have to press the brake pedal on the machine when you see red; the accelerator pedal, when you see green. Your ability to identify colours is verified by shouting out the colour on the cards that are held up in front of you. The depth perception test involves your aligning a moving cursor with a fixed point on the screen.

Farangs without a western or international licence have to take the same test as a Thai. This involves watching a video presentation on safe driving, maybe answering some written questions, driving around the test centre's circuit a few times while being watched by an examiner, and collecting your laminated licence at the cashier's window. There is no on the road driving test in Thailand.

I only watched the first five minutes of the driving video as the supervisor wanted to go to lunch. You will find that many official procedures in Thailand are either ignored or modified depending on the officer supervising or the region.

Most people pass first time or are allowed to have a few more attempts at the written answers or to make a few more circuits of the test track. Never seen anyone actually fail.

Before you leave the office you present yourself at the cashier's window and pay for your laminated licence.

19 June

Opening an account in a Thai bank can be difficult and time consuming. All the banks have laid-down criteria but one branch manager can interpret the rules differently from another. Some will require a work permit if the applicant is a *farang*. Some will require a certified proof of address. Neither is mandatory but once a bank officer asks for a document he would lose face if he accepts he is being over officious.

He won't change his mind. Try a different branch or go back another day. So long as you don't refer to the previous refusal, the bank may now accede to your request. Face will not have been compromised. That goes for many situations in Thailand, not just in the banking sector.

Account withdrawals at a branch other than your own Bank will require a proof of identity. The teller will ask for and make a copy of your passport. Because my passport is getting dog-eared from having been copied so often, I now give the clerk my driving licence to prove who I am. Even if they know me, they still go through the procedure of checking and copying.

Bank websites are not regularly updated with new product data or terms of business. It can be difficult to navigate and search for the information that you want. Internet security can vary from very tight to rather lax. One bank does not require you to log in with your password on each occasion you use its site. It remembers your password!

In marketing products, staff are inclined to think of making a sale without doing a thorough fact find of your needs. Investment staff undergo extensive training and have to pass tests to obtain a licence but Thai mentality is to think mainly of the short term. It comes back to the Buddhist philosophy that life is not permanent. Think of today not tomorrow.

Product knowledge is not always covered well in staff training programmes, whether banks or other sales outlets.

20 June

She smiled and was quite excited when her *farang* friend gave her a gaily-decorated box containing a present on her graduation day. Rattana did not open it though. She would only do that when she was alone.

She did not want to embarrass anyone if, on unwrapping the gift, she gave any visible sign of not liking the present. All the *farang* friends present were waiting eagerly to see what she had been given. They wanted to join in her happiness. They were in for a long wait.

Thais will smile and thank you and they are genuinely appreciative of whatever you give them. However, they don't want to risk upsetting you and making you think you had made the wrong choice of gift. That's a loss of face for everyone.

Two of her western friends had recently given a present to a Thai bride and groom on their wedding day. The newly married couple had mentioned previously in conversation that they both hoped one day to have a portable music system, it was something they had always wanted. Their guests thought it would be an ideal wedding gift for them. Something they knew they would like.

But the convention was to give a money gift in a sealed envelope. It was not a problem. Different nationalities have different customs and the Thais know that.

21 June

Turning up at the agreed time and being punctual is another non-essential to the Thai. There is some common sense in that when there is no real inconvenience involved. However, if you were waiting in for someone to turn up and they did not arrive or ring you to cancel, you would be annoyed. Well, *farangs* would. A Thai thinks in a more "does it really matter" way. *Mai pen rai.*

You will hear the words *mai mee panha* (no problem) quite a lot in Thailand.

22 June

Today we went to the umbrella village at Borsang, made famous by Princess Diana on her first visit to Thailand. The colourful umbrella they made in her honour is proudly displayed at the entrance. It is mentioned in the *Guinness Book of Records* as the largest umbrella ever made.

You can walk around, talk to the workers, and watch the various stages in the production of these intricately designed umbrellas. The artists will explain how they are painted and lacquered on paper and how they can incorporate your own design ideas into an umbrella while you wait.

Entire families are employed. Talented and experienced workers who have spent a lifetime honing their skills work alongside the children and junior members of the family.

In the workshops you can also see silverware, celadon, lacquer ware, and bamboo and teak products being made. Everything is hand-made.

23 June

I know Tong works hard at her job in the government office where she works. With twenty years' experience, she has a reputation as a dedicated employee, working late to finish the tasks she has set herself for the day. Her annual reviews have always been exemplary up until now.

The job appraisal system is complicated. The scoring method gives credit for exceptional skills, progress on training courses, adaptability, job knowledge, and teamwork. Her results are on a par with previous years.

Why does her new boss now give her an average of 50% when the individual scores range from 75 to 95 as in previous years? Is some envy creeping in because in the past she has had some very good salary increases? Tong's qualifications put her very close to the salary her boss gets.

Her husband, Oh, runs his own successful construction company and works long hours to ensure it succeeds. With Tong working just as hard, their joint incomes give them a good lifestyle. They went to Edinburgh last year and holidayed in Japan the year before. They work hard and play hard.

Government employees in Thailand need a confirmation letter to travel abroad. It's not been a problem before, but this year the application for traveling to France seemed to hit lots of administrative snags. She got approval eventually but it left a nasty taste in her mouth that her boss was being so awkward. *Khun* Sompanya, now very unpopular, has been in post less than one year and has never been abroad herself.

Do Thais have a jealous streak?

I suggested that Tong ask for a meeting with her boss about the delays to her vacation approval and more importantly her job evaluation.

"That would seem like a challenge to my boss's position, Matt. Everyone has a place in the office hierarchy. I will get some colleagues to drop a few well-chosen comments about my work and how it compares with the performance of others; but I can do no more than that. Thais like to use an intermediary to resolve a problem rather than going direct. I know that sounds strange to Westerners, Matt."

24 June

Outside dunnies, squat toilets, are still common in Thailand, in the poorer parts of Bangkok as well as in rural areas. Many schools and government institutions continue to use them.

Some restaurants, away from the tourist quarters, see no reason to upgrade to the western style. If the food is good, these eateries can be popular with both Thai and *farang* customers. The toilet facilities are perfectly clean and acceptable, though they may take some getting used to.

Practice makes perfect.

25 June

Mafias, organised crime syndicates, are well established throughout the world. No country is unaffected by their influence and power.

In Thailand it's big business.

Although drugs, prostitution, gambling, and human trafficking have formed the traditional base of their operations, they are also key players in legitimate businesses. They are run on formal managerial lines. They have finance and human resources departments. Lawyers and other professionals are employed alongside the heavy men that are needed to enforce how they run their profitable operations. They have business plans and strategy meetings. Mafias differ from other businesses only by their belief or creed that they are all-powerful and owe no allegiance to any government or society outside their own organisation.

Is it any different in Thailand? The short answer is "no." The longer explanation is "subtly yes"

Mafiosi don't wear uniforms and their businesses don't have "mafia controlled company" after their names. People can only suspect who are running the operations and who the big bosses are. Thais readily refer to them amongst themselves as *poo mee ithipon*. That is an interesting title. It can translate to "a person with influence." We would call them gangsters or crooks, we certainly would not respect them. Using the word *Poo*, however, is a mark of great respect. So, the populace are showing not only that these business people are influential in their communities but also that they are respected. That is certainly a major difference in attitude, created by the Thai's strong sense of hierarchy.

The turnover generated by mafias is not reported to the country's revenue department but can be estimated in hundreds of billions of Baht. A sizeable chunk of Thailand's GDP (gross domestic product) or national wealth. With such high cash inflows, mafias can influence stock and currency markets and are powerful lobbyists.

Wanchai Roujanavong, a distinguished Thai academic, has produced some detailed and well-sourced facts on the operations of mafias in Thailand and how governments throughout the world are trying to control organised crime.

26 June

A Thai lady lost a valuable watch in a shopping precinct in the UK. Passersby, sensing
something was amiss, asked what was bothering her. They suggested contacting the local
police station. She was visibly taken aback by what she thought was an absurd suggestion.
Most Thais would keep something valuable if they found it. She would have done so herself.
And surely the police would not admit to receiving lost property anyway.

Thinking it would be a waste of time, she did, however, go to the station. Someone had
picked up the watch, taken it to the police, and she was able to reclaim her watch. Even then,
she thought she would have to pay some money to the officers for their help.

Back in Thailand, she may have reverted to type. She had admitted that she herself would
have kept a watch if she found one. Such instincts may be hard to lose.

Tourists and foreigners will regularly be overcharged in whatever country they vacation. That
is a form of cheating. In Thailand, it is more open with prices being displayed clearly
indicating a foreign price and a Thai price. Somsee took a *farang* friend to a restaurant and
her Thai menu was changed to one in English. The prices were higher. She commented to the
server. "But, I am Thai."

"Yes, but he is *farang*."

They stayed, eat the meal, and paid the inflated prices. Somsee was unhappy and embarrassed
by what happened but didn't make a fuss. She won't go back to that eating place again.
Even state owned national parks engage in the practice. Foreigners don't usually realise the
prices are different because the Thai price is written in Thai and not Arabic numerals.

27 June

I listened to General Prayuth's weekly broadcast at 7.30 this evening. It's a P.R. exercise of
course and it comes across as a little propagandist. The NCPO (National Council for Peace
and Order) is, on the other hand, communicating regularly whereas previous elected
governments had done so only at election time or when they found themselves on the
defensive.

That actually applied to both mainstream parties as they were both trying to score political points off each other. The result was bickering, dysfunctional government, and, Prayuth would say, an abuse of democracy. During the recent anti-government protests, many departments were blockaded and Prime Minister Yingluck had difficulty in working in Bangkok.

Before the coup d'état, Yingluck had tried to avoid party political conflict by suggesting talks with the party which was in reality behind the anti-government protesters and their demonstrations. She told her followers not to rise to the bait that the opposition party was setting: encouraging violence, a likely intervention by the military, and blocking democratic elections. Her reconciliatory tactics were far removed from those that her deposed brother Taksin would doubtless have engaged in. Nevertheless, she was ousted.

Tonight, Prayuth's announcements lasted over half an hour and were more proactive than reactive. He said that the relevant ministries had been instructed to work together and coordinate work on flood prevention and drought avoidance measures. We saw video footage of dredging operations on some of the main rivers. The foreign media and many expats living here are not reporting on these news bulletins. We would be better served if they searched for all the facts, did not assume that "coup" is automatically a bad word, and "elected democracies" a cure-all.

The most talkative *farangs* on Facebook and New Mandala are often not even inside Thailand and do not have a large and varied circle of Thai acquaintances. Many only have their Thai wife or partner as a biased source of information (both pro- and anti-coup).

Although the overthrow of the government may not be the acceptable western way of achieving it, most Thais believe that the country is at least being governed and they can see decisions are being made and actions taken. They are, anyway, familiar with Thai's history of coups. This one has been nonviolent. No shots fired; no tanks on the streets.

The General is emphasising the NCPO's crackdown on corruption, improving morale, and boosting the economy before engaging in a fully consultative reform of Thailand's democratic processes (though not through a referendum). Some influential and powerful people were detained but most have now been released. Prayuth insisted that the arrests were for criminal and not political reasons and that trials would take place, albeit in a military court. In both the public and private sectors, key officials thought to be administering badly or corruptly have been replaced. That has included senior police and locally elected politicians. Large corporations have also not escaped scrutiny. Taxi mafias and excessive salaries and benefits in big business have been targeted. The police have been ordered to help deal with illegal gambling and human trafficking that has accumulated over time. The offenders' names have been disclosed in the regular bulletins.

It is interesting that Prayuth has referred to "persons of influence" (poo mee ithipon) when many of these names are announced. Poo mee ithipon is the Thai word for a mafia godfather. However, corruption is endemic in Thai culture and not only associated with mafias. As Singaporean experience has shown, it can never be completely eradicated. Some corruption will always remain, whatever anyone says.

War-grade weapons have been seized and political fundraising dinners which might enflame dissent have been forbidden. Prayuth claims he wants less bureaucracy and better transparency. He is asking for 400 "legal issues" to be reviewed and presumably for resolution to be speeded up. Work permits for unregistered migrants will be fast tracked so that many who have left can return.

The coup is certainly playing out very differently from that of 2006 and the General says he encourages Thais to come forward with ideas and questions. He has no problem with people disagreeing if done with civility. The NCPO has explained the reality to the EU and the USA and Prayuth says the States understands and is supportive. I have not seen confirmation of that in the western media.

He is hopeful that a functional democracy that accords with Thai culture can eventually evolve. The fact that the western models, which foreigners often quote, are tainted with interference and lobbying from big business, and short time frames within which political parties can make decisions, is not lost on the Thais.

28 June

Weerot is 33 and still lives with his 74-year-old mother. His parents divorced when he was fifteen. He respects his mother but she finds it difficult to control him. He cannot hold a job down for more than a few weeks at a time and he is mixing with friends who are experimenting with drugs. Weerot is not bothered about ignoring the law on drugs even though penalties are high in Thailand. He is no stranger to the local police. Drugs are big business in Thailand and the sellers have contacts.

Weerot will not openly go against his mother. Although he may sulk and has an awkward streak, he helps on their 3-rai lamyai farm. He sees that as his filial duty.

The police and the judiciary are not held in high esteem (they represent the rules). The elected village headman, the *pooyaibaan*, is regarded differently. Weerot, along with all his mates, respects him as a senior member of the community. Perhaps he'll have some influence.

29 June

Lots of cars parked on the side of the road and solemn music coming from one of the houses. Noticed there were red warning triangles on the road as I was driving along. Put up by the local authority whenever there is a funeral or whenever there is the likelihood of a lot of people attending an event.

The ornate coffin was elevated on an equally ornate platform; flashing coloured lights enveloped the whole raised area. There were many wreathes and flowers around the catafalque, together with a photo of the deceased. Mourners, friends and neighbours, were sitting on benches around a number of tables, no doubt chatting and reminiscing while having some light refreshments.

Funerals become social occasions within the community in Thailand. People don't die more in Thailand than in other countries of course. It's just that they are more visible as they are more public.

Just a few hundred metres further down the road, we passed a procession led by a very jovial and happy crowd, dancing and drinking. Again, there was music but it was loader and more jolly. Party time. A novice monk was being led to a temple for his ordination.

Fascinating to see two different events with music in the space of a few minutes.

30 June

At some point during his life every Thai male will enter the monkhood. By tradition, he would stay in the *wat* for several months during the wet season, the rains retreat. His time would be spent meditating, and learning the main teachings of the Buddha under the direction of the abbot and the senior monks. He would not leave the *wat* during that time except to walk in the alms round each morning to receive food from the local people.

Today, Sawat was to become a monk for a week. He is a computer software consultant and his firm was quite relaxed in giving him a week's paid sabbatical. His manager came along to this morning's initiation rites.

The day starts with Sawat, dressed in white, being led in procession to the *wat*. The crowd is made up of his family, friends, work colleagues, and any on-lookers who feel like participating in the fun. There is music and dancing as the procession wends its way to the temple buildings.

A few months ago I was stopped in traffic when a long procession of several initiates completely took over the narrow *soi* leading to a temple. The family beckoned me to join them. As there was no chance of my moving the car, I parked and walked over. Dancing, singing, smiling, joking. Then a whisky bottle is passed around. The only person seemingly not enjoying himself was the novice monk himself whose pending ordination was the purpose of all this merry making. Dressed all in white and with his hands in the *wai* position, his solemn face had no hint of a smile.

His term in the *wat* will only last a week or a month, so I am sure he'll make up for it when he returns to his day job.

There was no whisky at the actual ceremony.

The first part of the rite is to shave the initiate's head. Everyone present takes a turn with the scissors. The soon-to-be monk has his hands in the *wai* position and is not smiling. For him it is a serious and formal occasion. For the others it is no less serious but more of a fun occasion. Sawat was then led by two monks into the temple building where the abbot begins the ordination ceremony. Sawat makes his responses, which he had memorised over the last few days, in the Pali language. The main ceremony over, he is taken behind a screen where he takes off his white robes and is dressed in the saffron robes of an ordained monk by the two monks who will be his mentors and guides in the coming days.

Returning to the public area of the *wat*, his father presents him with a bowl which he can use during the daily alms round, and his mother and other members of the family give him gifts of soft drinks, toiletries and so on that he will need while he is at the *wat*. His mother also placed a basket of fruit on a cloth which her son then pulled towards him. Being female, she could not hand it to him directly. Friends gave some money in sealed envelopes which he will give to the temple authorities for the upkeep of the buildings.

Then we all have lunch together but with Sawat and the other monks at a separate table.

1 July

You will always find rows of orange buckets, filled with gifts, in the supermarkets. Rice, soap, toothpaste, soft drinks, and some snacks. People buy them to give to the monks in the *sang katan* ceremony.

Technically, they are not gifts; they are to show your merit. Men give their "gifts" first, followed by the women. The man can pass directly to a monk; a woman must place it on a cloth that the monk can draw towards him. A monk cannot touch a woman.

While those present are kneeling, with their hands in the *wai* position, the monk reads a blessing and sometimes sprinkles holy water, *nam mon*, over the people. He will also usually tie a white cord, the *sai sin*, around each person's wrist as part of the blessing.

Today, I saw a monk perform the *sai sin* by tying the cord around a woman's wrist. To comply with the "no touch" rule, that function is normally given to a layman, who ties the *sai sin* on the monk's behalf.

Buddhist rites and traditions can sometimes appear a little flexible. There is no standard form or procedure observed throughout Thailand.

Thai women will avoid even brushing against a monk when walking. They keep a respectful distance. Monks will sit in the front of a *sawngtaew*, (a truck used as a taxi) and not in the back with the other passengers. If the front seat is not available and they have to sit inside, they will select a seat next to a man. A woman will typically move to the opposite side of the *sawngtaew* to make sure he can do that.

Having said that, I did, on one occasion, witness a monk sitting next to a woman in a crowded *sawngtaew*. That was most unusual and irregular and I have never observed it since.

The monks can use the contents of the buckets. I understand that. But I have often wondered what they do with the actual buckets when they are empty. They can't possibly make use of them all.

One day, I'll pluck up courage to discreetly ask.

2 July

Sunantaa is a good cook and enjoys working in her kitchen preparing meals for her husband, *Surachai,* and their three teenage boys. He has bought her many labour-saving gadgets over the years.

They live on the same compound as *Surachai's* unmarried twin sisters. *Sunantaa* gets on well with them but does not want to go to their home every morning to collect purified water. She wants her own water softening machine. With a family of five, she uses a lot of water.

Surachai refuses to buy her the filter machine. It's not that they are expensive. Just a few thousand baht. No, his reasoning is that collecting water each day gives her an opportunity to keep in touch with family.

She would keep friends with them in any case, I am sure. That is the Thai way.

But her husband is adamant. She is not getting a water softener. *Sunantaa* tells her friends about it. She won't argue the point with her husband. *Sunantaa* avoided the issue when her father came to visit and asked why his daughter had to collect water every day.

3 July

Just seen a few *farangs* walking down a *soi* towards a bar with red balloons festooned outside.

The sign of a free party or at least a free drink. It's traditional to congratulate the host whose birthday or other event is being celebrated. But some foreigners don't do that. The Thais may still smile and make the *farang* welcome but they find it strange that Westerners can come across as impolite and selfish at times.

4 July

Although not a public holiday in Thailand, there are many festivities organised to celebrate 238 years of American Independence. Thailand has a high proportion of expats from the States. The two countries have had close links for 180 years and particularly since it became a favourite rest and recuperation destination for soldiers fighting in the Vietnam War.

Its strategic position in the Far East ensures America will always look favourably on its ally. "Two nations; one friendship."

When he was Secretary of State, John Kerry confirmed he was disappointed that there had been a coup and hoped for a return to an elected democracy. Military aid is, however, still being provided and no sanctions have been considered. Thailand holds a significant amount of America's bond debt.

5 July

The locals gathered at *Khun* Yai's again today. It has become a regular meeting place. The women potter around and start preparing food for lunch. They make sure all the volunteer workers have drinking water and bring hats round when it gets hot or rains. Awnings and chairs have been provided from the local *wat*.

I've never worked in construction, my DIY skills are zero, and my knowledge of building techniques wouldn't even fill a small thimble. I busied myself carrying buckets of cement to where they were needed and cleared away some rubble.

The concept of helping others is so strong in Thailand that it seemed natural to get involved. It's not just helping, it's engaging with the community. Getting on with people. The Thais are social creatures and like being in groups. They do not care for working individually outside a team. They are born team players who like company and not being alone. A couple going out for a meal or taking a swim in the local lake will invite friends or family to join them. They appreciate the company and it's more fun, *sanuk*.

Although there's a great deal of frivolity, joking, and gossiping going on; the work gets done. Though anyone who has ever seen Thai builders in action will be tempted to frown at some of their methods. Today, they were plastering the outside walls and left one area at the base un-plastered because the lower part of the brickwork was not in a vertical line with the rest of the wall. One guy started chiseling away to make it less noticeable. A large section of the wall then had to be re-plastered.

I know from previous observations that when they start painting, they may well do the walls in some of the rooms before the ceiling and there'll be spills on the work already completed. But nothing surprises me in Thailand: I doubt I will be proved wrong when decorating time comes around.

It's not a major issue of course though it would have been easier and less time consuming if they had got the wall straight before beginning to plaster. Time isn't too important to the Thai and they tend not to think that what they do now can affect a future part of the job. It does not bother them much; it's *mai pen rai.*

Broke off for lunch for half an hour. The conversation was friendly and happy though difficult to always understand as both the men and women were reverting to the local dialect. Hand gestures help when they use a *Lanna* word rather than a Thai word.

6 July

One of Tim's friends has decided to sell up and go back to Blighty. He'll probably get about half what he paid for his house, unless he is lucky enough to find a *farang* to buy it. Thais prefer to buy newly built houses or to build to their own specification on the family compound. They believe old houses may have ghosts. This pushes the value down.

They may buy if the price is right, but will usually demolish the building and re-build. Westerners don't always appreciate that real estate depreciates much more than in the West. Land itself holds its value but you can almost write off the building cost of the house.

Following the floods in Bangkok, the northern Lanna province is seeing a new interest in building homes here and land prices are rising. Tim's friend may be fortunate and find a buyer for his land and house, but he will basically only get the value of the land.

7 July

Rained off at *Khun* Yai's today, so just stayed half an hour for a chat. They kept offering food but I took just a little. There's a balance between their offering out of politeness and your being *greng jai* and either not eating or having a taste only.

Went to see *Pannee's* family in Maerim. It was not raining there and the new house build is coming on well since they started construction in January. *Pannee's* father checks on progress every day and approves all invoices. The family are buying the more expensive materials, which gives them better control over quality. He checks that materials are not being substituted for those of lower specification.

Thais trust only when they are given reason to do so. There's no assumption that there'll be no cheating going on.

Popped round to talk to Sandra and John. They both appeared quite glum and have not got over their swimming pool being overlooked from *Pannee's* home.

8 July

The boss had put a thick green line under the last entry in the office clocking-in book. Staff are allowed to be fifteen minutes late and the line is drawn after that time expires each day. But his watch must have been at least fifteen minutes fast because it was still not time for the office to open.

Nobody complained. That was not surprising, Thais are inclined to turn the other cheek. *Mai pen rai.* It doesn't matter. They like working with a bit of give and take, and dislike rules being followed too rigidly.

A few of the staff took exception and just turned round and went back home. Not going upstairs to the office meant avoiding any possible argument for technically being late. In a way, their idea of freedom is being able to do as they like. Life must not be too serious. The next time the boss wants a favour done in a hurry, he may not find the staff particularly cooperative.

You can go months in this country and still be taken aback by how Thais react to certain situations. Never underestimate a Thai's ability to be unpredictable.

9 July

I am sure it's only a minority of expats here that don't "fit in." The impression one gets from the internet forums and from some Facebook comments is that most *farangs* living here dislike what they perceive as unacceptable behaviour from the Thais.

The frustration of not getting straight answers, dual pricing, a cheating mentality, the difficulties of coping with Thai face, the confusing meanings of the Thai smile, and their propensity to lie to cover problems. All are well documented on the internet pages. Most are exaggerated. The majority of foreigners here adapt well to the Thai way of life and settle in to their local communities. Those posting on the blogs and forums represent a minority, albeit a vociferous one.

When I first came to Thailand I joined the local expats club and suggested to a neighbour that he did the same. He was married to a Thai, they had a two year old daughter, and he ran a small business delivering gas bottles to the locals. I thought it a sound idea for him to meet people other than Thais. However, he had been here three years and declined. He had got to know many Thais and made many friends in his local community. He said he had no need to join a *farang* club. At the time I thought there was every advantage in enjoying the best of both worlds: having Thai and expat friends.

Paul, on the other hand, is a regular at the club. That's fine but he socialises with *farangs* to the exclusion of the Thai community. Apart from his partner he has no Thai friends or acquaintances. He has zero tolerance for anyone missing an appointment and is very forceful in complaining when Thais don't do things promptly or in the way he wants them done. His partner gets visibly embarrassed. As with many Thais, he is reluctant to explain to him that Thais do things differently: that they have a different culture, lifestyle, and attitude to life than in the more hectic and serious west. I see Paul's frustrations. I just wish he could be a little more like his neighbour delivering gas bottles.

10 July

Even with the power of today's internet, being aware of what's happening in Thailand is not that easy or obvious. I recall, a few days after the 2006 coup, reading a respected observer of the Far East writing that anyone who knows anything at all about Thailand accepts that no one really knows what is going on.

He went on, "those that think they know what's happening are doing a lot of talking, however cautiously. Those that really are in the know aren't saying anything at all."

Most of the media have their own agendas. Thais, in any case, dislike reporting criticism, conflict, or unpleasant news that their countrymen do not want to read or would prefer to ignore. It is a cultural characteristic which is a little enigmatic when you see gory photos of road accidents on the front pages. Thai newspapers, including the English language dailies, openly self-censor. Sometimes there are legal reasons why information cannot be published.

It is not a uniquely Thai phenomenon. Leading up to the abdication crisis in England in the 1930s, the Prince of Wales' relationship with the American divorcée Wallace Simpson was known only to a handful of the élite in the UK. Some papers in France printed the news but copies were not available for general distribution in England. I tend to watch Al Jazeera, CGTN and RT. These programmes have different points of view and spin the news differently; by comparing them one can get a more balanced picture of events.

Only by having a wide range of Thai contacts, ordinary folk and maybe a few in higher places, and reading between the lines and listening carefully will you ever get a smattering of the truth and reality within the country. Browse the internet forums but check what you read from other sources, other Thais, and from your own observations.

11 July

It is not only in government departments that senior people get moved to other offices at regular intervals. Bank managers and supervisors are swapped between branches after a few years. Usually 3 years for managers, 5 years for other staff. In the West, promotions and sideways moves are typically the reasons for employees moving out of their current job. In Thailand, it is the fear of corruption developing and a manager or official getting too strong, powerful, or influential in his or her post. Relocation expenses are rarely paid.

It is this concept of lack of trust again.

Military and police promotions and changes are announced annually every October by the government though there is much discussion and probably compromise being made behind the scenes. Where there is no civilian government or where only a caretaker government is in place, ministers have no say at all.

Sideways moves or transfers to "inactive" positions are more common than dismissals.

12 July

Sometimes it is useful to try to bear in mind the value of the local money instead of thinking in your own currency.

By remembering that the average wage in Thailand is 300 baht per day, you can appreciate and understand just what Thais can and cannot afford.

Most Thais do not have enough money to afford lawyers, but if one has to be employed the fee is about one sixth of the rate quoted to a *farang*. That's quite a difference and is not the only example we will see of dual pricing directed at a foreigner.

If you try to consider what a Thai would be prepared to pay, given his income, you can often determine whether what you have been offered is good value for money or not. Ask whether you would buy the goods on sale at that price if your income was 300 baht a day.

13 July

One metre foundations have been laid along the roped off area around the *wat* next to *Sengdeuan's* property. The monks are obviously going to build a wall. The public telephone cubicle is inside the perimeter. Nobody will be able to get to it without walking through the *wat* and it's closed at night. No one feels able to comment.

Not that Thais walk any distance. Bikes, motor bikes and trucks are their preferred means of getting where they want to go, even over short distances.

Ever since the *wat* was built the land between the temple and *Sengdeuan's* house and factory has been available for public use. The telephone box had been erected on it without comment and *Sengdeuan* had planted vegetables on one side of the strip of land. The locals were free within reason to help themselves. No one took advantage. The piece of land was regarded as a *soi* for everyone's use as a short cut between two other roads.

14 July

Met with *Jaran, Tong,* and *Latdee* today. Three people from completely dissimilar backgrounds. *Jaran* has retired from the army now, *Tong* still has problems with her jealous boss, and *Latdee* has landed a good job with a foreign owned company.

It's unusual to get Thais talking together when they are from different sections of Thai society. They normally "know their place" and don't speak their mind openly. *Jaran, Tong,* and *Latdee* are rather exceptional characters whom I have known for a long time.

Conversations with them are always stimulating. It's refreshing to hear *Latdee's* unrestrained point of view as a younger person. Thais are, of course, as susceptible to propaganda and political spin as any other people.

Colonel Jaran could not understand the attitude of the foreign press and some of the social media towards the recent coup d'état. It was not, he said, a straightforward military takeover of the state, far from it. The armed forces had acted to put in place a temporary government that would now be able to function for the benefit of the country and democracy. They had moved, for example, against some well-known corrupt activities and many senior people in the private and public sector have lost their positions. Sideways moved to a non-job rather than being sacked. *Jaran* said that the military were right to act as they did to keep the country safe and avoid further strife and a continuation of a dysfunctional system of government. Not that the army is all powerful. Thailand has strong feudal roots that are not completely severed. Mafias, whether small local groups or larger and more powerful country-wide bodies, have great influence.

Tong and Latdee nodded in agreement. They said that he was factually correct in what he said but he was ignoring the fact that western ideology is anti-coup and pro-democracy and little had been done to explain to *farangs* that this non-violent "coup" was not an anti-democratic act: that it had taken place specifically to safeguard future democracy.

The problem, of course, is a misunderstanding between two cultures. To the western mind all coups are wrong. As indeed they may well be in other parts of the world: where violent and not universally popular regime changes take place. The Thai people, for the most part, welcome the changes they have seen, despite some reservations.

Historically, Thais have liked and respected strong governments. In the days of absolute monarchy, and given the Thai emphasis on hierarchy and people not being equal, beneficent and perhaps tough kings were totally accepted as the natural order of things.

Farangs (some commentators in the media and some expats) should take a broader look at Thailand. They should familiarise themselves with the history and culture and talk to as many Thais as possible, in all the provinces not just Bangkok. As Westerners, we have been brought up on a very different worldview on coups (always bad) and elected democracies (always good).

The reality is that there is no black or white. Some coups and some democracies are bad and corrupt; others are not. Maybe a solution to Thailand's problems could have been achieved without a military coup. Though it is difficult to see how. And democracies? Have we got it right in the West? Do banks and oil companies lobby and influence governments? Are electors able to put into power, through the ballot box, people they can trust to carry out the mandate on which they were elected? Or do powerful lobby groups and élites with vested interests hold more sway. It is not only in Thailand that one asks that question.

There is spin and propaganda everywhere. It was not this country that coined the word "spin doctor."

Jaran, Tong and *Latdee* agreed more should be done to explain more clearly to Westerners (the media and the ordinary people) the Thai thinking on these issues. They also stressed that the onus is on the West to get more up to speed on the circumstances that are prevailing at the present time.

Important for both the East and the West to try to understand the cultural differences.

15 July

Watched police checking for illegals on a building site today. One elderly woman worker did not have her Thai ID card, the *bat prachachorn*, with her. By law, you must carry these cards with you at all times. Rules are rules.

Law enforcement is flexible in Thailand. It was obvious from her appearance that she was Thai. Moreover, out of respect for an older person, they did not want to make a fuss. She was asked to sing the Thai national song to prove her nationality.

http://www.youtube.com/watch?v=djwY41a4lsA

Police do spot checks at the roadside in order to arrest workers without work permits and drug traffickers. Possession and selling of drugs trafficking is taken seriously in Thailand with convictions carrying severe consequences including the death penalty. The sentence is customarily commuted to life imprisonment for foreigners who may also be allowed to serve their terms in their own country if a bilateral agreement with the foreigner's country exists.

Thais are less lucky.

16 July

Very tired and exhausted now. Spent the day as a member of the "human chain" moving buckets of cement to the guys doing the floor of *Khun Yai's* house. Eighteen men, all volunteers. They see it as being neighbourly, normal activity if you're part of this small community. A dozen or so women were engaged in preparing food and supplying drinking water while enjoying their own company.

Better than staying in their own homes. Thais socialise more at festivals in the *wat*, house-warmings, weddings, funerals, and occasions like these than dropping in for a chat or a meal at a friend's house. They meet people and entertain in groups. At hospital visiting time, it's common to see a dozen or so friends around a sick bed. They may never have been to the patient's home though would certainly visit him when he is ill in hospital.

Thai industry and commerce is labour intensive. Relatively inexpensive labour compared with the West means there is little incentive to mechanise. It suits the culture too. Thais like working together or in groups. In one sense, that implies teamwork, helping one another. But Thais are also intensely individualistic and love individual freedom and doing things their own way. That's the exact opposite of working as a team.

Today provided an interesting example of that enigma. As ever, there is a jolly layback attitude when we're working. Laughing and joking is the order of the day. With so many people in the chain, the full buckets and the returned empty buckets are moving rapidly. It's labour intensive yet efficient.

The team changes order after short breaks. The guy standing two to my left started throwing the empty buckets towards the cement mixer instead of passing them along as the others were doing. It's not a capital offence but it slowed the operation down as the men near the mixer had to keep stopping and turning the buckets upright. What was interesting was that no one suggested he pass the buckets as everyone else was doing. It might have been a loss of face situation, however tactfully put or explained. He wanted the "freedom" to do it his way and that seemingly had to be accepted.

The *pooyaibaan* was working alongside everyone else. Not standing on ceremony. Dressed in ordinary working clothes, he looked nothing like the village headman dressed in his official white state uniform. Only when his clerk came round for him to sign off official documents did he stop for a few minutes.

We had lunch together, the meal provided by the women folk though they sat at separate tables and kept an eye on whether any dishes needed topping up. Just twenty minutes then back to the human chain. We got to a convenient point to finish at 2.30 so everyone cleaned up and settled down for whiskey and more food. Maybe in the West we'd have found a few jobs to do and broken off around four o'clock or so.

My glass got refilled a few times although I really wanted to get back home if we had finished for the day. You have to be ready to give a firm "no thanks" as the tradition is to keep your glass full unless you specifically say you've had enough.

As with all drinking sessions, the talking gets faster as one imbibes. When they are talking in dialect and not Thai, it's doubly confusing for the *farang*. I tried making a joke in my rather imperfect Thai in order to get back into the conversation. Thais love joking, so that works every time. Irony is appreciated and they take jokes against themselves in good spirit. Provided that the *farang* can take a joke himself, he'll fit in. Sarcasm though will result in a frown or a blank look.

17 July

In one sense, Thais dislike authority. Having the freedom to do as they want and not be openly criticised is important to them. We saw that yesterday.

Suggesting an idea or method unfamiliar to them can be quite difficult. They can have entrenched views on subjects they have learnt from family or teachers. One technique is to quietly demonstrate or illustrate and hope they will copy. Making a fuss, being forceful, or being direct are less likely to have any positive effects. *Farangs* in teaching posts have learnt that making a Thai think that it is his idea is a sound approach to getting your point across and avoiding any suggestion of loss of face or self-esteem. That can work in the West as well of course. The longer you stay in Thailand, the more you appreciate following the golden rules of being layback (*mai pen rai*), not criticising openly and of observing their unwritten values of hierarchy and status.

18 July

One hell of a racket this morning. All the wild dogs at the *wat* were barking and howling. Something had upset them. Of course, that set our dogs off.

In rural areas, dogs are kept to deter burglars. Many Thais can't afford insurance and police don't patrol at night.

The dogs are rarely trained or even exercised. They can be quite vicious and, if they have not been immunised, can pose an even greater danger.

In his Thai wife's name, because he can't legally run the training school himself, Guillaume has set up a dog training centre. He has an uncanny way with dogs that gets them to respond to him quickly. He seems to understand how they think and react. Guillaume has built an agility course which dogs love and which is popular with his clientele. It helps in training dogs to be obedient and under control. Only one Thai family has joined his club and stayed. They see the benefits.

The majority of his customers are *farang* though he had a few hi-so Thais in the beginning as clients. His agility course includes jumps, tunnels, an A-frame and a series of poles through which the dog has to weave. He starts each training programme with basic obedience drills: walking to heel off-lead, retrieving a thrown object, getting the dog to sit or lay down with the handler out of sight.

His foreign customers and their dogs enjoy the regular practice sessions and some are getting to competition standard. Most of Guillaume's Thai customers tend to come for a few weeks and you never see them again. In their eyes, dogs are for protection and don't require training.

Thais won't put their pets down, and many unwanted dogs end up at the local temple. They live off what the monks can give them and scavenge around the local *sois*. You need to watch out for them when you are driving.

There are cases of strays being poisoned, but generally the locals will not harm dogs or even shoo them away. They thus become confident when lying on roadways and will not move out of a car's way as readily as they would in the West.

19 July

Only one volunteer worker at *Khun* Yai's today, so I became Noi's plasterer's mate for the day. Mixing cement and carrying buckets. It was easier when there was a gang of neighbours to share the heavy work. However, this is *lamyai* harvesting season and many people have not got their fruit to the local wholesalers yet. More rain and wind may damage the unpicked fruit.

Then around 10 o'clock the "cavalry" arrived. One car, one truck, and several motor bikes pulled up outside. Help was here at last. I recognised the *pooyaibaan* and a few others, they had rolled up their sleeves and got on with whatever needed doing on more than one previous occasion. There were two ladies whom I had not seen before, both wearing the uniform of the local *amphur*, the district office.

They gave *Khun* Yai a basket of fruit. A whip round amongst the staff at the office, I would guess. The guy I did not recognise, and being suited and booted was clearly not here to get his hands dirty, called everyone to order so that a photo could be taken of him giving a cheque to *Khun* Yai. He was *Gamnan* Pichart, the head of the entire district. He and his staff had gone round to the *pooyaibaan*'s to find out where her new house was being constructed so that he could pay a visit and formally make a donation towards the build costs.

Then they all left. I got my shovel. Noi reached for his plasterer's trowel. I thought better of making any sarcastic remark about their not staying to help. Though I am sure I would have been tempted to do so if I were in the West.

Everyone understood that the visit and photo opportunity took place to reinforce the status quo in the village. The *pooyaibaan* being next to the *gamnan* whenever the cameras were pointed at the group, showing the respective positions of the two leaders in the community. Displaying the photo at the *amphur* will be a way of communicating *Khun* Yai's plight and what the community are doing about it.

When I first came to Thailand, I thought it was a matter of Thais showing off as usual. Yes, they like to brag a little, but I can now see the positive aspects of this feature of Thai life. It was communicating what had happened to *Khun* Yai to a greater audience and therefore strengthening community spirit.

Some Thai concepts take a little getting used to. Tourists rarely get the chance to see events such as these. It's a pity because it is difficult for visitors to absorb these aspects of Thai culture during a tight holiday schedule which includes so much else to see and do.

The even greater pity is that many long term expats, living in secluded housing projects (sometimes resembling foreign ghettoes) and not associating with the ordinary Thai, miss out on not understanding the realities of everyday life in Thailand.

20 July

Although Sengdeuan's partner is Taiwanese, he speaks both fluent Thai and the local dialect. He has been in Thailand for 15 years and has built up three businesses, mainly exporting quality bamboo products overseas. Tonight, he was explaining the difficulties for a foreigner working in this country. Thais, he claimed, are not even-handed in dealing with non-Thai business owners.

Despite the Taiwanese being similar to Thais in appearance, he is still a foreigner and seen as competing with Thai entrepreneurs while living in a Thai village. Lee and his Thai wife support the local community. They make donations to the local *wat*. Sengdeuan paid her respects at Dta Sompet's funeral (*Thailand Take Two: End of a Life,*) and her husband opened up their factory parking area for the mourners' cars. Yet Lee would still be referred to as *kon taiwan* by those who do not know his name. (*Farang* is used only for white-skinned Westerners, *kon* plus nationality for Asians)

When *Lee* first arrived in Thailand, there was some local opposition to his setting up a small factory even though he would be recruiting local labour. He dealt with the bureaucratic paperwork which he knew would be tiresome but inevitable. He did not appreciate some locals throwing stones at his factory roof. The *pooyaibaan* did not seem too keen to involve himself in a dispute with a newly arrived foreigner. Lee threw the stones back at them. The trouble stopped though atmospheres were strained.

Taiwan is economically more developed than Thailand and Lee thought some jealousy was creeping in when the locals saw his hard work and long hours paying dividends as his business steadily grew.

There is a mood of distrust and suspicion in all Thais. Although *Mai pen rai* is a strong force that sometimes means it does not matter what others do, some Thais resent the fortunes of others. There can be an attitude of jealousy when people are more successful than you are.

Thais generally accept their place in society and follow the rules of their country's pecking order closely. A hint of resentment is always in the background. It is never discussed openly and facial expressions will not betray what the Thai is really feeling. Much of the gossiping that habitually takes place in Thai society revolves around the jealousy of others.

Sengdeuan agreed with Lee that it was an unfortunate feature of many Thai people. Thais are fervently patriotic and can resent foreigner success.

She added, "I am Thai, but I am uncomfortable with the envy I see every day in some of my fellow Thais."

21 July

Driving around a bend tonight, I saw a red light flashing in front of me. It was fixed to the tail of an elephant. He was quite a big beast so I'm glad I had some warning as I approached. Always drive in Thailand at a speed that allows you to pull up within the space that you can see ahead of you.

The mahout is looking for gifts of money. He will sell you sugar cane to feed the animal and let you take photographs. The practice is being discouraged because of the risks involved but the regulations are not often enforced. Too much sugar can, in any case, make elephants hyperactive.

Police generally ignore mahouts leading their elephants into restaurant car parks to beg for money. The patrons, Thai and *farang*, usually give generously. Sadly, that perpetuates a dangerous and often cruel practice of bringing elephants into crowded areas.

The best way to interact with these creatures is to visit the sanctuaries where they are well looked after and don't have to parade on the streets or perform at circus-like shows. Always more interesting to see them behaving naturally in safe conditions.

22 July

At first glance, some expats who have settled here seem to have an attitude that is poles apart from those who have immigrated to western countries. I know several families that have settled in France and I had an interesting conversation with Robert and Denise yesterday evening when they seemed to hit the nail on the head by saying it was because some expats in Thailand appear to be outside the Thai social circle. They both know Alex and Samuel.

Robert's view was that Alex has made no attempt to involve himself in his Thai community even though he lives with *Ae*, his Thai boyfriend. Alex finds fault with the Thais who service his car and the servers who bring food to his table. He hangs out with his circle of *farang* friends, will not learn or speak Thai, and is a little condescending in conversation. He prefers the company of expats. Robert often wondered why *Ae* did not help him meet and get friendly with their Thai neighbours and explain how Thais must feel about his attitude. Maybe it's the age difference. *Ae* is forty; Alex, seventy-two. They're happy enough together.

Denise regularly talks to Boong, Samuel's wife, on Skype and commented on how Boong had tried to get new friends for her husband. But his interests were solely looking after his condominium business and surfing the internet. Again, there's a thirty year age difference between them though that's not unusual in Thai - *farang* marriages. Boong continues to try to get Sam to socialise.

As some other western nations, the French can be a tad xenophobic and arrogant towards foreigners and, of course, it is not easy to integrate quickly into *any* foreign culture. Once you make the first move and show you are prepared to fit in and adapt to a different way of life, your new French neighbours will warmly accept you.

Robert and Denise had found no difficulty in participating in French life and there were few obstacles to overcome. There was the usual bureaucratic nonsense associated with buying property: that was the same whether you were French, English, or any other nationality. They both enjoyed getting to know the people in their community and joined in the local fêtes and dances. They quickly found a circle of friends. It's a matter, Robert said, of sincerely wanting to fit into the culture of another country. It makes for a better and more rewarding lifestyle.

Robert insisted on having his English full roast dinner every Sunday and fell in love with the idea of taking a short siesta after meals. He got used to the French style of driving in France while disliking the way they drove relatively faster and seemingly always in a hurry. However, he did not complain and get angry about something he could not change.

Denise found it strange at first that you can handle and select the fruit you want at food counters but appreciated the very wide choice of fish, meat, vegetables, and fruit on the shelves compared with that on display in English supermarkets, particularly those outside London.

There were things they liked about France and the way of life; there were features they did not like. They felt they could live with that and found they had integrated easily during their nine years in France. They quickly crossed the culture gap.

Having listened to Robert and Denise, I think it's true that most expats in Thailand enjoy living in the country, have settled in, and make attempts to integrate and be part of Thai social life. Those that do not, a minority, do tend to be forceful in their views whether on social media or in the bar. They can be either staunchly pro-Thai or pro-Thailand; or they can be very anti-Thai, finding fault in everything that a Thai does or is Thai-related.

The Thais will smile and be friendly. They won't force a strong friendship on you. You'll have to initiate the first move and take it slowly. It worked for Robert and Denise.

23 July

Builders have completed the wall around the temple next to *Sengdeuan's* house, closing direct access to the telephone booth. Whether the booth had been erected on temple land or not is still unclear and nobody wants to start any argument or conflict. I doubt the telephone company or *amphur* will get involved. They don't want to risk causing any dispute or conflict.

Sengdeuan has checked her land deeds and can see that her family own 3 metres of the land outside their factory wall. There is just enough room for pedestrians and small vehicles to move along the short cut between the two *sois* if they use the 3 metres of Sengdeuan's land and the land that still remains outside the temple wall.

Only in Thailand would matters like these be left unresolved; the logic being that it's best to leave well alone and not cause a fuss.

24 July

People can't be dying that often surely? A lot of firecrackers have been going off at the *wat* every night this week. The usual sign that there has been a death in the village and the need to frighten away evil spirits.

My neighbours knew of no people recently passing on. Pigeons. The problem was the pigeons. The monks had tired of them shitting on the newly painted roof of the *sala*. And were using firecrackers to scare them away. Monks can't take life, so shooting them was not an option. Would have damaged the building anyway. They don't have sparrow-hawks in Thailand. That might have been a solution.

25 July

I noticed on the World Economic Forum website today that Thailand is well down in the international league tables for English teaching. Both Indonesia and Vietnam fare better. Until recently, when computer tablets were introduced into most primary schools, little was spent on resources other than teacher salaries. The government's initiative is certainly a step in the right direction.

There are some extremely dedicated teachers, but their levels of English are mostly poor. Some schools employ *farang* teachers that are qualified, but many are backpackers with no experience of teaching and who do not have a good command of English.

A new head has arrived at our local school and, ahead of an inspection that starts next week, his first task was to get the kids painting murals on the perimeter wall and making brick borders around some of the trees on the entrance drive. The school grounds now look good, the kids enjoyed being away from the classroom, but I'm not sure it has improved Thailand's scholastic reputation.

To catch up with other Asean countries, some fresh thinking is needed on teaching methods in Thailand. Top of the list should be training teachers to speak and write English to more acceptable standards. My choice for second place would be encouraging children to *think* about what they are being taught. Even at university level there is a reluctance to challenge a lecturer or professor.

26 July

Cakes in the office. Drinks all round in the pub lunchtime. An established English tradition when it's your birthday though it is not followed in Thailand.

It's strange the things you notice and miss if you live in another country. Thais are not bookworms. You'll see few books in Thai homes. If there are children in the house, there'll be a few student texts on the shelves but little else.

Libraries are rare and not well stocked. Thais are more interested in people than in books.

27 July

Driving too close to the vehicle in front is a major cause of accidents in many countries. It takes away your margin of safety if the vehicle in front of you makes a mistake and you are unable to stop within the distance you can see to be clear and avoid a rear-ender.

Today, two motor-cyclists collided and one is seriously injured. It is not clear whether they were riding in parallel or one was overtaking the other. Perhaps they were racing. The situation worsened when, rounding a bend, a following car crashed into one of the bikes and somehow made it somersault into the air. It then landed on the other rider.

The driver of the car drove off. It is reported on a Thai radio channel that the police checked ownership of the vehicle to a senior government official but he claimed his son was driving at the time. The son denies that he was responsible.

28 July

Enjoyed an invigorating cycle ride this evening. Early mornings and evenings are the favourite times for Thais to exercise. I often pass joggers and other cyclists as I ride along.

In the main towns and cities, Thailand has a large number of cycle lanes for those with bicycles or motor-bikes. It makes cycling that much safer and pleasant. You get the occasional car parked in the lane so you need to be careful when you then pull out into traffic. The lanes sometimes abruptly end without warning or, as you turn into a bend, you find a lamppost or advertising board right in front of you. Planning regulations exist but are rarely enforced if the problem is not seen as serious. *Mai pen rai.*

The present military government are more concerned than the police and have, in extreme cases, made businesses move boards that are obstructing pedestrian and cycle access. You can't slip a few baht to soldiers carrying out some of the popular initiatives the new regime have introduced. Fewer blind eyes are being turned now.

Exercise parks are popular and are free to use. They are well maintained with modern equipment provided by the local authority. Unless it's raining, there'll be at least half a dozen locals keeping themselves fit at these parks.

Outdoor aerobic dancing under the arches of a road flyover is becoming a favourite pastime for both young and old. The music draws more people into the group. I think participation is free or there may be a small charge. There must have been around fifty there tonight as I cycled past.

Saw a crew from the telephone company moving the telephone kiosk today to a position outside the *wat*. (See 29 April and 23 July)

29 July

There was an article today in one of the English on-line newspapers advising that taxpayers who have to wear uniforms in their jobs are entitled to claim the cost of their cleaning against their tax bill. Technically, washing your company car falls into the same category as the car is not your own asset. Provided that the employer requires you to keep the car clean, the revenue department in the U.K. would have to give way and accept your claim.

But this is Thailand.

With the exception of specialised weaponry, police officers have to provide their own hand-guns. Only ammunition is provided. The government provides traffic police with patrol cars and trucks while the officer on the beat uses his own motor-bike. He may on occasion be fortunate to use a bike that has been confiscated and is parked in the vehicle pool.

The handsome white uniforms you see being worn by government officials are not Government Issue. They are bought by the individual officer. Any decorations or braid worn on the uniform are similarly the responsibility of the wearer. Even the government brown uniforms are not issued by the state. No tax relief for employees here.

The costs of attending appraisal and promotion interviews - invariably in Bangkok - are met by the candidate. That often means an overnight stay. The officer is allowed to take the two days involved as duty days so that they do not impact on holiday entitlement, which is anyway not generous by western standards.

Training and seminars are becoming more commonplace though again they are usually in Bangkok. A contribution is given towards travel expenses; full costs are not met. Ordinary Thais don't get rich on expenses, commissions, or perks. I knew a purser working on a UK passenger liner who owned two race horses. He could by no means have made enough money in Thailand to do that unless he was very well connected.

30 July

The current government announced today that they have approved the building of two high speed train links. It had been mooted before by previous governments but agreements had not been reached and there had been disputes with the Chinese who were co-partnering the project and insisting on owning that part of the track that was on Thai soil.

Planned to be completed by 2021, the main link will be from Rayong to Nongkhai and onward into China. The current single line between Bangkok and Uttaradit will be converted to two tracks and extended through Phayao and Chiangrai to China. As well as improving rail connections between Bangkok and northern Thailand, the improved infrastructure will benefit trade links between the two countries.

The average speed at the moment on the single track between Bangkok, Uttaradit, and Chiangmai is 50 km per hour. Delays are commonplace, particularly in the rainy season when the track gets flooded. It's not unusual for arrival times to be two or three hours behind schedule. Derailments have also occurred on track which is decades old and has not been well maintained.

There has always been a historic struggle in Thailand between those that want infrastructure improvements outside Bangkok and vested interests in the Thai capital that favour wealth remaining where it is. Successive governments in the UK, of course, have similarly shown more interest in developing London and the South-East to the detriment of the economy in the regions.

31 July

Tuk jai; mai tuk tong. A common Thai saying, literally – "all heart; not all correct." Everything done with love in one's heart, but not correct or proper.

His girlfriend had visited him at a government establishment. "Polite" dress was mandatory. Siriporn's short trousers were leaving nothing to the imagination. *Mai tuk tong:* not correct, totally not acceptable.

But Peter obviously liked it. Hence, *tuk jai,* all love in the heart.

Quoting a well-known saying was the Thai way of giving a tactful reprimand. It was their way of making their views clear without being personally direct.
Tuk jai; mai tuk tong.

Peter and Siriporn got the message. It won't happen again.

1 August

Thailand sent 1300 volunteers to France in July 1918 to fight against the Axis powers, just before the First World War ended. They formed part of the occupying force in Germany after hostilities ended but were not involved in front-line service most of the time. No Thai was killed or wounded in action. The timing of their entry into hostilities meant they had little opportunity to show their valour. (In the Second World War they had sided with Japan and Germany and declared war on the Allies.)

The decision to side with the Allies in 1918 was not without controversy as both England and France had previously annexed large chunks of Thai territory. In retrospect it proved the right decision as Thailand's reward for their support and loyalty was a seat around the negotiating table when the Treaty of Versailles was being drafted. Thailand now had an influence in western affairs.

Each soldier was given a hero's welcome on returning to Thailand. *King Vajiravudh,* Rama VI, was "deeply gratified" and after the Supreme Patriarch sprinkled holy water over them they were received at the palace to be told that their service and duty had shown the world "that the Tai race still retained their old fighting blood."

Of the foreigners in Thailand at the time, many volunteered to serve with the Allied forces. The German engineers working on the *Khun Tan* rail tunnel between Lampang and Chiangmai were interned and work on the tunnel only re-commenced after the war was over.

2 August

Although the police and the army are not at daggers drawn, they have never seen eye to eye in Thailand. (I know that's two metaphors in one sentence, but this is a diary!)

Thaksin Shiniwatra, who led the *Thai Rak Thai* party, was a former police colonel and maintained close links with senior officers after he made his billions in business and was elected prime minister. His younger sister *Yingluck,* who ran *Peua Thai,* seemed to have maintained those connections.

It's an open secret that the police service in Thailand is open to corruption. Typical of all less developed countries where bribes are seen as supplements to poor salaries. The military own banks, businesses, and large tracts of land but are not engaged in petty extortions. The May 2014 coup put the military, however undemocratically, in a strong position to encourage some changes in police procedures.

Many senior officers have been replaced or moved sideways. 90 day reporting for foreigners, required to report their address to immigration police, seems to be slicker and faster. Routine searches and checks at police check-points appear better organised. Passports and ID cards must be carried at all times to ensure illegal immigration can be more effectively controlled.

The rule that backpackers and retirees must have a work permit to teach English is being more carefully looked at, though still not always enforced. Casual teaching that is not of poor quality appears to escape the full force of the regulations.

Carrying a passport at all times is inconvenient – I used to carry my driver's licence as a means of identification – but these regulations have a purpose and need to be upheld.

Most Thais see the benefits of tougher and logical enforcement and welcome the moves against corruption. It will never be eradicated but it is a step in the right direction and hopefully it will not just be a short term initiative. The Singaporean experience taught us that there are limits to removing all corrupt practices despite that country being the least corrupt in the Far East. Their zero tolerance policy may be too severe for Thailand.

A pity that these initial benefits resulted from a coup and the temporary suspension of elections. Most *farangs* and western bloggers are anti-coup and pro-democracy. I hold the same principles but observe and appreciate the pragmatic changes that have taken place. In the longer term, reform and return to the ballot box are promised.

For the moment, Thais, brought up on a strict feudal system where everyone knows his place in society, accept what has happened. As Westerners, we do not have that same worldview and don't always appreciate how strongly Thais feel about their class structure.

It's remarkable that the foreign media are not conducting secret straw polls amongst average Thais or even talking to them. They'd do well to listen to the views and feelings of the majority of ordinary people and understand why they are accepting the changes being made. In the long-term, of course, the Thais want open and fair elections to push forward Thailand's democratic constitution.

The media don't mention that the coup was popularly acceptable and bloodless. They don't mention there have been no international sanctions and that military aid and joint exercises from America are still taking place.

3 August

Thais do have a habit of telling tall stories. Walking along the *soi*, I met Adoon, (the banker). There was a lot of noise coming from the village loudspeaker system. It seemed to irritate Adoon. "We have to do that in Thailand, as most people can neither read or write."

That really is nonsense.

The daily announcements are to let people know what is going on. Someone having died, a school concert coming up, giving notice that the water is being turned off for an hour so that the pipes can be cleaned. That sort of thing. The speakers are used several times a day and often announcements are made after the 8am playing of the national anthem.

Today, for example, the village headman, the *pooyaibaan*, made an appeal to villagers to help a family whose outside wooden shed had been destroyed in a storm. A group of us made light work of rebuilding a temporary wooden structure.

Thailand actually has a relatively high literacy rate, 98%, well ahead of Burma, India, Cambodia, and Laos. On a par with Indonesia and 1% below Vietnam.

It's a western trait to take on trust what people say until you have reason to think otherwise. Thais will trust you only when they are sure about you. A big cultural difference. Better for Westerners to be a little sceptical in Thailand and not believe everything you hear or read. I have friends who have been told you can't have a bank account or register a car in your own name in the country if you have no work permit.

They will accept all the propaganda about Taksin, the former prime minister exiled after a coup, as being the most corrupt man ever to have held office in Thailand. He was no saint but he did not have sole claim to corruption.

I was surprised that Adoon made the comment about illiteracy though. He is an educated Thai who should have known better. No excuse for him to get his facts wrong.

4 August

Although everyone thought that it was his, Lit did not own the 1/4 *rai* of land on which he grew his bananas. It was land that had formed part of his divorce settlement but had been discretely transferred to his sister without his knowledge to stop him ever selling it to fund his drinking habit. He never tried to sell it, so he had assumed the land was his.

Soon after the transfer, the sister sold the land to Sengdeuan who had allowed Lit to use the land as if it was his own for the rest of his days. He never knew of that sale.

Lit died at the age of 59 and Sengdeuan has started to merge the land with her own adjoining property.

Things are never what they really seem in Thailand. The Land of Smiles or the Land of Secrets?

Our *pooyaibaan* told me that the land had been sold to Sengdeuan following Lit's death though he did not know to whom. I could hardly tell him what had in fact taken place. There had been some jealousy between him and Sengdeuan's husband because his factory was doing so well.

To his dying day, Lit believed the land belonged to him. Sengdeuan told none of the neighbours. She supports the festivals and events at the *wat*, she pays her respects at funerals.

She otherwise keeps her distance socially.

I was probably one of the few people in the village who knew the true story. Sengdeuan has always been very open with me about happenings in the community and she showed me the land documents. I think that is because she does not see me as part of the "jealous group" as she calls it.

5 August

Some western friends of ours met up with two young tour guides. University students in their final year earning some pocket money to help with their college fees. The girls knew some local places of interest which were not well publicised, and took them there. It had been a long day. Surely, they must be thirsty. "What would you like to drink?"

Both of them declined. Even asking what their favourite drink was had got no reaction. Our friends had apparently asked the restaurant owner how they could get them to accept a well-earned drink.

"Guess," he said. His answer was spot on. The deep-rooted Thai concept of *greng jai*, not wanting to be too forward or excessively pushy, was so strong that they would not ask for a drink. The only solution was to get some glasses of coke or other light refreshment, which is what they did. The two youngsters accepted that, but they would have died of thirst before asking.

The visitors were learning fast how cultural differences between Westerners and Thais can be fascinating but not always easy to get a grip of.

6 August

Visited Tong and his wife today and looked at the house his daughter, Pannee, and her husband are building on their land. The build started last July and is due for completion in three months' time. It is of high specification. All four bedrooms have an ensuite bathroom and a balcony.

Adjacent to the master bedroom is a large walk-in wardrobe. There are two large high-ceilinged reception areas, one with terraces overlooking a full length swimming pool. One room will be for Tong and Noi. The maid's quarters are better appointed than most maids would expect. Instead of a single small room with toilet and shower, the unit is self-contained with a sitting area and balcony complementing the larger than normal bedroom.

Pannee now has a one-month old daughter and they will live in her parents' house until their new home is finished. Both Pannee and her husband are doctors and easily obtained a bank mortgage for their 7 million baht house. With the land, the value is likely to be in the region of 10 to 12 million if they ever wanted to sell it, even more if it was purchased by a foreigner.

It's quite typical for sons and daughters to have a home on parental land when they marry. If that is not possible, the children will find accommodation very near, keeping in close touch with family is important to a Thai. Mike, the elder unmarried son, will continue to live in the parental home until his parents move into Pannee's home when it's finished. He will then have the house to himself, the whole extended family living in the same compound.

Tong is retired and his wife retires next year. Both are in good health and keep fit. He keeps himself occupied with his garden, his duties as *pooyaibaan* of a nearby village, assisting in the temple, and helping with the household chores. Now, Tong will be happy to add lending a hand looking after the new arrival to his daily schedule.

Family culture in Thailand encourages children to look after their parents as they age, paying mum and dad back for caring for them as children. The doting grandparents are more than keen to babysit and generally look after babies as they arrive. Hiring nannies and putting the aged in old folks' homes is virtually unheard of. The children of divorced or separated couples would be cared for by grandparents or relatives until they can fend for themselves and are of working age. There is a higher incidence of boyfriends and husbands leaving their partners when a child is born than in the West.

Visitors aren't able to see this side of Thai culture and expats are often unaware of it.

7 August

Khun Yai's *pooyaibaan* did a lot of organising for the rebuild of her house. He had ensured the local *amphur* had been kept informed, arranged for some soldiers to clear away debris, and he was not afraid to get his hands dirty when jobs like mixing cement were required.

All the former and now retired *pooyaibaans* came round at various times but, because of their position in society, they were not expected to do any physical labour. They would have given a donation in an envelope. Similarly, teachers and the more well off people in the village helped financially rather than practically. Nobody thought any worse of them for that. Everyone was aware of their status in the community.

The house is not luxurious but it has been built well, to Thai standards. The volunteer labour would not want any criticism of their work.

8 August

What the hell. The traffic light has turned to red but the police officer is calling me forward. Cars from the left and the right are obviously obeying the green light that they have now been given.

This is becoming a free for all. Just drive on slowly, I suppose. That's what everyone else seems to be doing. We are only complying with a signal given to us by the strong arm of the law.

Apart from when they are on crash helmet or seat belt purges, the country's finest don't routinely go after motorists or riders driving carelessly or dangerously. Three or more people on a bike, driving without lights, parking on a blind corner. *Mai mee panha.* No problem. Freedom of the individual to defy the occasional contravention of regulations. No need to make a fuss.

Goong told me this evening that she was in a hurry to get to work this morning and didn't stop for a police helmet check. She just smiled and said she was late for work. He beckoned for her to go on her way. Personally, I think he should have at least made her put her helmet on.

9 August

All countries have their *nouveau riche* as well as those who come from families that have always had money and see no reason to flaunt it. The nicest people to be around, in Thailand as elsewhere, are the un-pompous rich and the ordinary folk. Neither pretend to be what they are not.

Thais that have come into new money try to live above their station. Often the money and their standard of living results from marrying a *farang* or from obtaining an inheritance from a foreigner. Most will enjoy the luxuries that westernised ideas bring: holidays abroad, a maid, a gardener, a private education for the children, and designer clothes.

Others get stressed and cannot cope living a non-Thai lifestyle that is so different from what they were used to living in a normal Thai family. Not everyone can, in the long term, make or want to make the transition from living on 300 baht a day or less to having a limitless spending allowance.

They lose the real friends they had since childhood. They have a fashionable show-off lifestyle but may be unhappy deep down inside.

Gaaneegaa seeks solace in alcohol and nightlife. Her background has made her self-centred. She moves in circles where her friends, a mix of *farang* and Thai, have the same attitude.

Benjawan is from a poor family in Isaan. She likes the lifestyle which marrying a *farang* brought her. She can cope with the changes and is not stressed. She has disowned her old friends and become conceited. It does not bother her.

A friend asked her what she did all day long when she had a maid and a gardener in the house every day. "I tell them what to do."

Ordinary Thais will not show it but they dislike the "hi-so" type as they are called in Thai.

10 August

Spoke to Surachai this morning. He said he has to check his building workers constantly. He won't let them backfill soil in the foundations or paint over surfaces until he has checked them. They try to cover mistakes by going on to the second stage before their work has been approved. Surachai checks all wiring and plumbing connections before the pipes or channels are covered in.

Neither he nor his employees think that it is strange for him to be so untrusting. They do not lose face, he does not belittle them. Surachai did not disagree when I suggested it was because of the Thai acceptance of *mai pen rai*, that it doesn't matter. If you can get away with it, get away with it. If it looks okay, then it is okay: the customer won't complain.

Surachai does not get angry or criticise. He never lets them think he is criticising. He just tells them what needs to be done. He's the *wanna*, the boss, so it is accepted. All Thais respect hierarchy.

In one short example, we can see how *mai pen rai*, face, and hierarchy are always present in the lives of ordinary Thais. It's not easy for Westerners to appreciate this different Thai way of thinking. It took me time to understand it.

I'm going to ask Surachai if he's interested in making some modifications to my outside kitchen. I'll be watching the work closely but will only comment to him and not to the workers if I see corners being cut. No loss of face for the builders and I'll be as tactful as I can be with Surachai. The trick with Thais is not to make it look like blame. They'll resent that.

It made me think about Pomelo. He did some excellent work on the patio, measuring and re-measuring until he was satisfied it was absolutely right. He even watered the loose stones into the pathways and put a roller over them to fix them into the ground. He was a good worker when he started working in the garden. Then he started coming a little late in the mornings, and leaving early. He didn't seem so bothered about paint splashes on the walls when he did some decorating. Initially Pomelo taped surrounding areas with paper to avoid the paint splashing. Then he seemed to tire of doing so.

It was not laziness: I think the strong Thai concept of *mai pen rai* was taking over. Surachai could prevent that because he was the boss; not so easy for a foreigner who is not seen as being part of the Thai class system and therefore not able to "pull rank" on his employees.

11 August

Thais can be very agile. Pranom is 65 and still climbs up his *lamyai* trees to take down the fruit. He and his wife have 70 trees on their farm in Lampang. He keeps busy and fit. He has no need of exercise machines or visits to the fitness parks so favoured by other Thais.

Men from the electricity companies don't use ladders or cherry pickers, they put on boots and use the spurs attached to them to climb up the poles, the spurs fitting securely in the holes drilled in the posts. It looks deceptively easy. Thailand's wiring system looks so tangled, lots of loose wiring on posts that are not always upright.

Inside houses, it's best not to rely on the colour codes when repairing or changing wires. The live, neutral, and earth wires may be connected properly even though they may be of different colours. Another example of *mai pen rai*, I suppose. Provided you are careful and check what you are doing, it doesn't matter. Just don't rely on the colours.

12 August

Don't normally ride my bicycle at night but I had been visiting a friend and was not that far from home. Stopped on a corner and put my left foot down only to find there was no kerb. Ended up in a ditch and had a faint recollection of the bike somersaulting over me. Scrambled up the bank and could only see a flickering red light coming from the bottom of the ditch. My poor bike signaling its discomfort.

A passing pick-up truck stopped and we got the bike out eventually. They offered to put the bike in the back of the truck and drive me home. I felt okay to ride but it was a nice gesture from them. Thais can be so helpful and caring.

Thais don't always stop to help. They know only too well that sometimes it is better to just pass on by at the scene of an accident rather than run the risk of being attacked or being stitched up as being involved in the accident. Best to take stock of situations and make a quick decision on whether to get involved or not.

They'll usually help *farangs* provided they are not speaking loudly or getting annoyed.

13 August

Had a look at that ditch this morning. It was about 7 foot deep. I think I had a lucky escape.
Last night I had not realised how far down I must have fallen.

Bancha came round to check on the workers laying a concrete path. Tried to be as persuasive
as I could be to get him to get the workers not to rush the job and to keep the path wet so that
the concrete would not dry out too quickly. They don't take enough care in curing concrete in
Thailand.

My offer of coffee got the usual Thai *greng jai* response. They don't like to impose. But
when I said I was having one and would like him to join me, he changed his mind. We had a
nice chat. Thais respond to light conversation and even a bit of joking. They hate seriousness.

His wife wouldn't join us though. She just sat in the truck. He didn't find that odd and I've
learnt to accept that reserve and shyness from a Thai. She'd have been kicking her heels if
that happened in the West, not waiting half an hour in the front seat of a truck parked in full
sun.

Socialising with a smile is a good way to get things done in Thailand. The workers did a
reasonable job on the path in the end when they saw me chatting to the boss.

14 August

Was running late to get to my petanque game today at the *Alliance Française.* I go most
weeks as they are a friendly and welcoming crowd not at all like the starchier and formal
expat clubs that have sprung up in some cities and towns in Thailand. The emphasis is on
enjoying the game and the social interaction among friends. There is no commercialization. It
is run as a club should be run with nobody trying to sell you unwanted financial advice or a
condo.

I wanted to turn right at a busy junction and the car ahead of me made the turn when he saw a
gap in the traffic coming towards him. I followed, copying the Thai way of "following my
leader." Thai drivers accept that when one goes, the rest will follow. I noticed the four or five
cars behind me did the same. You don't see that in the West. To be safe, one needs to adapt
to the driving style of a country's drivers and not drive as one would at home.

There's no on-road driving test in Thailand. You're asked some questions, drive around a
short circuit with the examiner supposedly watching you, carry out some reaction tests, and
collect your licence. That's not a recipe for good driving standards. One feature of Thai
driving that I do like, however, is the use of lights as a warning of presence and an indication
that you are coming through. Flashing has no other meaning and significance as it may have

in the West. I have only seen a few drivers, whom I suspect are *farang*, flash their lights to call you forward to proceed.

It's common in rural areas to use hazard lights to indicate you are going straight across at a road junction.

15 August

Bancha came round and wanted to take out the shuttering on the sides of the path. It's too early for that but he eventually agreed to come back tomorrow when he can remove them and I can pay him.

Then he started re-measuring the path. I hope he's not thinking he can raise the price from what he agreed with me.

16 August

Bancha sent a worker round to take down the shuttering and to fix a few minor snags. The previous workers had partially cemented over a manhole cover and it could not be opened. He needed to break up the concrete and re-build around it, but he did not really know how to tackle the job either. He kept looking at the half cover that was still exposed.

He wanted to take the *mai pen rai* view that it did not matter. I suggested he get Bancha to come round later and look at it.

Bancha came round with three men and he explained what they had to do while I poured some soft drinks and chatted with him.

He did not raise the matter of the enhanced price and I gave him what we had agreed. But he had been trying to pull a fast one. Better to sweet talk, *pootwan*, than to argue or make anyone lose face.

I've seen discussions go on for twenty minutes when a few sentences would have sufficed to make one's point in the West. But that is not the Thai way. So smile and master the art of *pootwan*.

17 August

Amazing how Thais park their cars and bikes wherever they like. A few motorbikes had some near misses this morning on a corner where two cars had double-parked. Thais aren't the most careful of road users.

Driving tests are done off-road in Thailand and last only a few minutes. They watch a safety video but are not subjected to a particularly rigorous Highway Code test with a high pass mark.

Reminds me of an 80 year old uncle – he was an undertaker in a village in Devon – being asked by a driving examiner where road users should not park their vehicles. Presumably, the correct answer includes: not on a hump back bridge, not near a zebra crossing, not on a bend etc. etc.

His reply always made me laugh.

"Don't know about any Highway Code Book. Never been a keen book reader. I only ride around the village on my moped. If I stop anywhere, I'd just park it in a hedge. I've no intention of riding in big cities like Exeter anyway."

18 August

Thais seem to think one step at a time. The builders had run the overhead electric wiring into Leon's new house and started the internal connections. Then they started erecting the garage where the wires were leading into the house. They moved the wires to the side, which was better cosmetically in any case. It was not regarded as a mistake, it was natural for them not to have thought of the next stage in the build. They were concentrating on one thing at a time.

The architect had not allowed for the size of the washbasin and cupboard in the bathroom when he designed the room. The plan showed the basin right next to the door. That was no problem but the intended built-in cupboard underneath would not have opened. It was agreed to leave an open space under the basin unit. Although it was not ideal, it was a minor point and in Thailand you tend not to insist on rectification if the issue is not serious. This *mai pen rai* attitude can get quite contagious.

I would imagine Thais don't use critical path analysis as a planning tool to schedule the sequence of events for any project or design. They'd be expert at using the statistical theory of Markov Chains, though, where each outcome is determined only by the previous action or event!

19 August

In rural areas there are usually irrigation canals between properties. Farmers can draw water from them to irrigate their crops and they act as a flood prevention measure taking surplus water away from the rivers which feed them.

To one side of my property is a disused canal, *klong*, which has been filled in. The 3 metre strip is owned by the local authority but has been planted with bananas and *lamyai* by the owners of the adjacent land. Normally that would pose no difficulty. I was not bothered and certainly no Thai would give it a second thought. The owners, however, intend constructing a house on the land and would most likely build on the 3 metre strip. They would be building on land that did not belong to them and that upsets most Thais. The owners said that they had contacts in the Land Office.

Although I said I wasn't worried so long as no building was erected, my neighbours were concerned they won't be able to use the strip as a right of way if it were fenced in. The usual gossiping and comments in the village have resulted in the owner paying for the Land Office to send four men to put in marker posts establishing the *klong* boundary. The previous markers had oddly disappeared. All six of them.

No formal representations or complaints were made to the authorities. The solution was arrived at through the usual chit chat and gossip taking place throughout the village. The owners didn't feel aggrieved at what the neighbours had engineered and everyone is still on speaking terms.

(Addendum: there have been developments on this which are recorded later)

20 August

All the families around here are busy picking *lamyai* (longan) from their trees. The big farms are recruiting contract labour and the workers are harvesting the crop from early morning to sunset. The largest landowner in the area has 200 rai of orchard surrounding his very opulent house. The younger men are climbing the trees or using bamboo ladders to take down the crop. Others are taking the bunches and stripping the fruit from them at high speed. A lot of chatting and gossiping while they work.

The baskets full of fruit are taken to one of the local wholesalers who grade them according to size before the fruit is taken to the canning factory. The hopper machines are working flat out. It is a busy time of year.

We only have ten trees but have made a little money this year. Prices range from 7 baht to 30 baht per kilo. Ours averaged 25 baht.

21 August

The best Thai restaurants with authentic Thai menus and good value for money are undoubtedly those in the mid-price range and where you see lots of Thais eating and empty plates going back to the kitchen.

Another tip is never visit a restaurant where there are menus translated into English. The prices in the English menus are usually higher anyway and the food more westernised.

Chanced on an extremely good restaurant today for lunch after visiting the local plant market. The very bubbly and friendly waitress was keen to explain the dishes on offer, all traditionally northern Thai.

We got chatting and I learnt a bit more about the lives of waitresses. Her Thai was very clear and she spoke slowly. That was a giveaway that she was from a hill tribe and had learnt the language from school and not family. Her home was too far away to commute each day and she boarded at the restaurant with a few others, visiting her parents once a month and giving them a large slice of her earnings. That is very typical of young girls here.

She works ten hours every day and gets a salary of 300 baht – the legal minimum wage – per day. With customers rounding up their bill by a few baht to include a tip, she probably makes a few hundred baht on top of her salary each week. Her rent is 500 baht per month and includes electricity and water in her room. These one room apartments are basic but clean, with a bed, table, and a chair. Each has a separate toilet and shower area.

You can get to know much about Thailand and the people by taking the trouble to converse with the ordinary Thai.

22 August

General Prayuth's broadcast tonight concentrated on education. A family man, he appears to be in touch with popular feeling. He is certainly charismatic though there is some spin in his announcements. What he is doing, however, is communicating with the people. None of the political parties have done this or attempted to kept citizens informed.

Manifestos are debated before election time then forgotten when whichever party wins and is in office. Political parties in the West are pretty much the same.

He wants more emphasis given to the needs of children and students and more career direction given so that when they leave school or university they can find satisfying and useful employment. He is emphasising meritocracy. Prayuth also drew attention to the need for Thai students to learn more about their country and heritage.

He is reviewing with Immigration the complex visa rules for foreign teachers to make sure common sense and not bureaucracy is taken into account. He wants no artificial barriers in place stopping the talented foreign teacher from working in Thailand. He did not specifically mention it but Prayuth seemed aware of unqualified backpackers taking advantage of current rules which allow low quality teaching in the classroom.

He details the actions the NCPO has taken, naming and shaming both officials and corporate bodies that are not being effective. Corruption won't disappear but it is being tackled, at least for now. He asks for all Thais to speak up and be part of the reforms and changes which are needed. He openly encourages debate and says he is listening to the popular voice. Elections are promised once there is a stable climate for them to take place.

That is why anti-corruption measures, which are being made very transparent through the bulletins, are such a basic initial requirement in the changes the regime is making. A long way to go, of course, and not all corruption is being tackled. Let's hope the momentum is not lost in the coming years with any change of government and that it will be possible to hold free elections. Corruption is partly cultural in Thailand and will not be totally eradicated. Some powerful groups may find they are immune from scrutiny.

The foreign press do not even report these bulletins, which is apparently why so many foreigners in Thailand are not fully conversant with what is going on. They have only to read the English subtitles during the broadcasts or get them translated by a Thai partner to be better informed (whether they believe the promises will be kept or not.)

It may not be the majority but many *farangs* seem content to regurgitate bar gossip on social media, such as Facebook and New Mandala, even when the facts are readily available. Neither site is banned in Thailand for its inaccurate propaganda. Those re-tweeting or re-posting are not being prosecuted unless a serious libel is perpetrated. Even so, Thais are targeted more than ordinary *farangs* unless the foreigner is high profile.

Prayuth's broadcasts can come across as a bit one-sided and his delivery is rather "flat." In naming and shaming he may be being a little selective. Even he has to watch his p's and q's in a country so immersed in the importance of keeping the levels of hierarchy intact.

Let's hope the education agenda will be achieved. A promising start has been made. The UK's Prime Minister Blair made impressive promises on "education, education, education" in 1996 which proved to be false starts.

23 August

Geng had suggested getting a palm tree from a nursery he knows. They delivered it this afternoon with the roots wrapped in Hessian. They usually plant without taking off the wrapping but I asked them to cut it off so that the roots had a better chance to grow. No problem, but they couldn't understand why *farangs* always make that request.

Plants grow so quickly here that they just replace any that die. I call it *mai pen rai* gardening. It doesn't matter if it does not survive, just plant another.

24 August

Weerot turned up this evening a bit flustered. He wanted to see his elder sister and tell her their aunt was not sharing all the proceeds of their *lamyai* sales. He and his mother had worked hard on both pieces of land, his mother's and his aunt's. The aunt had taken the baskets to the wholesaler but had kept most of the money.

Direct confrontation being out of the question, Weerot's sister rang the aunt, chatted generally for a while, and then asked how much her mum's share of the *lamyai* sales would be.

No arguing. No raised voices. The aunt had been trying it on. She said she would give Weerot the full amount due when she goes round their house tomorrow.

Weerot had ridden 30 kilometres to see his sister; she had spent fifteen minutes on the phone with her aunt. It all seemed quite normal practice to both of them. Thais amaze me every day.

25 August

Spoke to a monk this morning who has transferred from Wat Dhammakaya near Bangkok. He told me that during the allied bombings in the Second World War the monks prayed for angels to divert the bombs so that they fell in the sea. He seemed convinced that the prayers had been answered.

It is true that not all bombs hit their targets but I'm not convinced the angels had anything to do with it. Always difficult to discuss superstitions with Thais. I like debating and putting forward a point of view. Nevertheless, Thais can often take that as challenging them. I tend to move the conversation on to something else if I see that happening.

26 August

It's the egg-laying season for pond-life. Frogs, toads, bullfrogs, shrimps, and other sea creatures breed at this time of the rainy season. A selection of the amphibians and fish are trapped and put in a small holding pond at the local school in preparation for a mass "wedding ceremony" to be conducted with all the usual pomp and high-spiritedness associated with Thai rituals.

The day starts with a procession led by monks and villagers carrying a gaily painted pole to which envelopes containing cash are pinned. The donations, *tamboon*, are presented to the monks for temple use. Those making merit in this way have a sacred white cord, the *sai sin*, tied around one of their wrists by the monks.

After the "wedding" the creatures are released into the wild with a blessing and good luck for a fertile mating. Frogs and toads are popular delicacies in Thailand. And the ceremony ensures that they are protected from being caught and eaten! Yes, amazing Thailand.

27 August

A local paper, with advertising links to the leisure and tourist industry, reported today that the military government has introduced some new regulations curbing alcohol advertising and had held a press conference. One attendee made it sound as if it was a summons rather than an invitation. He may have been right. Whether there was any debate about the detailed regulations and how they could be sensibly enforced was not mentioned. Maybe there was little or no discussion with representatives of the industry. Maybe there was. The style, officially anyway, of the current administration is to encourage deliberation and to listen to pragmatic suggestions.

Those at the receiving end of some of the government's new measures sometimes report a more negative version of how decisions on bringing in new rules and regulations are reached. Vested interests are unlikely to give a balanced account of what the military are doing. The basis for the "new" rules is actually a statute enacted six years ago. As with many regulations in Thailand, it had not been strictly enforced by previous political parties. No doubt blind eyes were turned and money changed hands.

A 70 page handbook was handed out at the conference which went into minute detail on what could and could not be allowed in advertising, promoting, and selling alcoholic beverages. There was room for some interpretation though essentially the handbook clarified and strengthened the 2008 law. Its aim was to remove any doubt and to close any loopholes that may have been used previously.

It's understandable that businesses making a living from the hospitality sector were worried at stricter regulations and enforcement hitting their bottom line. The initial reaction from one member, quickly followed by others in the audience, was to start posting on social media. The language on Facebook was getting more and more emotive. Would prohibition be next? Why were such "draconian" measures being introduced by a "junta" which seemed hell bent on destroying the freedoms enjoyed by both clients and providers? Why were "debilitating fines being introduced willy-nilly?" They were not of course, this was all journalese.

There were a few comments that there was some anti-junta journalism creeping in and that the full facts of the legislation and the reasoning behind it were not given as much prominence in print as the restrictive and complex rules. Most of the comments were self-serving and protectionist in nature. Attendees realised that the gravy train they had enjoyed for so long was being moved into the sidings.

The English language newspapers and magazines cater for a niche market. With a *farang* readership, their comments pages are full of sarcastic comments. That's usual in the western media. It's frowned upon by Thais.

Thailand has a serious drink-drive and alcohol abuse problem. It is tackled in other countries; it can be tackled here. That does not mean a ban on alcohol sales. It does mean discouraging anti-social drinking by regulating advertising. Having said that, the devil is always in the detail and the legal draughtsmen seem, in my opinion anyway, to have over complicated what should have been a sensible working set of regulations which would eventually have been seen as reasonable and workable.

How many of these do you think are over the top?

Drinking banned for those under 20 years of age, health warnings to be placed on all alcoholic products similar to those on cigarette packets, "happy hours" to be made illegal, promotions giving three drinks for the price of two to be outlawed, bar staff must not wear t-shirts advertising beer or spirits, no brand names or logos to appear on beer glasses or even ashtrays.

No drinking in bars and restaurants after midnight, no posters on display advertising alcoholic products, no drinking near schools or temples, no drinks to be sold on religious holidays, photos in magazines which show alcoholic beverages must have the brand names blurred out, and the employment of girls by the big beer companies to promote their products in bars not being allowed.

I've not seen binge drinking near schools and temples. I suspect sense will prevail when it is realised that girls promoting products when punters are already in the bar won't alter their drinking habits. Wearing a uniform showing the logo of one of the major beverage companies owned by the élite is unlikely to be challenged. A bartender giving his suggested mix for a cocktail to a customer, which is technically advertising, surely won't result in prosecution.

Rules and regulations in Thailand tend to be linked to the "flavour of the month" and are modified in practice or ignored when a new idea is thought of and takes over as the latest enforcement gimmick. I suspect in a month or so this will all be forgotten and we'll quietly go back to the status quo, Thai style. Rather like the stage actor in Macbeth.

"that struts and frets his hour upon the stage, and then is heard no more: it is a tale .... full of sound and fury, signifying nothing."

28 August

Not all land in Thailand is freehold and owned outright by way of a *chanote*: many houses are built on land for which no legal title can be traced. The local authority will allow you to buy the plot and build on it though you cannot be sure if it will be taken back later when someone makes a claim. The matter is then decided by weighing up the evidence of purchases and sales of the land over many years, proof of previous occupation, and any supporting documents. Memories can be unreliable, transactions will almost certainly have been for cash.

Records may be scarce or of dubious authenticity. An exercise carried out in Samui some years ago collated the total acreage of all land titles issued. It came to 200 thousand *rai* (an area of 1600 square metres). The total land mass of the island is 150 thousand *rai*!
The fact that your local *pooyaibaan* and elders in the neighbourhood believe you have a strong claim to ownership and paid in good faith may become irrelevant.

There are six main types of title and a few forms of title with limited validity as they are issued by government departments other than the land office. Yes, you read that correctly. Just for information, I give them below.

Lawyers must love the opportunities that this mish-mash of legislation provides. It is best to proceed only when a *chanote* is produced or when your seller undertakes to complete all the formalities of upgrading to a full title of ownership.

Naw Saw1: Indicates ownership of the land though evidence of an occupier may prove a stronger claim. New titles have not been issued since 1972 and cases are usually limited to farmers who are using the land.
Naw Saw2: A temporary permit to occupy and use the land. It can be upgraded to stronger forms of title but even then can only be transferred by inheritance and not by sale.
Naw Saw3: Shows occupation and use though not necessarily ownership. There are no boundary markers and the plot can only be sold if there is no public objection.
Naw Saw3 Gor: Some small technical differences to *Naw Saw3* relating to how the land was measured.

Naw Saw4 Jor: Commonly called the *chanote,* the safest and strongest title of ownership. Mortgages can be given on this title deed and rights of occupancy can be attached so that foreigners, who cannot by law own land in Thailand, have some degree of security and right to stay on the land, the cost of which they would most likely have funded anyway. Even with a *chanote*, squatters' rights will allow a claim after 10 years of occupancy to succeed.
Naw Saw5: This title only gives a right to use the land.
Saw Raw Gor 4 01: Not issued by the Land Office. It allows occupation and transfer by inheritance only.
Saw Raw Gor (STG): As *Saw Raw Gor 4 01* but applies to forest land.
Naw Kaw 3: A deed allowing use only and limited to self-help communities. Cannot be sold.
Paw Baw Taw5: Merely shows tax has been paid for using the land. Not an evidence of ownership.
Gor Saw Naw5: A deed showing use by a cooperative. No ownership title.

Because Thai land law is such a minefield, many foreigners rent a house or buy a condominium of which they can own 49 per cent. (51% must be Thai).

There are large areas of land in Thailand with no documentation at all. They can be claimed by the government. Some wealthy individuals have accumulated acres and acres of land where there was no documentation.

29 August

A photo of a Thai bank employee went viral on Facebook and YouTube today. An attractive girl, smiling and laughing to camera with her skirt hitched up. The problem was she was wearing her uniform so the bank, the oldest bank in Thailand, was clearly identifiable. Apparently she was also selling shoes on bank premises.

Adoon said other banks had also sent out memos and emails to all staff forbidding them having their photos taken in uniform and spreading it around social media. What surprised me was the speed in which the banks reacted.

30 August

Got caught in a traffic jam today. It looked like there was an accident up ahead. Cars and trucks were moving at a snail's pace and there appeared to be only one open lane on the bend in front of us.

Getting nearer, we realised the congestion was caused by cars and motor bikes parked on both sides of the road close to a newly set up market stall. Street markets are usually at designated places and police attend in order to control traffic flow. Here, a stall-holder had taken the initiative to put up hoardings advertising his low prices and was selling his goods at a busy interjection. Too much of a bargain for people to pass by.

Police may or may not come later and move him on.

31 August

Quite a few letters arrived this morning even though it's a Sunday. The postman went to a house warming, *tamboonbaan,* yesterday so could not complete his deliveries. I was not surprised when I saw his motor bike pull up outside. It's happened several times before.

Thais often feel a deep satisfaction in their work when there is direct contact with a customer. He did not want those he saw and chatted with on a regular basis to miss out by their mail being delayed.

This attitude seems prevalent in rural areas and where the employee wears a uniform. Workers and staff know uniforms get noticed and they are worn as a badge of pride and reflect on the organisation they work for.

1 September

Lots of traffic and police presence around the local *wat* this lunchtime. A member of the royal family is attending a funeral on the King's behalf. Must be someone important. The pyre will be lit from a royal flame brought from the palace.

In fact, all government officers are entitled to this privilege when they are cremated. The flame is transported from Bangkok but usually no member of the Thai royal family attends.

2 September

The ink is not dry on the contract and the builder is still trying to re-negotiate the terms we've already both agreed. The signatures do not appear to mean much to him. Bancha does some good work but, like many in his line of business in Thailand, he's on the look out to increase his profit at every available opportunity. Although it does not happen only in this country, the tactic of trying to change a contract and increase the cost is very prevalent in the Land of Smiles. You can either refuse to accept the changes or, if the amounts are small, you may think it better to go along with them.

Taking the matter to court would be slow and expensive. You are unlikely to receive costs even if you win and they are awarded. Collecting any sums due from the defendant would normally involve bailiffs, lengthy delays, and travelling to a legal execution office to pick up a cheque. There will be lots of hoops to jump through on the way to get your money. Thais use a direct approach and use contacts rather than proceed along the legal route.

Because of possible loss of face, workers may just walk off site if you disagree with new terms. They know how the system works. Sometimes one needs to be pragmatic and accept some compromise and not hang out for the sake of a principle. Lawyers will quote hourly rates or offer a fixed fee. Choose hourly rates and the case will drag on and on. Choose a fixed fee and you will still be charged for extras such as translation services of an outside translator. A fixed fee also takes away the incentive for your lawyer to achieve your desired result. You may win or lose the case. The defendant may win or lose the case. It's a win-win situation for both sets of lawyers. A good tactic may be to offer a gratuity for a successful outcome.

An air conditioner was included in the specification and shown on the plans but the builder would not fit it within the price. Bancha said that the wording meant supply only and not fitting. He was charging what he thought the market would bare. He knew that I assumed, as anyone else would have done, that the fan would be properly connected.

Bancha would have tried it on with a Thai as easily as with a *farang*. He saw my reasoning in the end. Thais watch out for these extras and sometimes they get caught out too.

I remember Anoon telling me not to expect builders to do remedial work once they have received final payment, always hold a little back whatever promises are given.

3 September

Duangjai is still waiting for a resolution on her dispute with the owners of the paint spraying facility built next to her home. Saw her today. Lawyers would not be of any help; Thais prefer to sort things out face to face or with an intermediary like the *pooyaibaan*. She still awaits his decision.

She and her husband have planted some vegetables in her tiny 2 by 6 metre garden, and they have bought a few items of furniture for the home. The bedroom, though, still only has a mattress on the floor for sleeping and a metal rail on which to hang their clothes.

I'm sure they'll get more furniture when they can afford it. Certainly could not pay any lawyer fees on their joint income.

4 September

Many khaki uniforms on show today. It's Thursday. Both school children and their teachers are in Scout uniform. There won't be any special ceremonies or activities but there is a strong sense of bonding when all are dressed alike.

It's a change from school attire and Thais love uniforms. When visiting Thailand you'll notice different colours being worn on different days, yellow on Mondays, for example, as the late King Bhumibol's birthday was on a Monday. In the North, traditional *lanna* costume will be seen on Fridays.

5 September

Prayuth's Friday broadcast this evening concentrated on how in the past it was acceptable for small private enterprises not to pay tax. It's clear he intends to change that situation so that all businesses, small or large, pay their share. By quoting figures by industry sector he showed a sound grasp of how the Thai economy ticks and how it can be encouraged to grow. Elected parties, perhaps because they want to be re-elected and are therefore reluctant to impart bad news, have never done this.

That is not solely a Thai phenomenon. Presidents and Prime Ministers, nearing elections, tend not to make tough decisions which may in fact be necessary for the long-term well-being of a country. Short termism and the power of strong pressure groups usually prevails. That's hardly democratic.

Tax rates are not high in Thailand and allowances are generous. Corporation tax is at 20% while tax for individuals, the bulk of the Small Medium size Entrepreneurs, only starts when income reaches 150,000 baht after allowances and then only at 5%. You would have to earn over 4 million baht to start paying at the higher rate of 35%. VAT is at 7%.

Prayuth commented on the floods that are ravaging the extreme north of the country and has set in place emergency measures. The situation was aggravated by China releasing water from a dam on the Mekong River. Unless he is complaining through diplomatic channels, which I doubt, he outlined no action for dealing with that.

Thailand has an extensive network of small canals, *klongs*, which could be used if sluice gates were opened to lower the water levels in the main rivers flowing into Bangkok. That didn't happen two years ago when the capital city was heavily flooded. My view at the time was that there was political pressure not to open the gates. The Thais that I know would not comment but neither did they disagree with what I had said.

The general's broadcast leans towards a public relations spin on occasion. He has to get people on side. By continually giving details of the NCPO's attacks on corruption he is, however, justifying his use of unelected power. A pity this was not achieved through the ballot box. Both political parties had their chance and flunked it.

6 September

Weelai took us to see some of her friends today. Both their husbands are quite ill. One seems to have dementia and the other looks very frail. Had an enjoyable lunch with one couple.

Nevertheless, it slightly spoilt it for me when the husband was excluded from the conversation and just sat in the corner with a glass of water after the meal. He had obviously worked hard all his life but was no longer the breadwinner. I am sure that he was well looked after but it was sad and strange to observe their attitude towards him. He did not seem to mind.

We took the other couple out for dinner with the family, but although he was sat at the head of the table, he was not being included in the conversation.

Thais and Westerners view things differently.

7 September

We saw how customers wanting a bargain at a market stall will park on a bend, not being too bothered about any inconvenience or danger. The point is of course nobody minds. It's acceptable.

Keeping strictly to rules where no sense is seen in them and no harm is done holds no importance to a Thai. What Hollinger called in her book *Mai Pen Rai Means Never Mind,*" "freedom to spit."

They weigh up how significant something is and if they can ignore it, they will.

8 September

Mana's wife went into the maternity wing of the local state hospital today. Not completely free as in some western countries. She will pay a flat fee of 30 baht. That's reasonable but it's still 10% of the minimum daily wage. Visitors to Thailand, and even expats, often think in dollars, pounds, and euros. And see the country as an inexpensive place to live. For the Thai, even 30 baht can be significant if there are many visits to doctors or hospitals.

When Alex talks of things he has bought or meals he and Ae have had, he always mentions the price in dollars.

9 September

Went to hospital this morning with a stomach problem. Waited only a few minutes. Had the usual blood pressure, temperature, pulse, and weight checks carried out by a nurse and then was directed to the doctor responsible for stomach ailments. I signed a few forms and there was no other paperwork. All the clinical details were entered into the central hospital computer so that all medical staff could have access to my medical records.

Third in line to see the specialist who carried out the initial examination who recommended an x-ray, blood test, and a CAT scan. Thai doctors tend to send their patients for tests before confirming their diagnosis. Sometimes that may be overkill. There are reports on the internet of insurers believing hospitals in countries like India and Thailand are artificially inflating costs by recommending unnecessary tests and procedures, and by overprescribing medications (particularly antibiotics and painkillers.)

Doctors in the UK, in the public sector anyway, generally diagnose, select a procedure, and await results. If symptoms persist they try other medication, request specialist advice at a different hospital, or arrange for further tests.

Thailand offers more of a "one stop" service. When they form a diagnosis they do so with the benefit of the detail amassed from the numerous tests they have asked hospital technicians to carry out. There's no attempt to make an initial guess from the symptoms presented. There is also no "triage" system where you pass through levels of examination to determine a priority for being seen by a doctor. Emergencies are seen as such and dealt with speedily. No time is wasted with doctors asking similar questions and passing on their notes to the doctor that will eventually be responsible for your case.

Triage was set up because of the strain on state hospital resources. The system became more popular in the last decade of the twentieth century in the UK but some hospitals particularly in the north of England have reverted to a less complex and more common sense approach to assessing priority enabling most patients to be seen by one specialist doctor without going through what is really a screening process.

They have found that it cuts down waiting times.

I had great difficulty in explaining triage to my Thai doctor. I doubt if I succeeded: he felt, as the hospitals quoted above clearly realised, that a patient should go directly to the specialist doctor that had been determined at the registration stage on arrival.

As in England, Thailand has both private and state hospitals. For Thai nationals and, until recently, for some expats who could elect to pay an annual fee, health care costs around 30 baht per visit or admission. Most Thais would go to a state or private hospital and not a private GP clinic, the advantages being the increased facilities available and there being specialists on site.

The CAT scan had shown inflammation of the colon which had a 90% chance of healing with medication and I was admitted. They were right to ask for further tests though having an ECG test on the heart and an x-ray were not procedures that were necessary given the symptoms as presented. I can see why health insurers are wary of hospitals.

On the other hand, no harm is done (other than to one's wallet and an insurer's profit and loss account) and it's best to be safe than sorry.

10 September

Private hospitals have 8-bed wards as well as private rooms. Doctors visit three times a day on average, whether you go privately or not. They see you before they start their patient surgeries, then after lunch before their afternoon appointments, and finally before they go home for the evening. Emergency doctors are on hand throughout the night.

Nursing care is faultless. Caring comes naturally to a Thai. Examples of uneaten meals being removed because a patient can't self-feed are unheard of. A Thai would have difficulty understanding that such incidents are not uncommon in western hospitals. The patient-staff ratio varies between 6:1 and 12:1 depending on how many beds are occupied. Unless there is a serious road traffic accident or a natural disaster, beds are always available.

A member of the family is encouraged to stay with the patient overnight and a flatbed is provided. Visits during the day do not suffer restrictions and can be of psychological benefit. Thais love talking and gossiping. They also know when the patient needs rest and quiet.

Friends and colleagues often come in groups and it became clear that they see it as an automatic cultural response rather than as a duty. It's a difficult concept to explain. Thais see hospital visits, funerals, house-warmings, and other functions as a chance to socialise with friends and neighbours, and to show a caring attitude. Some fruit and snacks are routinely brought. You'll see your acquaintances more at functions and situations such as being ill in hospital than at organised dinner parties.

In the West you entertain your friends at home and they reciprocate. In Thailand, Thais meet up with people they know outside their own homes, normally at a restaurant or, as in this case, around a hospital bed. Your visitors may bring food for themselves so that they can share a meal with you. It's a social occasion. You visit people's houses of course though not with the same frequency as you would in the West.

11 September

Only one other patient on the ward was a *farang*. He said that Thais visit only to show off, they are only acting as if they are compassionate. They only sit and chat to each other and don't come specifically because you are ill as they would in the West.

He certainly had a lot of Thai visitors, friends and relatives of his wife. Some had come quite some distance to see him. Robert has been in Thailand a year, having lived and married his Thai wife, *Tong*, in England where they stayed for twelve years. He's looking at their reasons for visiting with western eyes.

12 September

I have "survived" many coups in Thailand, having emigrated here a few weeks after one particularly controversial coup d'état. A very down to earth Thai told me at that time not to worry. "These things happen every now and again."

It's mainly business as usual after a coup. Few things change; life goes on but with a different government in place. New brooms always sweep clean and that is manifested by a couple of high profile announcements and promises. The underlying theme is to almost always to reduce corruption and cheating, blaming the previous administration for all the perceived damaging actions perpetrated during their period of office. Sometimes there is truth in that; sometimes there is not. Changes are largely cosmetic and the Thais are not overly swayed by what they read in the press and on social media. Even if they are careful not to comment, they don't believe every piece of "news" they've been fed.

Foreigners don't have the luxury of being able to converse freely with Thais in their own language, they don't have access to close-knit family groups who can be trusted to quote accurately how and why previous coups have acted as they have. Westerners generally do not observe events impartially as much as the Thais do. They take too much of what they read or are told on trust. Thais distrust until they have reason to trust; foreigners tend to more easily accept what they read. My advice always is to check as many sources as possible and to work at gaining trust with some of your Thai friends, those you know who will eventually open up and talk frankly with you.

Do Thais like coups? The answer is "yes and no."

They like coups in the sense that they appreciate strong leadership. Thais do not question their parents or family elders; they don't like to take individual responsibility, preferring others to make decisions on their behalf. They may not like what a government does but they do not see that they have a role to question it. They respect the strength that family, their "betters," and the government in power are displaying. They believe it is not for them to challenge that right. Others will do their thinking for them.

Theirs not to make reply, theirs not to reason why, theirs but to do and die.

They dislike coups in the sense that they would wish there was an alternative way to having an uncorrupted government in place. They want to use ballot boxes but do not want the people they elect to work in an undemocratic or corrupt way. So, for the voters, it is a matter of accepting the least bad option.

13 September

Quite a few *farangs* here carry out do-it-it-yourself jobs in their homes. If the work is extensive and you are taking away trade from a Thai it is technically illegal though you would be unlucky indeed if it became an issue. Most prosecutions, resulting in a fine paid to immigration police, result from other foreigners making a report about their neighbour's activities.

Edward has built a western style walk-in wardrobe in the master bedroom. He had been quoted 150,000 baht for the job but did it himself for 50,000. His 4 days labour has saved him a hundred thousand baht. He had been prepared to pay a Thai worker to do the job. At that inflated price, he was prepared to take a chance on not getting caught.

Tool hire shops for DIY are not common in Thailand. Many *farangs* have built up a collection of useful tools they have purchased and which they can share amongst themselves. Provided they are used only in their own homes and no one is aware of the work being done there is rarely a problem.

What the eye does not see....

Prices to the expat community are usually higher than that quoted to a Thai family. Although labour rates are linked to the 300 baht minimum wage, construction projects in Thailand attract high gross margins. Owners make higher percentage profits than in the West because of low wage rates. A major disadvantage in the low wage concept is that it encourages labour inefficiency. Quality of labour is not of significant concern to businesses as labour cost is not a main component of total cost.

Over-manning is rife for the same reason. Department stores in the big malls have more staff than customers most of the time. Unemployment can be minimised when labour rates are low. High staff complements, however, encourage slower working and the production of a lot of unnecessary and duplicated paper work. Open a bank account and you will see what I mean.

14 September

Fancied a beer this evening. Passed a fair at the local temple where music was playing, so stopped to take a look.

Very much like old-fashioned church fêtes and fairs. A shooting gallery, throwing darts for a goldfish. Kids laughing and enjoying the bouncy castle. They had a trampoline there too. That did not seem so popular.

Many food and snack stalls. No beer tent – well, it is a *wat* – so bought a refreshing cold chocolate drink. Later, there'll be dancing and singing right up to midnight. Nobody I spoke to knew what the *wat* was celebrating by hosting a fair. Provided the karaoke machine does not blow a fuse or the stalls run out of food, I don't think it matters. People use *wats* a great deal in Thailand to meet people and enjoy themselves.

The temple will get a donation at the end of the night from the money made by the stallholders.

15 September

Had a lazy day today and relaxed re-reading Hollinger's *Mai Pen Rai Means Never Mind.* I'm always astounded when I realise how her observations of Thais in the 1960s are still so relevant today. She put Thainess in a nutshell and was brave enough to question the sometimes entrenched views her fellow compatriots held of Thai people and their culture.

She spotted quickly how stratified society was. That has not changed. Thais over many decades have been used to powerful feudal-like class systems and dictatorships. Where they have been benevolent and helped the ordinary Thai, they have been welcomed and accepted.

Hollinger saw through what she called "humph" *farangs* – those who stayed in fancy hotels and *moobaans,* always travelled with the air conditioning on, and saw very little of the real Thailand. They did not understand the Thai; the Thai did not understand them.

She was able to step outside her own nationality and see foreigners as Thais saw them. She could adapt her western worldview.

16 September

I was awake at 5.30 this morning. After an invigorating shower I put on my blue overalls, tied a sash around my waist, and donned my white bell-shaped hat. The uniform I would be wearing as I experience being a Thai mahout for the day.

The first challenge was getting on my tall and heavy elephant. Fortunately *Naam* was in cooperative mood. One command of *sawng soo* and she raised her foot so that I could mount and sit astride her neck, my legs behind her ears. *Naam* is well over two metres in height. Moving and changing direction are achieved using a combination of verbal commands and applying pressure to the sensitive parts near the elephant's head. A firm, though not in any way vicious, kick behind the left ear made *Naam* turn to the right. It was not difficult to learn the basic aids or commands though they must be given in a strong voice and with determination.

It is said that a good mahout does not need to use the sharp metal hook to control his charge. However, I have never seen a mahout without one. In any case, the hook is not used as a punishment. The foot-long instrument enables the mahout to reach the pressure points which control the elephant's movements.

A mahout stays with the same elephant throughout his life and a bond and mutual trust develops. When the animal is in "must" and sexually aroused, or when a female beast is with her calf, great care must be taken. It is rare but not unknown for an experienced mahout to be killed by an elephant who has been with its keeper for maybe 40 or 50 years. Elephants are wild animals and should be respected as such.

Naam loved being bathed and it was difficult to imagine she could get violent quickly. I had no such problems with her during the whole day. She immersed herself (and me) several times in the water to get the dust off her body, and used her trunk to spray water on her back. We ambled back to camp, *Naam* stopping occasionally to pick up food with her trunk while I admired some of Thailand's breath-taking views from my high vantage point.

I will not forget *Naam.* I'm looking forward to spending another *sanuk* day with her soon.

17 September

Waited patiently at a junction for a motor bike to pass along the main road so as not to inconvenience him. And he turned left into my *soi* without signaling. Great. He smiled the usual Thai smile.

I would have been annoyed if that had happened in the West. I'm used to it now, sometimes I even smile back. It's what the Thais would do.

Such inconsideration for other road users would not give them a second thought.

18 September

Just been reading some comments by Dr Ubolwan, the Thai academic who claimed that the reason early Christian missionaries failed in Thailand was because they completely misread the culture.

Thais are not easily swayed by rhetoric or speeches; they look for illustrations as proof of an idea. The missionaries should have taught by giving examples that were relevant to an individual's life experiences. You reach a Thai through emotion. Quoting religious rules, or biblical texts without reference to everyday life does not work. Parables and stories would have been better.

Even propaganda has to be well managed to influence a Thai because he is encouraged to accept only views that relate to his own environment and circumstances.

Academic ideas and formal concepts will fall on deaf ears. The approach must be personal and not clash with the Thai views with which he has been brought up and with which he is familiar.

19 September

Invited to a Lanna wedding today. No monks attended and the ceremony was conducted by the same village elder who officiates at all local weddings. The marriage is symbolic and regarded as more important than the signing of documents which will take place later at the local *amphur* registration office – maybe months later – when the marriage becomes legal.

The hands of the bride and groom are tied together with a white cord signifying the bond to which they have both now agreed. They are led, with cheers from all the guests, to a bedroom. Despite the obvious implication of going to a room away from prying eyes, they have only time to change into less formal clothes and join their family and friends for a celebratory meal.

There are many surprising customs in Thailand.

20 September

If you get a chance, watch a Thai soap when you visit the country. They seldom have sub-titles though you can easily get the essence of the action. Judge for yourself, but the plot is a little contrived and there are not the usual Thai smiles from the actors. Their expressions are serious and movements can appear a little unnatural and stilted. You see frowns and looks of bewilderment, pained expressions of surprise. Faces can freeze during dialogue with eyes looking into space. Situations look very unreal and contrived.

So unlike the friendly smiling and unassuming Thais you see around you every day. Thais are good at controlling their emotions in real life. Maybe soaps allow them to show anger, surprise, vengeance, and hate which they must otherwise hide.

Western films mirror the lives of people in different situations which closely resemble reality. We can associate with them. Thais watch this very unrealistic version of life. An escape mechanism?

21 September

Apparently, they are building a new *sala*, meeting hall, at the temple. Bancha won the contract. He has built a metre tall brick container a metre square and filled it with sand ready for the foundation ceremony later this morning.

It has been decorated with flowers and garlands and some decking has been laid around it. There's been music playing over the last few days at the *wat* and I was told they were having a fair, being opened by a general from Bangkok, at 10 this morning.

Went along just after ten and found a few soldiers waiting for his convoy to arrive. Three or four of the local *pooyaibaans* were there in their best clothes. I'd come along in shorts expecting a fair to be in full swing.

I had to join the *pooyaibaans* in the line up to be introduced to the great and the good. But the general, I think to everyone's relief, gave up after meeting the first half dozen dignitaries, and walked swiftly along the red carpet. Being the only one dressed in shorts, I too was glad.

He then placed flowers and holy water on the sand while the monks were chanting for good luck for their new *sala*. By the time it was my turn to sprinkle holy water it had run out. *Mai mee panha*, no problem. A bucket of water was brought; I filled up the silver jug, continued the sprinkling ritual, and passed the jug to the next person. Didn't seem to matter that it had not been formally monkly blessed.

I chatted and had lunch with some people who had come up from Bangkok. I think they knew the general who now works as a consultant in the defence ministry. He had not been in uniform.

22 September

Paused for a beer alongside the River Ping this evening and watched three or four young lads splashing water over themselves in the shallows. Dressed only in their underpants, they were enjoying the fun of being totally free to do as they pleased and keeping cool into the bargain. The Ping is not a particularly polluted watercourse though no canal or river in Thailand is pollution free. They'll shower when they get home.

On the other bank, guys, waist deep in the river, were casting their nets near an open sluice gate, a favourite place to fish with water gushing down the slope. Every few minutes they would pull in their nets to see what they had caught and, if lucky, hold up the fish for all to see. Putting the catch in a submerged holding bag, they would cast off again.

I asked one of the fishermen how many fish he normally catches. He said he came every evening when the sluice gate was open and the number of fish varied. Usually just one or two over a three hour period. Sometimes he went home empty handed but that did not matter. He enjoyed spending time in the cool waters and fresh air, laughing and joking with his mates.

I imagine the scene would have been exactly the same a hundred years ago. The only difference being there would have been bicycles and not motor-bikes on the side of the road. Thailand has not changed greatly.

23 September

In the bar areas of Thailand's cities and towns you'll often notice a few *farangs*, either sitting alone or in small groups, nursing a beer and contemplating how Lady Luck has dealt them a weak hand in Thailand. Some have lost a great deal of money in the country by buying a house in the name of a wife or girlfriend only to find that the relationship was purely a scam to obtain property for the family or to be re-sold.

Some have suffered crippling hospital bills which include overpriced services and the cost of unnecessary procedures. Hospitals are businesses and you need to choose those that the ordinary Thais use. For all expensive purchases get a Thai you know well to give you advice on where to shop and the places to avoid.

Financial frauds are prevalent world-wide but the majority, and check this from reports on the internet, that are perpetrated in Thailand can be traced to foreigners setting themselves up as advisors who see only rich pickings from an expat's pension fund or from his life savings. Regulation is as weak in Thailand as in the rest of the world with mere "slap on the wrist" type penalties applied even to the big institutions. The *farang* advisors may sport out of date qualifications or wrongly claim they are regulated overseas.

Occasionally foreigners in the bar will get up and play a game of pool with the girls. More usually they'll complain about the inscrutability of the Thai who never say what they mean, never mean what they say. They'll relate stories of the cheating they or a friend of a friend have experienced from a Thai, the detail being embellished every time they describe what happened. They don't always tell the full story.

Nobody can deny that cheating exists in Thailand and a *farang* is seen as an easy target since he is perceived to have come from a rich developed country with an endless source of cash. You'd be lucky indeed if you succeeded in convincing a Thai otherwise.

Many *farangs* have had a raw deal. Away from the safety net of a welfare state, they find themselves in a culture they do not understand, in a country whose people they barely know, speaking a language they are unable to learn.

Their daily life revolves around the various bars. Drinking and surfing the net being their sole comforts. With bridges burned, they resign themselves to staying in Thailand and making the best they can of their lives.

24 September

The children were all wearing coloured armbands while waiting for the buses to take them home from school. I didn't take much notice at first, then realised they were to make sure the teachers and security guards put them on the right coaches. Schools are very security conscious in Thailand.

Hospitals tag their patients to safeguard against nurses giving the incorrect medication or food to a patient and is a failsafe precaution so that surgical procedures are carried out on the right person. Newly born babies have armbands with their mothers' names on so they are returned to the right mother in the ward.

Tagging may seem a bit dictatorial or authoritarian but one can see the benefits. Paul had been very critical of children and grown-ups being forever labelled with their names on.

"We don't do that in Texas. It's undignified and de-personalising," he said.

"Yes, I know. In Texas you brand them, don't you," the nurse replied.

25 September

Noticed again today that when parents speak to their very young children they don't use the strictly correct forms of *ka* and *krap* at the end of sentences.

This polite particle has no meaning; *ka* is used by a female speaker and *krap* by a male. Lady boys use *ka*. The rule is determined by the sex of the speaker and not the person addressed. A mother talking to her son will end her comment with *krap* as a way of teaching him to use that word when he himself speaks. Children learn a language by copying what they hear. A father would say *ka* to his daughter when she is very young.

In parts of rural Thailand elderly women will sometimes use *krap* and not *ka* when speaking to a *farang* male in Thai. That is the same logic. She is teaching him how to speak her language!

Western children are always taught to say "please." In Thai, you will never hear that word in ordinary speech. Politeness is achieved by closing a sentence with the *ka* or *krap* words. To be more polite, and when talking to strangers, you could say *na ka* or *na krap*. With very close friends of your own age or younger you could drop the closing particle altogether, but usually add *noi* at the end of your sentence. *Noi* literally means "small" but has no meaning in this context. *Kin noi*; would you like something to eat.

Thais like their language to come over as being polite. They do it by using these specific words. In formal loudspeaker announcements, you will hear the word *garuna* (please), as when a flight attendant is reminding you to fasten your seatbelt. You won't hear it often and never in everyday speech.

26 September

You can hail taxis from the street in Bangkok but in other towns and cities they are not so widely available. Small converted trucks ply the main thoroughfares and *sois* and will stop when you flag them down. If they are going in your direction, they will charge a flat fee but pick up other passengers en route. It does not slow the journey down a great deal. They do not have set itineraries and are restricted to nominated areas within the town. In Chiangmai, red "taxis" will take you anywhere within the city. To go to Lamphun or Maerim, they will take you to Wararot market to connect with a green or yellow pick-up.

Most of these taxis are not privately owned. They are controlled by syndicates who ensure their drivers keep within their assigned areas.

There are some local buses though they are few and far between and don't keep to their timetables. *Tuk tuks* are more expensive and not so comfortable and you need to barter the fare before you climb aboard. The lack of formal taxis can give conference organisers a headache. They usually do a deal with private motorists so that they can ferry the participants around in relative comfort.

27 September

It was a community event, everyone was free to come along and join in. I think they were celebrating their niece's graduation. *Fon*'s husband had rigged up a karaoke and there was space for some dancing. *Saa* was chatting with her university friends and, although I'm sure everyone was pleased with her achievements, the party was about enjoying the company of one another and having a good time eating, singing, dancing, and singing. An opportunity too to catch up on the local gossip. There was again speculation on how Sengdeuan had bought *Lit's* land.

I saw no one congratulate or give *Saa* a gift but everyone had brought some food, fruit, or some drinks to share. They had a few English songs on the karaoke so we had some fun trying to follow the sometimes oddly worded sub-titles. Laughter outweighed any seriousness.

The karaoke cut out occasionally and I saw *Fon's* husband climb a ladder to adjust the wiring to get it working again. Everyone realised mine host had connected his loudspeaker system to the village electricity supply! Well, it was a community event in which everyone could share.

28 September

Had to take a second look at the cafe sign this morning. Apart from using a "G' instead of a "K," the three letter sign looked exactly like that for a Kentucky Fried Chicken outlet. An identical logo featuring someone remarkably resembling a smiling Colonel Sanders with his goatee beard and red and white apron.

Copying and counterfeiting is common in Thailand. The small restaurant may or may not be challenged by the owners of the Thai KFC franchise.

You might notice something similar in the supermarkets and large out of town stores. You will see two brands of paint on the shelves: Berger and Beger. Only one is made by the established and well-known Berger Company. Not easy to spot the difference when looking at the can.

29 September

The military government is regularly emphasising its work on anti-corruption measures, No one believes it will be eradicated but it's a welcome step forward. In their nightly broadcasts, which can come across as indoctrination at times, they list officials and businesses, especially in the tourist spots of Phuket and Pattaya, which they have targeted and removed. Whether this is a short-term public relations exercise or is a genuine attempt at cleaning up the more obvious scams, depends on how jaundiced a view one takes on current events.

Overpricing does seem to have been reduced. Cases of Jet Ski owners wrongly claiming damage to their skis and demanding recompense, often aided by officials, are certainly fewer. Corruption is endemic in Thailand as in all countries of the Far East. It has acquired a cultural acceptance. Most Thais want it reduced so long as it does not mean not being able to make the occasional bribe themselves to avoid a police fine or to pay to move bureaucratic procedures along more smoothly.

The Thai attitude can be guessed from a law passed in the 1960s which made corruption illegal IF the amount was in excess of 200,000 baht!

30 September

The pace of life is much faster in Bangkok than up-country. Jumping on a bus smartly because you know it will move off as soon as you have one foot inside, hanging on tightly at corners, bracing oneself for abrupt stops at traffic lights.

The driver and ticket seller on Thai buses are on commission. The more fares they collect; the higher their earnings. Moving off quickly after picking up a passenger is of the essence. The driver may not even pull in to pick up a sole person waiting at a stop if he knows he can pick up several people at the next one. He has every incentive to get there before a rival bus does. It can be annoying when he decides to take a short cut, missing out some bus stops. It does not happen often but it does occur. You just get off at the most convenient stop near your original destination or catch another bus going in that direction. Passengers don't object. They take it in their stride, *mai pen rai*. It's no big deal.

Most buses are not air-conditioned, so the windows are open unless there is heavy rain. Fans also help keep the passengers cool.

Tuk tuks can carry two or three passengers, and are more expensive than the buses. You negotiate the fare. The standard practice is to start by halving the amount he suggests and accepting when it's about one third less than his first price. They take you directly to where you want to go. Well, not always. Sometimes he may think it would be better to take you to his brother-in-law's gem shop for some tourist bargains. Smile, say *mai ao* (no thanks, I don't want to go in) and he'll proceed with the journey. He'll accept that. Just don't get annoyed.

Taxis are metered and it is usually best to insist that the drivers use them. Pick another cab if they refuse. Unless you know the area, you may find some drivers will take you on a scenic tour to boost the meter total. But most drivers do not do that. Some are from up-country, so genuinely may not know their way around Bangkok.

Taxis at hotels and airports may add a charge for picking you up there. The drivers often have to pay a fee for queuing in the taxi rank. There is little you can do at an airport. But at hotels, you could easily walk a few metres down the street and hail a cab. The majority of taxi drivers are honest and work hard. The best rule, if in any doubt about whether to take a particular cab, is to flag down another. That was what a Thai once told me to do in such cases. Applies in all countries, not just Thailand.

Motor cycle taxis are faster and cheaper. But their weaving in and out of traffic may or may not appeal to you.

Outside Bangkok, the usual form of transport is the *sawngtaew* (literally, two benches). They are converted pick-up trucks that carry around ten people (more, if you want to stand on the rear platform – but do hang on tightly.) They normally charge passengers the same fare irrespective of distance and plan the journey depending on where passengers want to go. Because they don't run on fixed routes, they may decline a fare if they are not going your way. You won't normally have to wait long for another *sawngtaew*.

In small villages, you can see motor cycle sidecars that can take two or three passengers for short distances. Pedal rickshaws are slow and not as popular today as they were; but they are a pleasant way of taking in the sights if you are on the tourist trail. Lampang has horse drawn carriages used by tourists and locals.

For longer distances, travelling by air, coach, or train are options. Trains are slow and often run on single tracks, so delays of several hours are not uncommon. Buses are faster but do not have good safety records.

1 October

Even Thais need to take great care in dealing with lawyers in this country. Anoon reminded me that many had obtained their positions through family or other contacts in the old boys' network. Giving a cash present to gain advancement in a legal practice is not unheard of.

Thai society prefers conciliation and compromise rather than conflict. Plea bargaining and out of court settlements are not uncommon in the West; it's a way of life in Thailand.

The confrontational and assertive style of an English barrister would be out of place here. A Thai lawyer would not be as keen to examine an opposition witness in the same adversarial way that his colleague in the West might.

A western advocate puts forward all the points that favour his client: it is for counsel for the other side to make its own case. The judge and jury will balance the extreme opposing arguments later. The logic for this adversarial style is that it brings out all the facts, anything not pertinent can be questioned in cross examination by counsel. The judge and jury have the final say on the guilt or innocence of the client after the arguments have ended. Note, however, that there is no jury system in Thailand. The judge decides.

Every lawyer is looking to maximize his fee. Anoon suggested avoiding a contract quoting an hourly rate and advocated making a fixed fee agreement. With no incentive to drag a case on unnecessarily, resolution may be quicker. Once the fee is agreed, discuss including a significant bonus for a successful win. That will avoid there being negotiations between the two lawyers resulting in some compromise being reached with each side partly giving way. In the West that may be questionable ethics; seeking concessions is a Thai peculiarity. A fixed fee with a bonus for winning will get the lawyer working solely on your side as it maximises his income.

Your lawyer still won't be as adversarial in court as his western counterpart, the judge would frown at that, but he will try to win your case.

2 October

"Monk chats" are becoming popular for tourists throughout Thailand. The *wats* don't charge though donation boxes are not hidden. The monks are keen not only to explain and answer questions on Buddhism and to give insights into Thai culture but will also discuss any other topic, including the latest football results, that you want to talk about. In a friendly and informal atmosphere you can learn what monks consider their role at the temple to be.

Almost all temples have set times aside for these programmes which are meant to broaden the monks' knowledge of other cultures and religions as much as to impart knowledge to the *farang.* Although the younger novices are eager to improve their English, they may not be able to answer more intricate questions on Buddhist philosophy and thinking.

Of the temples in Chiangmai, for instance, there are two temples worth an hour or two of your time. *Wat Suandok,* the most popular, is more structured than others with a larger number of monks, both novice and more senior. *Wat Umong,* located on a hillside overlooking the city, is in an idyllic forest setting. They have a library which has a section with books in English and some thought-provoking Buddhist sayings posted along the walkways around the temple grounds. Many *farangs* visit even though the temple is not on the main tourist trail. You'll see no tourist buses at *Wat Umong.*

3 October

Is it face or *mai pen rai*? My visit to immigration took longer today. The procedures keep changing and the left hand does not seem to know what the right hand is doing.

Spoke to a French expat who has been here since he was 20 years old. He accepts it is getting worse. When he first arrived, he said, reporting every 90 days was not strictly enforced. Now, you are fined if you are over 7 days late. In addition, the number of expats has increased several fold, many are workers from Burma and other Asean countries.

To be fair to Immigration, it cannot be easy or keep staff motivated while dealing with the current large numbers of "aliens."

There are no signs to indicate where to obtain a queue ticket or which counter is for which type of application. When you arrive and get your plastic queue card, you sit and wait until your number is called. In fact, they call out a range of numbers.

Numbers 1 to 15 to the Information Counter.
The first person to get to the counter is seen first, even if his number is 15!

You are then given a further paper queue number relevant to the purpose of your visit: 90-day reporting, visa extension, exit permit etc. There are about five categories in all and it's not clear which counter you should attend. So, you sit again and wait.

The high volume of work has resulted in management making incremental changes to procedure. That is very much the Thai way. Changing one procedure without considering its impact on other parts of the operation.

To speed processing, three people now man the 90-day counter. One clerk checks your documents and forms and places the papers in a pile for her colleague. She puts the next person's documents on top of yours! Her colleague then takes from the top of this new stack of papers. If that 90-day report involves a fine, he has to stop and go to the cashier before proceeding to the next case. Meanwhile, you wait.

You cannot comment on it. Thais don't like any kind of confrontation. Some members of staff probably know there are faults in the system, but they too can't easily suggest changes to the big boss. Too much loss of face. Or, is there an element of *mai pen rai*, that it does not matter and there is no incentive to improve or change.

In a further 90 days' time, the procedures will probably again have changed. (Addendum: There is now just one queuing ticketing system, not two. One officer does a quick check on your papers before you proceed to the main office.)

4 October

Cycling over the bridge, I pulled up by a small group of people peering over the edge. They were watching several men tugging at a rope trying to pull up a small truck that had slipped down the bank of the river. Only the front wheels were on firm ground. Eventually they tied the rope to a lorry, whose driver had stopped to help. It was still a long process to drag the truck right up.

My fellow watchers started talking about *karma*, a strongly held belief in Buddhist countries, being the reason for the misfortune. They said the driver was a well-known local villain. I thought the predicament was caused by a bit of bad luck when the truck had been driven too close to the edge.

They were adamant. It was the driver's bad karma.

5 October

7-11 franchise stores are common in this country. In Bangkok you'll notice several on the same street. Selling most convenience items including snacks and drinks.

You can have a meal virtually anywhere in Thailand 24/7. You can find stalls and small eateries wherever you go. If a Thai is hungry he'll stop at the first one he sees, eat his meal, and be on his way. Ask a Thai what he missed about visiting or living in the West and he'll list not being able to find somewhere to eat whenever he wanted.

Office and outside workers will break off for a few minutes to have a snack while their colleagues continue to work. It's accepted and not regarded as unusual. In places where the public may be present, for instance in banks or government offices, the practice is more discreet but not outlawed.

6 October

Tim realises now that he has to watch the workers on his house build very carefully. They had badly scratched a worktop and covered it with papers so that he would not notice. Fortunately, he moved them to check and got them to repair it. If he had waited until the next day, they would probably have blamed him for the scratches.

He's got used to their not cleaning up after they have finished a piece of work. Nevertheless, he had not bargained for the way they tried to cover their mistakes.

His wife was out shopping and Tim speaks little Thai, so he couldn't tell them that the hole they were digging should be at least half a metre deep in accordance with the plans. They went down only six inches as they laid the concrete. He explained to Somsee when she got back but she assured him that they confirmed they had gone down the required depth.

"I saw them doing it with my own eyes," Tim replied.

They were adamant. Tim got the foreman to use a drill to go down half a metre to prove what they had done. When the drill was removed, the foreman showed Tim that the whole half-metre length was covered in concrete not soil. Proving, he said, that his workers had followed the original plans from the architect.

It proved nothing of the sort of course. On withdrawing the drill, it would pass through the six inches of concrete and so would indeed be covered with traces of concrete. Both Tim and the Thais knew this but there was no point arguing. He won't use that particular team again. Put it down to experience. His friends have had similar problems.

7 October

Thai street markets can be lively places. Thais shop every day, often early in the morning to buy fresh food for their breakfast. Although fridges are quite common and can be used to store food instead of doing the daily shop, nothing beats going to the market each day and having a natter with the neighbours and spreading a bit of local gossip. How else would you keep up with local events?

Dropped in to my local market this morning – to buy a kilo of tomatoes not to chatter – and selected (you can choose your own fruit and vegetables in Thailand) those I wanted. Entirely by luck and not judgment, I had picked exactly 1 kilo. The stallholder was startled at my accuracy. I just smiled and paid. Then she put a few more tomatoes in my bag.

English market traders often did the same. The baker's dozen; paying for twelve, getting thirteen.

If you have a problem with a builder's work (and if you are a foreigner in Thailand you will have problems with builders – take a look at www.coolthaihouse.com) and he is unresponsive in correcting his faults and mistakes, you drop comments to the local *pooyaibaan* and to those you meet in the market or at work. You don't keep arguing with the builder, no more direct contact. He'll get to learn of your annoyance soon enough.

In the West we are more direct and get things out in the open. In Thailand it's best to adapt to their ways to keep your own sanity. It's less stressful. That does not mean you lower your western standards or go native; it means you cope with frustrations by assimilating to Thai lifestyle.

8 October

Thais love Karaoke. Some even have good voices. Quite common to rent a private karaoke machine for a private party at your home. The men usually do more singing than the girls. For a night out, a group will often hire a room for around 400 baht at a local bar, and enjoy singing and drinking together. Meals can be ordered by telephone from the room, brought in, and shared. The rooms are frequently themed: sporting trophies and pictures, a romantic Parisian theme, an outer space atmosphere.

There are indeed karaoke bars that are public but the Thais prefer singing in private rooms or parties at home.

Foreign visitors going in a group need to be cautious when ordering food and drinks as the bill can quickly run up without your realising it. You may be asked if you want some girls to sit in with your party, work the machine, and sing along. Not realising that you will be charged per girl per hour, and be responsible for their lady drinks (usually watered-down coke on which they get a commission.)

If you are into karaoke, chat with some local Thais and get their advice or suggestions. Better still, join in with their fun.

9 October

Never tell a joke in a foreign language. This is an established rule and a useful piece of advice when you are new to a language. A funny story can fall flat when you try to say something amusing in a country other than your own. Their sense of humour can be poles apart from yours. Sarcasm, for example, does not travel well across the borders to Thailand.

Imitate the humour style of your host country. Break the ice first and watch the body language of those you are with. You may still get it wrong but it won't be disastrous.

"Pai nai kap" (where are you going?), I shouted as Geng got up from the table where we were all sitting and drinking cold pints of the local brew. Thais tend to just get up and go without any explanation. I found it strange at first.

We all knew where he was going when he walked towards some bushes in the garden. We were having a reasonably heavy drinking session, so it was not hard to guess. He turned round, laughed, and went on to water the shrubbery.

That sort of joke would work well in France. Other countries may be more serious. It would not even raise a snigger in Russia, but your attempts at another type of humour would bring the house down. The rule holds true: be careful telling a joke if you are unaware of the culture of your listeners and their reactions to humour.

10 October

It's an old survey but the latest one conducted in 2012 by Durex. They claim that Thailand has the largest number of unfaithful lovers in the world. The Land of Smiles certainly leads the field in "love hotels," ranging from seedy motel-like drive-ins to up-market suites which can be rented for 1500 baht per hour. These VIP suites have a Jacuzzi, soft drinks cabinet, and a full entertainment system: TV, videos, music centres. Everything you need to get in the mood.

Discretion is the key word. Popular with Thais, these rooms are called maan root, "drawn curtains." You drive in, pull curtains around your car, and enter your chosen themed room.

You don't wait around in reception areas. You agree and pay the room rate. Well away from prying eyes.

11 October

Dao asked me to check and explain the standard deviation calculations that she had been asked to do by her boss. She had downloaded an SD calculator from the internet and completed a table showing the results of the staff appraisals for each of the company's employees. There were twenty classifications to determine merit and the total score for each worker was correct. The average attained by each employee over the 20 classifications was also correct. She had input the figures accurately and the computer had of course produced true results. A quick back of the envelope calculation proved that.

The standard deviation calculation was however a nonsense. Somehow she had interpreted the figures spewed out by the computer as an SD for each employee when they were only part of the calculation for the standard deviation of the group. The computer printout was certainly misleading; it should have given just the one figure and not a column showing the calculation. I could see her confusion.

It took two minutes to correct her report. It took longer to convince her that the computer report was showing a working calculation not a result.

Thais learn by rote and accept what teachers and computers "tell" them. They don't want to question or check something out for themselves independently. They don't want to appear to be losing self-esteem or challenging authority, whether that is a teacher or a computer.

It's happening in the West too. We over trust computers. They are only tools and reports need a human overview. Algorithms are useful but do not let them take over. If you query the result of an algorithm, you cannot discuss it with the "computer." Sadly, you may find you are unable to get in touch with a human being either.

12 October

I found Thailand's opening hours unusual when I first came to the country. Most department stores stay open late in Thailand. 9 or 10 o'clock in the evening would not be unusual.

Though you may find they don't open until 11 in the morning. Small family run shops will often open from 8 until 6, but do not necessarily open every day if the owners feel like a day off or have some business or a ceremony to attend.

Banks in tourist areas may open for limited hours on Saturdays and Sundays. Food stalls open from first light each day.

No one goes hungry in this country.

13 October

Looked at some brochures this afternoon on Bhutan, the Himalayan mountain kingdom famous for its breath-taking beauty and its unique culture. Their people carry on their daily lives in identical manner to their grandparents and great-grandparents. Visitors feel they are stepping back a few centuries.

The Bhutanese believe that happiness is more important than economic measures of performance. Their government uses the term Gross Domestic Happiness and not gross domestic product when it considers the country's wealth. The Thais have a similar strong belief that life is for living and enjoying. Everything must be fun for them, *sanuk*, including work. The Thai smile is the outward expression of *sanuk*. So, in many ways, the two countries are similar.

Improving GDP (in the economic sense) is of great concern to the Thai government, with its high reliance on tourism and foreign earnings. It has always been a difficult balancing act to maintain ancient cultures and traditions while improving the standard of living and, to some extent, accepting inevitable Westernisation.

Thailand, as a result of its close links with America during the Vietnam War, is a favoured western country with privileges and reciprocal arrangements not given to the nationals of other countries.

Wealthy Thais shop in exclusive London stores, own property abroad, and send their children to western universities. They love what the West has to offer. The Bhutanese have until recently shunned the outside world.

Only since 1974 has tourism in Bhutan been seen as an essential factor in gaining wealth to improve the standard of living of the ordinary people. The industry is, unlike in Thailand, strictly controlled by the government so that ancient cultures are preserved and what are seen as the worse aspects of Westernisation kept out. Tours, which are expensive, have to be organised with registered agencies and tourists must spend at least $250 a day while in the country. A quarter of that goes to the government to fund social improvements in Bhutan. The rules thus ensure that only well-heeled visitors get to visit their country.

Thailand is more accommodating, I suppose. You will see both rich and not so rich western tourists here. Many are here for the culture and enjoy visiting the famous sites of Thailand.

But in Bhutan you won't see call girls plying their trade and foreigners spending their days relaxing in bars.

14 October

Some of the richest men in the world are Thai and live in Thailand. The wealth of big businesses is concentrated in the hands of relatively few families. It is not surprising, therefore, that a "hi-so" culture has developed with playboys (and girls) hitting the fashionable nightspots. We find the super-rich in all countries, whether their money has come from their own efforts or from generations of wealth creation.

Because Thailand has a strong class structure, upward mobility is not as common as it is in the West. There is a frame of mind that guarantees that both the élite and the not so well off move only in their own circles. Thais accept this structure: they yearn for a fairer though not equal society.

Buddhist teaching reinforces the belief that karma has determined your position in today's society. Thais will wait for a better life in the next. The playboys don't accept that; but most Thais do.

Gaaneegaa worked long hours and used family connections to get where she is today. Benjawan got her money by marrying a *farang*. Both now live a "hi-so" lifestyle.

The true élite don't work, they have access to family money that increases at a rate higher than they can spend. Karma has been good to them. Pomelo has got a job as a chauffeur to the 20 year-old son of one of Bangkok's richest families. I don't know how long the job will last, Pomelo does not stick at jobs for long. Maybe he'll stay a little longer this time. He's getting almost three times the minimum wage with food and accommodation provided. He is, however, on call at all times.

He told me that he more often than not has to put his young boss to bed in the early hours after a night of partying. One of his other duties is to look after the cat which has its own air conditioned room and is fed meals from its monogrammed silver plated dish.

The boss's car was impounded abroad for some motoring infraction. He promptly bought another for cash. The news hit the western press. It did not appear in the Thai media.

15 October

I wouldn't say Thais were tidy people. Sweeping and hosing down with water every day. Fastidiously clean, but not tidy.

While they'll brush their homes every day, giving the house a thorough spring clean does not occur to them. Carol Hollinger, in her excellent book "Mai Pen Rai Means Never Mind," quotes a fellow American complaining that her servants don't clean under the refrigerator. Hollinger, who understood Thais, was embarrassed that Westerners would worry about what was under a fridge when the house was otherwise clean and posed no health hazard (in her opinion and that of most Thais).

If you only read one book about Thailand, read Carol Hollinger's. It's the most accurate account of Thai life.

Thais are great hoarders and throw little away. You'll see stacks of papers piled high on shelves and in cupboards. Shoe boxes and containers for cooking utensils may be placed on any vacant chair or table.

Clippings from garden shrubs and the broken boughs of trees remain where they lay. Not everything will readily compost down. It matters little. *Mai pen rai.* At the end of the *lamyai* harvesting season, *Fon* always has to clean up after her labourers. They don't see the necessity. They get paid for harvesting the fruit and go home.

16 October

There is a fusion of Buddhism and Animism in Thailand. That is really the only way to describe the Thai attitude to the religion. While ninety five per cent of the population are Buddhist, almost all the lay members will practice what we would term animism – ancestor worship – to a lesser or greater degree.

Because of the robust respect for family in Thailand it is easy to understand why members of one's family who have passed away are venerated by placing incense, flowers, food, and drink in the spirit houses erected for them.

You can see them in the gardens of homes, public parks, hotels and even shopping malls. The spirits defend those who live in the house and the land on which it stands. Drivers of cars, and sometimes coaches, passing such shrines on roadways will sound their horn as a mark of respect.

Taking the hands off the wheel to *wai.*

You will also notice sacred trees garlanded with a saffron belt around the trunk in your journeys in Thailand. Pavements will be built around them and the trees may be pruned. They will never be destroyed or moved.

17 October

Many believers, in all the main religions, practice some form of meditation. In Thailand it is an essential part of being a Buddhist. It is the path to enlightenment and seeking eternal truth. Monks will tell you that by meditating regularly and deeply you will realise the impermanence of life and become aware of a more important goal: stopping the continual cycle of rebirth and reaching Nirvana.

Worshipers in the *wats* may not comprehend the complexities that are being rather mystically explained. They are unlikely to be able to discuss them with you. They will tell you only that life is not permanent and emphasise the importance of acquiring good karma so that they can be reborn in better circumstances. Few members of any religion are that knowledgeable about their church's teachings, they rely on a sense of faith.

The techniques of meditation taught in the *wats* varies. Most will instruct novice meditators to try to achieve a calmness of body and mind, shutting out all thought and worries from the outside world. Repeating a mantra, either aloud or in your mind, will have the effect of blocking any other thoughts. The mind becomes focused and concentrated on nothingness. Visualising an object to the exclusion of everything else brings the same result. It could be a Buddha image or any other object. The monks encourage you to contemplate the image as appearing in turn at one of seven points in the body starting at the top of your head and finishing two fingers width above the navel. Their instructions are quite precise but they cannot explain the reasoning.

My guess is that the point represents a body's centre of gravity though you would be fortunate indeed if you ever found a monk to state that. When your mind is at that point above the navel you are told to repeat the mantra and visualize the image to the exclusion of all other thoughts for as long as you can. One hour is not unusual.

Attending *Wat Dhammakaya*, the most formal place for learning meditation techniques, can be an experience that is both thought provoking and a little mysterious. Unlike most *wats,* the buildings and grounds are in immaculate condition. The monks do not walk the daily alms rounds, there is an on-site kitchen and refectory. The *wat* broadcasts on satellite TV and has overseas branches. The emphasis in their headquarters near Bangkok is on the two meditation halls and the teaching of mediation techniques. Although the *bot*, the central part of most temples, can be visited, it is not near the main buildings and you will not see many people inside.

Six evenings a week the abbot gives a sermon on Buddhist teaching, invariably it is linked to a meditation topic. Foreigners are regular visitors and are provided with headsets to enable them to hear the abbot's words in translation. On Sundays, the hall where the abbot gives a sermon is packed with both Thais and a significant number of *farangs*. Most of the thousand or so people are dressed in white and each sits cross-legged in a one metre square chalked out area facing the abbot.

Free coaches bring adherents from the centre of Bangkok and those arriving by car are able to park their vehicles in the *wat's* own underground car park. There is some meditating, chanting, and prayers but the main focus is on Buddhist teachings, the abbot's sermon, and his public interpretation of dreams experienced by others during their meditations.
When it is time for the congregation to make a financial contribution, the people who are present form a line to hand-over their donations directly to the abbot. It is regarded as making merit rather than making a donation. After about half an hour, with the line still forming, a saffron coloured strip stretching from the abbot's hand to the centre of the hall is laid out so that those whom the abbot will not have time to see individually can place their offering on it. Symbolically, he is able to accept each person's merit before leaving to return to his quarters.

The services are unlike anything we see in the West.

18 October

A pick-up truck with a loudspeaker drove along our *soi* this morning. He was advertising the opening of a new hardware store in a nearby town. I didn't give it much thought but we have never had them come down our lane before.

Then I realised. Our *soi* is very narrow and is a dead end. How was he going to get out? He would have to reverse all the way back. I opened my gate so that he did not have to back up all the way along our three hundred metre lane. A Thai would not dream of asking if he could reverse in your driveway. Too much *greng jai* for that.

You will see and hear many of these loudspeaker trucks in Thailand, whether they are advertising local goods and services or canvassing for votes in local or national elections.

19 October

Road accidents in Thailand are the second highest in the world per capita. As we have seen, the police often turn blind eyes on regulation infringements. There is no "on the road" driving test. Formal training and instruction is rare.

You will see small kids sitting in front of mum or dad holding the motor-cycle handlebars. That is a Thai child's first experience of motoring. They learn how to ride and drive on Thai roads from that first experience. They copy how their parents ride. They see how the rules of the road are ignored and they keep that knowledge with them for the rest of their lives behind the handlebars of a bike or the steering wheel of a car. No wonder then that, combined with no real training and lax enforcement, they have the reputation of being among the world's worst drivers.

However, there are some very skilled drivers. Watch some artic drivers maneuvering and reversing on small *sois*. Those working on VIP protection duties are trained to high standards to be able to cope with driving their passengers away from any emergency which occurs. And they do that fast and safely.

I knew a lady, keen to improve Thai driving, who spends some time every year advising groups of police officers on western techniques of safer driving. Unfortunately, she does so using a lot of technical language and buzzwords. That is a dated way of training in any modern country but is worse than useless in Thailand. Thais learn by observing and copying and not from books and formal lectures. She once told me that good driving methods were universal and there were no differences in driving methods in individual countries.

My own view is that you adapt your driving, but still keeping safe, to the style of motoring in your host country. Anyone who has driven in say, France, Greece, India etc. will appreciate that.

20 October

Sengdeuan has a Chinese background though she has Thai nationality and regards herself as Thai. Her husband is Taiwanese and from a wealthy business family. Both have worked hard to make their business successful. For the most part they employ hill tribe people or workers from Myanmar (Burma.) Some have lived and worked in Sengdeuan's factory for a few years. That is quite unusual. Migrant workers commonly, after sending some money back home for any family remaining abroad, save the rest of their wages until they have sufficient to set up a small business for themselves and their families when they eventually return to their native land.

But Sengdeuan and her husband look after their workers well. They have their own communal kitchen and can pick vegetables and fruit from the gardens.

Some migrants from Myanmar are more likely to want to stay in Thailand longer term than other nationalities because of the political situation in their own country.

Thais, whether hill-tribe or not, like to go back to their family villages regularly, some may stay for only a few days, some for a few months, and some never return. One factory worker was away for seven months and neither she nor Sengdeuan batted an eyelid when she arrived one day and sat at her usual work station!

There is a happy atmosphere in the factory. Workers chatting away amongst themselves or listening to the radio. It could not be less unlike a western working environment. Getting the job done and enjoying the work at the same time is how they see the work-life mix.

On Mother's Day, one worker's entire family came to spend two days with their daughter. They shared her living quarters and eat with everyone else. A few weeks later, Sengdeuan took her employees out to a roadside barbeque. All sitting at the same table as if they were one family. I can see why her workers respect her and stay longer than most Thais.

21 October

I don't believe it. Saw some imported veal on offer at 499 baht. Not cheap because of the high import taxes. But it's okay to spoil oneself occasionally, so I popped it in my trolley.

I don't check every item when I get to the checkouts, but noticed it had been rung up on the till as 520 baht. I queried it and customer service called a staff member to check.

"No, sir. It's correct. The bar code reads 520 baht." I went back to the shelves to check, but the price was clearly marked 499 baht. So, back to customer services. "No, sir. The price is 520."

We walked down the meat aisle together, as I wanted to show customer services the large sign pricing the veal at 499 baht. But someone had taken it down within the last few minutes. I just could not believe someone could do that.

No one accepted that it had been removed. I asked them to raise it with the manager. Making a mistake is one thing; deliberately covering it up and pretending it never happened is another. I had to sign some paperwork but the manager had relented and I got the veal at the 499 price.

During all these "negotiations", they poured me a cup of coffee and I had a pleasant chat with the customer services staff. I was intrigued that the store was making the correction of a mistake so complicated. Would a Thai have challenged the price, I asked. I learned much from their reply. "Thais don't like to make an outward fuss even when they are quite annoyed inside. A Thai customer would smile and pay up. But they wouldn't come back to our store again. That sounds odd to a foreigner, doesn't it?"

I had to admit that it sure did.
http://www.youtube.com/watch?v=mLNrLI3OBwg
(If ctrl and click does not work, copy and paste into your browser window to watch the video)

22 October

Spent the day with a Thai friend who is a keen photographer. It's Saa's principal hobby and she produces work of a high professional standard. Her main camera cost over 100,000 baht.

She took as many photos as possible to complement and illustrate the events and observations covered in the diary and which could be posted online later. We can't include them here though they appear on my webpage at www.BestThailandBooks.com

The written word cannot always convey the full significance of what is observed. Photos tell a good story. My webpage also includes up-to-date articles on Thais and Thailand.

23 October

Fon got talking this evening about the *farangs* that frequent the girly bars. She wondered why they don't seek genuine dates. Is a girl in a short skirt and displaying a lot of thigh really someone with whom you want to form a relationship? I didn't answer though the truth is that many foreigners do seem to want to associate with sexy looking bargirls and do not want any lasting friendship. I thought Fon's comments odd as she must know that Thais accept their husbands and boyfriends sleeping around as being as natural as the male gender standing up to pee.

There are Westerners who marry former bargirls believing they can change and settle down. Some do, some don't. And every *farang* I speak to in that situation says, "Ah yes, but my partner is different."

Respectable Thai women like being bought gifts and will make subtle hints if they want something. Asking directly for money or a gift is a tell-tale sign that she's not interested in a future with you. The question to ask yourself is whether her request or hint is for services to be rendered or whether she wants a genuine association where you care for each other.

As well as being *greng jai,* not wanting to appear forward or demanding, the average Thai woman is modest. Sex is for the bedroom with the lights out. Trying new positions or experimenting with what would be regarded as mutually satisfying activity in the West between consenting adults, is seen very differently in Thailand. A no holds barred approach to a couple's sex life happens here but would be unusual.

Although Thais dislike the immodesty of the girls who work in the sex industry, they understand and accept their reasons for choosing that vocation. The girls in the bars have no respect for their clients; they know the men have no caring attitude, *namjai,* towards them. That outlook is not easy to comprehend given that the girls themselves have shown no sense of modesty in their blatantly inviting approach to their clients.

Deep down the girls want support and respect. Maybe even love eventually. They know most customers will never give them that. "Caring" is a better description for "love" in Thai culture. Most Thai females who engage in the trade do so in order to send money home to parents, repaying then for bringing them up as children. Longer term, they want security and a caring attitude from men rather than love. As you can see, their attitudes to relationships and prostitution is not the same as those in the West.

24 October

Sab has been out of Thailand for a few years now but came back on a visit last week to see her family and to spend a day meditating at *Wat Dhammakaya.*

Like many Thais, she believes she benefits from meditating. That does not mean she's intensely religious. Technically she's a Buddhist though she admits she visits *wats* only to meditate or to join with others enjoying a festival. Sab told me she was a little disillusioned during this last visit.

After attending a class session with a senior monk, those attending were asked what they experienced when they were in deep meditation and were fixing their attention at the seventh base of the mind where they concentrate on reciting a mantra and visualising a brilliant and sparkling object. Everyone saw something different and one meditator asked what the monk saw. He said he could not tell her. What was so secretive?

Sab had seen an image of a person dressed in white moving slowly amongst the columns of what appeared to be a Greek or Roman amphitheatre. It had made a lasting impression on her. She felt fulfilled after her meditation. Then nagging doubts started to enter her mind. Was her brain simply associating people and events already in her memory? Her car was parked in the underground car park with its many pillars supporting the roof. A large number of people at the *wat* were dressed in white.

Sab told me she was finding some of the monks' ideas hard to accept. However, she'll continue meditating in her own way. It relaxed her and made her feel good.

25 October

Electricity and water supplies can be unreliable. Perhaps once a month on average the service will go down. Water pipes and pumps are old and we have all seen the tangle of electric wires hanging from leaning poles. Services are, however, quickly restored. The longest period without supply may be a quarter of an hour or, rarely, a half-hour. Every few months water towers are flushed out to be cleaned and that may take a few hours. You are given plenty of warning through the loudspeaker systems.

Power surges will shut down computers for a few seconds and internet speeds are notoriously slow whatever the computer marketing men tell you. In rural areas, which is most of Thailand, mobile phones are more commonly used than land lines. And you may find that the mobile phone numbers of your contacts get discontinued when your contact changes provider, which Thais frequently do.

The owner of a newly built house has to pay for the erection of all overhead telephone and electricity posts to his property, telephone and electric. It's not the responsibility of the utility providers. Once he has done that, he may find his neighbours will decide to link up to supplies; utilising the posts he has already paid for.

26 October

Read an interesting piece in the papers this morning. One of Thailand's most outspoken commentators was observing that the standard of education and the patronage culture were the two forces holding Thailand back.

Ajarn Voranai, who teaches at Chulalongkorn University in Bangkok, and is a frequent guest on Thai TV, was pulling no punches about attitudes in the country. By patronage, he seemed to be referring to the hierarchical nature of Thai society. He said you have to do what your superiors tell you. "It's not a place to argue, according to the teachers, but I say do it anyway, but do it with a measure of respect and a hint of smile."

Critical thinking does not come naturally to a Thai because they are hot-wired to be deferential at all times. They shy away from making even the most tactful and diplomatic comments. That is a generalisation, of course, but there are very few people like Voranai who can enter into a logical debate on social problems that affect everyone in the country.

The unwritten rules of not arguing with the boss can make it difficult, for example, for a co-pilot to challenge or correct an error made by the captain. Valuable minutes may be lost with the pilot trying to find the right words to use without causing offence or loss of face for the more senior person on the flight deck.

Some western educated teachers encourage open discussion and argument, but even they find it difficult to get students to forget their inhibitions and let themselves really get their teeth into an exchange amongst themselves. It's hard work. Away from the lecture hall, when a lecturer or professor is not present, they might open up a little more. They would not find the oppressive yoke of the very stratified structure that is Thai society on their shoulders. They would not need to be so politically correct.

Perhaps the answer is to be respectful, but not to over-play being deferential to the point of coming across as being completely submissive. Constructive discussions won't work in those circumstances.

I agree that the smile is important. That can take away a lot of the bitterness that the person you are talking to may feel when he disagrees with you. A student may even win an argument with the *smile of avoiding conflict*.

27 October

The Thai outlook on *greng jai*, wanting to be considerate of the feelings of others, is a problem when you want to find out what they think about an issue or idea. They'll instinctively tell you what they believe you want to know. I try never to ask leading questions and continually seek balanced and truthful answers, emphasising they are not going to upset my feelings. They find it odd that I don't necessarily want them to agree with me.

It took me some time to encourage Saa to suggest ideas of what to photograph to illustrate the essentials of Thainess. Although she understood what I wanted, she was initially reluctant to come up with what turned out to be some excellent photo opportunities. You have to work hard at getting a Thai's confidence and getting him or her on the same wavelength.

We chatted about her ambition to immigrate to America and it opened her mind a little when we compared some of the topics she was photographing with their equivalent in the States. She's thinking more deeply now of her future plans.

I think she'd settle in well. At least now she has some idea of how much of what she takes for granted in Thailand: the lay back lifestyle, the lack of enforced regulation, and the lack of seriousness, does not exist in the West.

28 October

There are different dress codes for Mondays, the day of the week linked with the late King Bhumibol as he was born on that day. Every Monday, government officers and teachers usually wear formal uniform to show their rank and position. Many people will dress in a yellow shirt or blouse, yellow being the colour associated with Mondays.

There are regional variations. In the Lanna provinces in the north of the country, traditional dress is frequently seen on Fridays. And that can be the opportunity to show one's position in society by wearing the latest addition to your wardrobe.

Snobbery is often about showing off and trying to make yourself appear important. More important than you really are. There is some of that in Thailand, but the Thais do not see it in a negative light. What we may consider snootiness is their way of indicating their position in society. They will show their material wealth in order to draw attention to their place in the hierarchy. The way they dress, the size of their house, and the car they drive are very important indicators for them of their standing in the community.

In western cultures snobbery exists but is not regarded as good form in polite society. It occurs, not to indicate class or position, but purely to show off.

29 October

The *wats* organise visits to other Thai provinces and hire a coach to take those who support the temple on a two or three day tour. They never start at the appointed time and include half-hour to hourly stops at temples en route. Photographs are taken, donations are placed in the offering boxes, and snacks are bought at every opportunity. Stops will be made at any busy market or food stall that the coach tries to pass. Nobody starves through want of food. At lunchtimes everyone will eat together at a pre-booked restaurant, the monks sitting at a separate table. At dinner, a local eatery will be chosen though the monks will not be present, they do not eat a main meal after midday. Overnight accommodation can vary from sparse rooms at a temple to ordinary hotel accommodation.

You can talk to the monks during the day though they generally keep to themselves and won't in any case initiate a conversation. Rarely are films shown on long distance coaches as would be usual on public service vehicles. Occasionally a religious themed film might be shown. The journey is taken up in the main with talking.

The tours tend to be well organised and the charges are at competitive rates compared with the tour companies. It's a source of income for the *wat* and allows people to give merit. The monks enjoy visiting other parts of Thailand, its scenery, and its temples.

30 October

Tourist guides correctly advise not touching Thai people on the head. It is considered the most sacred part of the body while the foot is the dirtiest. So you should avoid pointing your feet at anyone. Sitting in front of a monk, keep your feet pointed to one side. These rules are seen more as marks of politeness than superstitions to be heeded. A friendly pat on a child's head won't raise any frowns or objections in my experience though some books suggest you avoid any head contact. One of the few parts of the body you can't hit in Thai boxing, *Muay Thai,* is the head.

Thais not visiting hairdressers on Wednesdays is a popular superstition. You'll never find an authentic barber's shop open. Cremations are not held on a Friday. No one seems to know why. Not having sex on your birthday or a Buddha festival is said to be an important superstition. I've never had the courage to ask and establish whether Thais follow that or not. They'd lie to me anyway, I'm sure.

I queried the superstition of not giving handkerchiefs as presents. Some said they'd never heard of that one. Two said it wouldn't bother them. That may be due to modern thinking or a subtle hint that they were looking for a gift. Thais may tell you they don't believe in these old superstitions; in practice they take care to observe them.

We have superstitions in the West. I've always thought the rule of not inviting thirteen guests to a dinner party was less to do with the number of disciples at the Last Supper and was more likely due to most canteens of cutlery being sold in boxes of twelve. Some superstitions have rational explanations.

Not taking plants or images from a *wat* is said to be a superstition. It probably has more to do with not creating bad karma. I know of one temple in Chiangmai which suffered a spate of such thefts then found the broken idols and statues returned a few days later. A twinge of conscience or the result of a strong belief in superstitions?

Others that I have heard of: hearing the sound of a gecko during the day brings bad luck, don't destroy a bees' nest if built in your home, accidently touching the hand of another when passing food forecasts the arrival of a guest.

31 October

Visited Graham this morning. I like to keep in touch and meet up with fellow *farangs* (foreigners) occasionally. We can talk about the latest news from England, and it's refreshing to have a conversation in English now and again. It stops us expats going completely native. Often friends, Americans, Aussies, and Dutch, will sometimes pop round for a coffee and a chat.

Like many *farangs* in Thailand, Graham lives in a gated community, a *moobaan.* There is usually a private security guard on the main gate 24/7, and visitors are checked in and out. There are some pleasant communal garden areas and the development is kept clean and tidy. Even where there is shade from trees, these areas are not well frequented but they make the park look attractive.

The annual maintenance fee covers street lighting, road maintenance, and garbage collection. Electricity and water supplies are provided by the *moobaan,* though you pay a much higher rate than if you were allowed to deal with the utility companies directly. Many *moobaans* boast a swimming pool and a clubhouse. Some will have a fitness area and a children's playing quarter. The greater the facilities; the higher the yearly fee.

In some *moobaans,* particularly after the developer has sold all the units, services can suffer and the park can look pretty run down. Not all owners will pay their fees, and the developers find it more profitable to concentrate on selling houses on a new site. Often security is withdrawn.

Many foreigners choose to live near one another, and some prefer to socialise only with fellow expats. The well-off Thai also live in these *moobaans,* they are not solely *farang* ghettoes.

From the outside, their houses look very posh and expensive; there will often be a new top of the range Audi or Merc on the drive. But apart from a flat screen television, the inside of the house won't usually have the luxuries associated with western living. And the car is likely to be on finance. Presentation is important to a Thai as it is a way of showing the way they perceive their own status in the community.

Thais rarely entertain in their own home, preferring a restaurant meal. Inviting you inside their home is not common, whether you are Thai or *farang.* Once you get to know them, you will see that even some of the so-called elite are down to earth people. It's rather endearing to see them stop off at a food stall at the side of the road, order some fried pork with garlic and rice, jump in the Merc, and enjoy the meal sitting cross-legged on the floor inside their home. But the hardened, dyed in the wool, "hi-so" may always come across as needing to show off rather than forming a genuine relationship. Ingrained views are hard to dislodge.

1 November

All nationalities drive differently. I remember driving from the airport in Athens and being stopped at a traffic light. The cars ahead of me were tooting their horns. It didn't make the lights change any more quickly but it was a common practice apparently. Not sure if that still happens.

Driving in Paris is an experience like no other. The French drive fast and seem to assume drivers will mainly keep to the rules. Everyone will have their own recollections of driving in other countries.

Thais don't keep to road regulations. Driver training courses are few and far between. None of the Thais I know have been on formal driving courses. Tests are not taken seriously. *Mai pen rai* is everywhere.

Kids are naturally curious and observant. So, perched on the front of a motor bike near the handle bars they pick up a lot of ideas on how to drive. When they themselves have a motorbike or truck they already have a host of driving techniques to call upon!

To turn right or go forward at a red light they'll regularly go left and do a U-turn then go straight on if they wanted to turn right originally or turn left if they wanted to go straight on. They won't do it if cameras are visible or if any police on duty are likely to take a note of their registration numbers.

The larger or more expensive the vehicle, the more the driver will flaunt the rules of the road. Never assume a large truck, coach, or "hi-so" car is going to keep to driving regulations. They'll do what they want to do. Motor cyclists will overtake on either side of you even if you're signaling to turn. A no-entry sign is not always observed; expect two way traffic on one-way streets.

2 November

Yee is a very experienced vet and is popular with all her clients, most of whom of course are Thai. She has built up a successful small animal practice and she shows a genuine love for her clients' pets. Her charges are reasonable, she makes a healthy profit but it has not gone to her head. She drives a small car and often comes to the surgery on her motor bike. She is not at all "hi-so" with the usual airs and graces and a showing-off attitude.

As Talley was due to have a neutering operation, we took him to the surgery last night for a blood check, the results of which will be available later today. Hopefully there will be no problems and the operation can go ahead next week.

Yee normally got on well with Talley. I am sure no pet looks forward to a visit to a vet but Talley has always liked Yee, wagging his tail whenever he saw her. Last night was different. She tried to wrap a piece of linen around his jaws to keep them closed when she took the blood sample. My dog does not bite and he has had injections before. It was a sensible precaution. However, Talley was having none of it. The vet had been too quick in trying to tie his jaws together. A few soothing words and a pat on the back first might have got him in a more cooperative mood. The more she tried to use the cloth to keep his mouth closed, the more he resisted. I was surprised she had no muzzle. All vets, wherever in the world they practice, have situations like this. I imagine they rack their brains to find a solution or perhaps get a colleague to see if he can regain the animal's confidence.

But Yee is Thai. She walked out of the consulting room without any explanation, returning a minute or so later. Took a look at Talley and then went out again. She was exhibiting the Thai trait of walking away from a problem which she did not know how to solve. And she also did not want to lose face. I've seen it so often in Thailand though I will admit to not thinking it would have applied to Yee.

I went to the local market to buy a muzzle and held Talley myself while he had his blood sample taken. It took about two minutes. When paying the bill at reception, I made a point of making a fuss of Talley and, more importantly, getting Yee to do the same. Talley was wagging his tail and that made her feel better about the entire episode.

By playing this little game of praising and patting Talley for being a good boy I was ensuring that Yee was not losing face. A Thai would do that instinctively. I'm slowly learning to do it too.

3 November

Saw a good example this evening of how the internet forums intended for expats in Thailand actually work.

The opening post gave details of a promotional offer at a Bangkok zoo. Their marketing department had contacted the poster saying that they wanted to encourage more foreigners to visit the zoo and were therefore offering a discounted price of 200 baht. Finances were limited and they wanted to increase attendance figures to raise revenue. Fair enough.

The resulting blurb sung the praises of what the zoo was doing. Talking about the new animal arrivals on loan from foreign zoos. Gave details of the more interesting exhibits. Everything seemed very positive.

Then someone asked how well the animals were treated. It was a reasonable question but it got no answer at first. Circuses and zoos throughout the world are regularly scrutinised in this way. Then the floodgates opened, as expected when responses appear evasive. Posters chipped in about cruelty they had seen in both foreign and Thai zoos. They spoke of tigers being put on show and visitors being allowed to enter their enclosures so that photos could be taken of them stroking and sitting alongside the animals. Arguments followed on whether they had been drugged or not. One poster claimed he had been assured by the owners that it was not the case; their tigers were trained and anyway were very well fed.

Quite a lot of off-topic flames on dual pricing then followed. Not a civilised debate.

A Thai commented that he could not understand why *farangs* were so naïve to think that wild animals would not have to be drugged when near humans. He asked why they seemed to accept so much on trust.

Provided that you don't treat everything as gospel, the forums can make interesting reading and there are some helpful and informative posters. The Drummond site is one of the better blogs to read. He does not mince his words but does concentrate on the negative aspects of Thailand. Given the number of travel blogging sites that only show the good side of the country, I suppose his site at least gives a different perspective. http://www.andrew-drummond.com

4 November

Thais excel at outward show. The cars in used car showrooms will be cleaned and polished until they look brand new. The engine compartment will be immaculate. There will be no trace of mud or dirt under the wheel arches. You may note exceptions though generally a lot of effort will have gone into making each vehicle highly presentable for sale.

They enjoy the marketing side of business. You will be looked after well. There will be smiles all round while you will be given a fresh glass of iced water and offered tea or coffee. Answers to more detailed questions about the specification of the car may not be so forthcoming. The salesman may have to think of an answer quickly or ring the car manufacturer. He will not tell you if the vehicle has been in an accident and it is for you to make sure that it is his to sell.

Any excuse for why he does not have the registration book should be treated with caution. Once you've bought and paid for your purchase you will be on your own if any dispute arises. Customer protection is not a prominent feature of Thai business, the few regulators that exist are unlikely to be of much help. Justice is slow everywhere.

While marketing is seen as essential in making a sale, the use of sound management techniques takes a secondary role. Companies will send staff on training courses and seminars but the results may not be as one would expect in the West.

Students don't question their teachers in Thailand. They'll take notes and sometimes listen. They won't discuss or debate if they don't understand a point. Face must not be lost; it's too embarrassing. The better teachers will try hard to involve the attendees and get them engrossed in the subject, often by encouraging role play. They may get one to play an angry *farang* customer and the other the sales person, then reverse the roles.

Thais find it difficult to be angry and how to respond to anger and complaint constructively. Their instinct is not to get annoyed; just smile and walk away.

The role plays are not successful every time. Face is a dominant cultural force in Thailand.

5 November

Although he was ousted from prime ministerial power in 2006, Taksin is still a favourite for the media's attention. He regularly pops up in the Thai press, often on the front page, despite his no longer having any political authority and no longer living in Thailand.

His younger sister, Yingluck, was PM from August 2011 to May 2014 when she was ousted in a coup, and though not of the same party as her brother, her government followed many of the principles that Taksin's *Thai Rak Thai* party established in the period 2001 – 2006. She went into self-exile in August 2017. Some sources say she "escaped" to avoid imprisonment but it is more likely that something was arranged. Yingluck's movements were monitored 24/7, she would not have been able to cough without someone observing and reporting it. She was no ordinary citizen and the Thai security services are notoriously efficient. (Not of the standard of Mossad or the UK's combination of MI5. MI6, and GCHQ; but effective none the less.)

The newspapers draw parallels, and there are suggestions that Taksin's messages from afar were far more than just brotherly chats.

Money under the table and business sweeteners to get contracts have always been features of Thai society. Tell me where in the world that does not occur. In Thailand, it is more open and transparent. Indeed, Taksin himself said you would never rid the country of corruption. His own downfall was based on fraud allegations.

Accepting that a little bribery is normal fits well with the Thai view of freedom, doing what one wants within reason. It smoothes the path in many commercial transactions and is really part of the price of doing business.

Larger scale corruption and operations run by organised criminal gangs are the areas that need to be addressed. But it is a way of life in under-developed countries.

6 November

"Where is your labour?" *Kroo* Art asked me. I was about to make some concrete steps into the garden pond and had borrowed a spirit level from my neighbour, *Kroo* Art. I wanted to make sure they were level.

He could not grasp that I was perfectly capable and willing to do such a small job myself. We both laughed when he asked, in all seriousness, where my labourer was and I replied that it was me.

I'm sure though that he did not fully appreciate why I did not get someone to do the job for me. That's what he would have done.

7 November

Thailand has never been colonised. More practical solutions avoiding colonisation were found through the signing of treaties and playing one country off against another. The Thai's strong slant towards nationalism and the rigid class system would never have sat well with living in a colonial structure. Thais respect and respond to their own national identity, not to those of other countries.

During the Second World War, the Thais decided to accept Japanese occupation as a practical solution, but they never felt at ease with the situation. Thailand sided with the Japanese but did not deliver a declaration of war to the allies. They had signed the document but it could just as easily be said that, as it was not delivered, they had not officially done so. Welty called it "doing but not doing at the same time."

Bending like the bamboo in the storm; giving a little now to gain much later.

They cooperated and took advantage of Japanese assistance in gaining some territory from neighbouring Burma and Malaysia. They saw opportunities for collaboration and took them. Always the Thai pragmatic approach.

Many businesses in Thailand are owned by Thais who are from Chinese stock. CP is probably the best example. In that sense, some have commented that the country has been "effectively" colonised economically. I spoke a few days ago to an Indian businessman who was born here, as indeed was his father and grandfather; runs a successful number of enterprises; owns large tracts of land and property in exclusive areas; and is fully integrated and accepted in Thai society. He mixes with all the "right" people and makes it known that he is a prominent supporter of Thai charities.

8 November

Got a fair price when I enquired about a teak desk and some shelving at a local woodworking shop. It was made to measure and about a quarter off the retail price in the city's more expensive stores.

I'd seen their work and had ordered my furniture a few weeks ago. It was delivered yesterday and I asked them to design a TV cabinet and give me a quote.

They rang this evening. For the amount of timber and labour involved, they were about 25% over what one would expect to pay. I explained why I thought their price was high but they made no comment. Although they seemed to realise that I had a point, the craftsman could not lose face by coming up with a more realistic figure. Using reason and explaining why the price is high gets you nowhere.

Thais can rarely get over this cultural barrier of not losing face. Although some foreigners see losing face as a negative attribute of the Thai, it is really just a case of different cultures thinking differently. Who is to say that one way is better than another?

Negotiating in a market is fun to them but in that situation they know a fair price below which they will not go. But, this was an example of trying to inflate the price because they felt they had a captive foreign customer. Nothing wrong with aiming for a price that the market would bare, but poor business practice not to close the sale by suggesting a more reasonable price.

Losing face is unacceptable. Losing a sale seems to be less important.

9 November

Wat Po, arguably the temple in Bangkok which attracts the most foreign tourists, is raising its entrance fee for *farangs* to 500 baht. Thais can enter free whether they are ordinary folk or rich businessmen arriving in a chauffeur driven Mercedes. Chinese and other visitors from the Far East enter freely if they have Thai features. Western Buddhists going to the temple for religious reasons have to pay. Showing a Thai driver's licence or work permit cuts no ice with those on duty at the temple entrance.

Although dual pricing is illegal, it is commonly practiced even by the state owned national parks. Internet comments range from suggestions that Thailand should adopt the western practice of not discriminating between locals and foreigners to observations that it's just greed associated with a capitalist culture that seeks to get the most money out of foreign tourists.

I recall a lay reader of a local church being asked for an admission fee at St Paul's Cathedral when he wanted to attend a service. He was stopped as he looked like a tourist from out of town. After a rather heated discussion he was allowed in to participate in the service. However, they insisted that he sit at the very back. It left a sour taste but shows that all countries try to maximise revenue, even in religious institutions.

Other posters on the internet forum, all *farangs*, raised questions on where all the money goes. There were no convincing answers.

10 November

We are all justly proud of our own countries. The Thais are no exception. We cheer when our country's team gets gold in the Olympics; something may stir inside us when our national anthem is played after winning the Five Nations rugby tournament. But we tend not to be as nationalistic as the Thai. Most of us can take some harmless banter or a joke against our nationality; we can argue openly on the way our railways are run or how our banks seem to be laws unto themselves.

The Thais don't openly criticise their own institutions. They are offended at any suggestion of disapproval by foreigners of their country and culture. Sometimes that can be a pity because often foreigners may have constructive comments which could help the country's development. Lessons could have been learned from the foreign experts and rescuers during the Tham Luang Cave rescue in 2018.

Their fervent nationalistic pride can border on xenophobia though their laid-back lifestyle does not make that immediately obvious.

It's fine to be patriotic provided that it's not a step towards jingoism and a dislike of foreigners.

11 November

I have always found the Thai tax inspectorate friendly and helpful. (Diary entry 8 March.) The officers will assist, with a smile, anyway they can. They will point out any reliefs and allowances which you have claimed or are unaware of.

Thai tax laws are not as complex as many other countries; they are certainly easier to follow than those of the U.K. Legislative changes in Thailand are not as frequent as those in the West. However, Thai officers are sometimes unaware of unusual or obscure tax laws that are on the statute books. In those cases, they make understandable mistakes. Everyone makes mistakes the world over, particularly with little-known legislation.

The difference, in my opinion and from observation, is that officers in the West will quickly remedy any mistake they make and apologise for any inconvenience caused. The far eastern concept of loss of face makes it more difficult for a Thai to do so. A mistake made on my return in March has still not been corrected and, under their guidelines, they have 90 days to correct it! It is actually one entry on the tax return (one dividend voucher.)

Product knowledge is not always that great. Bank staff may not be aware of all the products and promotions of their bank. They go on training programs but the Thai tradition of not questioning a teacher or trainer means they do not ask questions if they are unsure of something they are being told. The same can apply in the shopping malls when you ask for product detail.

12 November

My nickname is Waterfall; so call me Water. Thais only use surnames for official documents. Even the last female Thai prime minister was called by her first name.

Your boss may be called *wanna* (boss) or *pee* (a word meaning elder,) followed by the first name, never the surname. Thai telephone directories are listed by first name.
To confuse even more, Thais have two first names, an official name and a nickname.
A nickname is selected at birth by the parents. A small baby may be called *Goong* (shrimp) or *Lek* (tiny).

Thais can be very superstitious. Nicknaming your child *Oun* (fat) or *Moo* (pig) is supposed to discourage and frighten ghosts and evil spirits, and dissuade them from any association with the newly born child.

The official name is registered some days later at the local district office, usually after a monk has been consulted over the choice of name. The parents simply give the monk the time and day of his birth and he will decide a name. His suggestion will invariably be accepted.

So, from now on, I will call *Khun* Sonjai by his nickname, Water.

13 November

Someone has been placing poisoned dog biscuits around the grounds of the local *wat*. A few stray dogs have died. The monks would have had nothing to do with it. They do not accept the taking of any life.

They will only eat fish that is given them on the alms rounds if they believe that the fish had not been caught solely for their own needs. They will not eat the meat of any animal slaughtered especially for them. Seems odd, because they would never know the origin of the food they were offered or be able to check how it was obtained. They never ask.

Sad about the dogs, but Thais do often take matters into their own hands rather than talk through any trouble they may have with the owners or those who care for the dogs. Maybe it will change but it has been going on for centuries. Perhaps Thais are resigned to accept the way problems are dealt with here.

Some time ago, I was discussing police and court procedures with the head of the local police station. He opened the drawer of his desk and pulled out a revolver. "This is how we sort problems out in Thailand."

Road rage incidents can result in a shooting and disputes are often resolved without going to the police.

14 November

Not to everyone's liking, but northern Thai food can become an acquired taste. Dishes are served with an extensive range of different spices and herbs. Variety is in; blandness is out.

You select the food you want and put a little on your own plate. Or, more typically, someone on your table will serve you, particularly if you are the elder.

Sticky rice is the staple food of choice in the north. You roll some up in a ball with your hand and then envelop it around whatever food you wish to eat. Your right hand is always used for eating, never the left. That is reserved for toiletry purposes in eastern countries. Older people will give money with the right hand not the left.

Sticky rice is called *kao niao* (*kao,* rice; *niao,* sticky). Not to be confused with *kee niao,* which is Thai slang for stingy or mean, literally sticky shit.

Where cutlery is used, the spoon scoops up the food, with the fork pushing it onto the spoon. Dishes are generally served in bite sized chunks, but if cutting is required the spoon is utilised. For Chinese style meals, such as noodles, chopsticks are used. Unlike in the West, meals are brought to your table when each item has been cooked. The rest of the order will not necessarily come at the same time. Even plated meals, which are less common, will be served when ready; the server will not wait until everyone's order is complete.

By tradition, water and ice is provided free of charge, either brought to your table and regularly topped up by the servers or available for self-serve. Certainly true in the rural areas and where only Thais congregate.

Unfortunately, that custom of Thai hospitality is dying out, particularly in the tourist spots. A corkage charge may be levied if you bring your own wine or drinks, though if the restaurant serves food and does not provide alcohol, it is not usually charged. They may even get on a motorbike and get the drinks for you from a nearby shop.

A good rule in choosing a restaurant is to select one which does not have a menu translated into English. And check that all the dishes going back to the kitchens are empty. These are two useful tips.

15 November

Khun Yai's house is almost finished. Perhaps just one more day's work when people have some free time to help. The family have moved in so the urgency to complete her home is now not so great.

She's clearly delighted and grateful for what the community has done. A TV has been donated and she has a stove to cook on. There are mattresses on the floor of both bedrooms and an adequate number of fans to keep cool. As in most Thai houses there is little other furniture. She does need a few chairs to sit on. She dropped what would, to a foreigner, be a less than subtle hint. It would be regarded by a Thai as a natural response not to ask directly but to nevertheless make clear what she wanted.

16 November

Had lunch in a pub in Chiangmai's Night Market today. The area is busy in the evenings but can be a pleasant change for a drink and a meal at lunchtimes. I don't frequent foreign bars and restaurants that often, preferring local venues and meeting the locals. Everyone to their own tastes. It's more up market than the girly bars where many expats congregate but still has the feel of an English pub.

Imported beers and spirits are around three times the prices of their Thai equivalents but are of better quality. Import taxes are high and higher margins can anyway be gained selling to an expat community. The sign above the entrance jokingly proclaims "No riff raff."

The Thai staff know how to pull a pint of Guinness and the meals are at the same standard you'd expect in a typical English village pub. A chance to interact with Westerners occasionally is not a bad thing. As on the internet forums though, the bar talk can veer towards a bit of Thai bashing after a while, particularly from the older patrons.

17 November

There's a full moon tonight and there will be crowds of young foreigners at the famous Full Moon Party on the beaches of the island of *Gaw Pangang (sometimes written as Kaw Pangang)* at the southern tip of Thailand. There's never fewer than 10,000 revelers at these events. Around 30,000 around New Year's Eve.

Beer and Thai whiskey are sold in buckets and it's not difficult to buy drugs. A few decades ago, the island was a notorious hippy compound for foreigners with its easy fun-loving lifestyle. Tents would be set up on the shoreline and everyone would sit around the camp fires. Although it's more commercialised these days and the atmosphere has changed somewhat, it stills pulls in the young foreign tourists as if it's a rite of passage for all backpackers on a visit to Thailand.

The beach bars compete to attract their customers with the loudest music from the biggest loudspeakers. Stages are set up for fire-dancing while the less adventurous gyrate their bodies further along the beach or skinny dip in the sea. No one minds the nakedness.

There are no lifeguards and a few tourists have drowned in the past. Rapes and muggings are sometimes reported. Last year there was a murder following a drunken brawl. Ferries take those suffering from being high on drugs or having collapsed through excessive drinking to a local hospital on the mainland.

As everywhere in Thailand, there is some corruption where "fines" are demanded by officials for supposed misdemeanours.

After the ferry leaves for the mainland the next day, the huge operation of cleaning up the broken glass, plastic bottles, condoms, and other discarded debris begins. All to prepare for next month's Full Moon party.

http://www.youtube.com/watch?v=9RsvoN1PV_w

18 November

Had a mailshot from one of the banks in the post this morning. Blazoned on the front cover is a picture of senior management and some of the staff smiling happily and holding up the awards and trophies they had just been given.

There were seven other photos inside, all of dignitaries posing to camera. More prominence being given to the people giving and receiving awards than the details of the new products they were advertising. Marketing is different in Thailand.

We learnt of something similar on 19 July when officials and staff from the local *amphur* paid *Khun* Yai a visit and set up a photo opportunity.

19 November

Contravening lèse majesté is a serious offence in Thailand. The name of the King and senior members of the Thai monarchy must be treated with respect and dignity at all times. No criticism of the King or the institution is allowed and the police will always follow up on any complaint they receive. Dropping a bank note on the floor and stamping on it to stop the wind blowing it away, refusing to stand for the national anthem, and publicly throwing away an out of date calendar with the King's picture on it, is judged disrespectful and may land you in a great deal of trouble.

Senior politicians have claimed cases where LM has been falsely cited for political purposes and to damage a party's reputation. The courts have not always found the accused guilty and have thrown up the trumped-up charge. That is no reflection on the police who would have had no choice but to carry out their duty, fully investigate the case, and bring it to court.

A Thai would not shake the hand of the King or a member of the royal family. In degree ceremonies for instance, the hand is stretched out, the wrist is flicked, but the royal's hand is not touched. You receive the award, step back a few paces, *wai*, and then move away.

http://www.nationmultimedia.com/national/the-king-extends-help-to-ubon-ratchathani-girl-30241453.html

20 November

Thais find tongue twisters such as "She sells sea-shells on the sea shore" difficult and the sounds "th", "r", and "l" are regularly occurring problems. Repeating "Yellow lorry, red lorry" several times at increasingly faster speeds is good training and Thais appreciate learning in this fun way.

The thirty three thieves thought they thrilled the throng throughout Thursday.

Here are two Thai tongue twisters. *Yak yai tai yak lek, yak lek tai yak yai*
The big giant chases the little giant, the little giant chases the big giant.

Krai kaai kai gai.
Who sells chicken eggs?

The vowel sound is longer in *kaai* than in *kai* though not always distinguishable to a foreign ear.)

Most Orientals, not only Thais, sound the letter "r" as an "l". The practice is particularly noticeable in northern Thailand. They also tend not to sound the final "s" in an English word. *There are many "car" on the road today.* James would be pronounced Jame. The reason for that is likely to be that there are no plurals in the Thai language. The word for both car and cars is *rot*. There is also a symbol called *garan* which is placed above a Thai letter which is un-sounded. For example; Monday in Thai is *wan jan*. In Thai script it would be written with an "r *garan*" as the last letter, the "r" not being pronounced.

21 November

One week to go before the *Loi Kratong* festival and we already have the regular sound of firecrackers going off throughout the day, but more particularly at night. The dogs do not like it, but it signals to me the start of Thailand's most colourful and enjoyable festival.

Kratongs can be as simple or as elaborate as you like, hand-made or purchased. Schools hold competitions for the most beautiful *kratong*. Flowers, candles, incense sticks: all are skillfully positioned onto a hand-sized raft made from banana leaves. You make a wish as you ease the *kratong* into the flowing water.

It is a fun time with lots of music, eating, and drinking. On rivers and canals, you float your *kratong* in the symbolic gesture of banishing your troubles and fears forever.

Tomorrow you begin afresh. It will be the first day of the rest of your life.

The governor of the province has appealed, in the paper today, for people not to release their hot air lanterns (*khom loi*) near the airport or along the flight paths. These lanterns are about half a metre in diameter and two metres high. Each bamboo frame is covered in gaily-painted rice paper. When a candle is lit inside the lantern, the air heats up and creates sufficient lift to send the *khom loi* up into the night sky. It is not unusual to see thirty or more gently progressing higher and higher into the heavens until they can be seen no more.

You make merit by releasing the *khom loi*. You are also casting out all your worries and problems, sending them away with your lantern.

We will know next week whether the governor's appeal for restraint in launching the hot air lanterns has been heeded. But I think the Thai love of *sanuk* will win the day.

Let us see.

22 November

Look kreung, children of mixed Thai-*farang* parentage, can face more problems than advantages in Thailand.

Thai mothers tend to spoil their children because they have a strong maternal instinct for caring and looking after their offspring which can result in not wanting to punish for any naughtiness. If a child cries, mother or another female relative will rush to him. A crying child soon learns how he can get his own way.

If the father is a 50 or 60 year old *farang*, the infant probably thinks his boat has come in; he knows he has a virtual licence to be mischievous. A younger western father may not be so gullible to believe that his offspring can do no wrong. He is not such a soft touch. An attentive mother and a doting grandfather type figure is not a good combination when it comes to bringing up a child.

Most *look kreung* will attend an "international" and not a state school. Fees are relatively high considering the cost of living in Thailand. Teaching is in both Thai and English. Some of these schools have high academic standards and have the benefit, which state schools do not have, of being able to select their pupils. The teachers can therefore concentrate on children whose parents are keen for them to learn and who are typically of higher than average intelligence.

In the West, disruptive pupils can be a problem for teachers and can hold other children back. That's not such a difficulty in Thailand as there is a strong culture of respect (*napteu*) towards teachers and the hierarchical nature of society does not allow children to answer back in class or be disruptive. It does not follow though that they are necessarily listening to teacher.

Samuel and *Boong's* daughter, Mary, is not untypical of 5 year old *look kreungs*. She has to be told to *wai* or say thank-you if guests arrive, she can misbehave at table and go into tantrums if she dislikes her meal. All quite excusable behaviour as far as Samuel is concerned. Even *Boong* thinks he is being too lenient and treating Mary as if he were the devoted but all-forgiving grand-father and not the responsible parent the child surely needs. But, father or not, he pays the bills.

When *look kreungs* leave school they are likely to go to a foreign university or college. They improve their English skills and a western education can open doors closed to Thais educated in their own country. Western standards are seen as somewhat higher. There is some snobbery attached to saying you've been educated in England or the States and Thai employers cannot fail to be impressed. Paper qualifications and your background can be influential in Thailand.

Whether in school or after leaving university *look kreungs* seem to socialise more with other *farangs* than Thais. Sometimes it's the whiter skin which sets them apart, more often it's an attitude problem resulting from how they've been brought up.

Gaaneegaa is a *look kreung* in her late forties. After a university education in England, she set up a travel agency with funding from her father, a retired and well-off entrepreneur. She has a keen business sense, ruthless even, and easily outstrips her rivals. Gaaneegaa goes the extra mile to make her *farang* customers satisfied in the itineraries and travel arrangements she organises for them.

Her fluent English gives her clients confidence in her company and they recommend her services. As a result, Gaaneegaa can charge a premium over her rivals' fees. Her business is successful and she makes good money. She works hard and plays hard. Now divorced, she spends her evenings living it up in fashionable nightspots. Good luck to her, of course. It's her money and she has worked exceptionally long hours for it.

But success and her hi-so lifestyle has come at a price. Gaaneegaa looks down on other people, her staff resent her overbearing manner, and those who were her friends regret the change that has made her into an objectionable snob. Sometimes being born with a silver spoon in one's mouth and having all the advantages that having a foreign father brings can result in an unfulfilling and unhappy life.

Sab always wanted a *farang* husband and her three year old was born in the Netherlands where they now permanently live. Leon is only four years older than Sab and the way Louise is being brought up suggests she will become a well-adjusted young girl. Her parents don't spoil her. Perhaps it's the western environment, perhaps it's the relatively small difference in her parents' ages. (English nicknames are typically given to *look kreung*. The child's formal name would be in Thai.)

23 November

Surachai is fed up with the lack of action from the local authority in repairing the many potholes in the *sois* around his home. The roads are well used so the inconvenience is not just a personal one. Traffic gets slowed down and care must constantly be taken when motorcyclists swerve out at the last minute to avoid a big hole in the road. Rightly or wrongly, the rider would not be blamed. The motorist would pick up the tab for any damage or injury. In this country the person assumed to have more money than the poor motorcyclist pays.

Directly and formally complaining wasn't going to work; face must be maintained. After a night of heavy rainfall, Surachai sat on a chair next to one of the larger puddles and held his fishing rod over it. He was only there for one hour during which time he caused a lot of laughter and merriment from those passing along the *soi*.

Later that day a team of workers started filling in the potholes.

24 November

How old are you? How much do you earn? Why are you so fat? How much did you pay for the land you bought?

We'd find such questions extremely rude and bad form in the West. They are personal and not anyone else's business. The Thai simply wants to know. Partly out of their natural curiosity on what others are doing, partly to find out more about you. It helps them decide where in the social framework you are in relation to them.

Thais do not have the same ideas on equality as we do. They are aware that someone is superior or inferior to them and can be jealous but they take the view "that's life, put up with it." Good deeds today will get you good karma and you'll be re-born in a better position in the next life. Although I don't find it easy to accept that thinking, I do understand it. In any event, it's their culture and they aren't complaining.

Apart from with a person you know well, we would not ask a woman what contraceptive she uses. I've overheard a Thai ask precisely that of a comparative stranger. A perfectly reasonable question to ask in their culture.

As a *farang*, do as the Thais do. There are three options: answer the question, lie about it, or make a joke of it. The Thai will accept that you're lying to avoid the question. And that will be the end of the matter. There'll be no embarrassment.

25 November

The issue of advertising restrictions on alcoholic beverages is still being debated on social media and the Thai forums.

It's understandable that businesses in the hospitality industry are not happy about the regulations designed to lower alcohol abuse and drink-driving deaths. In reality, the measures are not as "draconian" as they are making out. Some of the initial rules were a little over the top – no alcohol brand names on ashtrays – but common sense prevails in the end and minor transgressions are being overlooked.

To lighten what was becoming a flame war I posted a clip from the UK comedy sitcom "Yes Prime Minister" on Youtube. It showed Paul Hetherington as Prime Minister James Hacker attending an international function in one of the dry Arab countries. Hacker is dying for a drink other than the soft drinks his hosts are providing him with. His aides devise a hilarious plan to quench his thirst.

They pretend he has to take an urgent call from Downing Street:
Prime Minister, sorry to disturb but Johnny Walker is on the line. Can you apologise to your hosts and take the call in the anteroom?

And later, *another call I'm afraid, Sir. Gordon wants to talk to you urgently.*

https://www.youtube.com/watch?v=F_vPvLlcUqM&pbjreload=10

The comical scene went down well in England. Thais watching the clip here found it highly amusing. It was their brand of humour. They dislike and won't respond to sarcasm or sarcastic remarks; irony scores a hit with them every time.

Only one person was not amused: the person who had first started the forum thread by exaggerating how the regulations would destroy his business. That was not unexpected, I suppose, he did not want to lose face.

26 November

I saw something quite unusual today. For ten minutes or so I witnessed, as did all the Thais present, a child of maybe 10 or 11 being scolded by a man I presume was an older relative. His voice was not loud and he was not shouting. It was, though, a firm reprimand for what was considered his bad behaviour. Wanting another ice-cream is more often than not dealt with either by submitting or by simply refusing and walking on. Being given a very public lecture was not what I expected to hear.

Onlookers seemed a bit perplexed but showed no disapproval of a conflict being aired for everyone to observe. The relative's position in the family chain of command was presumably his justification, nonetheless I found his dressing-down out of place in a country where people strive not to show their emotions.

Even in the West, we would more likely deal with the problem when we got home. I did, however, once watch an American kid being told off for jumping the line on a boat trip in Walt Disney World. The Disney employee repeatedly explained throughout the whole journey that line-jumping was wrong and how the boy had not achieved anything by doing so. It looked to me that he was educating the child in the rules of politeness rather than being annoyed with him. He did not raise his voice or get angry. Part of the Disney mission is to teach and communicate in a non-conflicting style. The boy's parents did not object and made no complaint or comment.

27 November

It's a pity the Thai bashers who frequent the forums get a wide audience. Most expats and visitors here aren't so negative. The silent majority.

A very radical Australian site is getting a poor reputation for unbalanced reporting. No one has a problem with academics holding deeply-held views. It can be healthy provided that contrasting opinions are allowed. Unhappily, that is not true of New Mandala. They seize every opportunity to denigrate and belittle Thais and Thailand.

I can only speculate on the reasons. Is it a syndrome-like attitude where grumpy old men find fault wherever they look? Have they had bad experiences of being cheated or defrauded by Thais, perhaps on land deals where they were misled into believing property could be held in their name? Or is it basically the fact that they are unable to convince the Thai that western values may not always be appropriate in Thai culture.

They question a lack of free speech in Thailand while not allowing its readers to air views other than their own on their web pages. Occasionally they will allow a poster to give an opposing opinion but it is always followed by vitriolic remarks and flames and the poster is voted down within seconds.

They do not accept, for example, that Thais have a different definition of coups and democracy. They can't see another country's points of view.

Their extreme radicalism and biased comments are not helpful. In the same way that Islamic terrorist groups claim fundamentalist ideas when they don't represent the majority of Muslims, New Mandala gives the wrong impression of how most foreigners think. These forums are still worth a look though if only to get contrarian views.

28 November

The snake sunning itself beside the pond was not a cobra but it was about two metres long nevertheless. I was not going to go near it and tried to get the dogs to move away. Unless cornered, snakes will normally keep out of your way. Just be careful if walking in long grass that you don't accidentally disturb them.

Some snakes have keen eyesight; others don't. This is why you often see them moving their heads from side to side to get better focus. They sense movement more from any ground vibration when you try to walk away than anything else. The best advice is to stand still, hold your breath, and not make any sharp change of direction. Easier said than done. If you don't pose a threat to a snake, it may slide away. Make a mental note of its colour and other distinguishing features. If you are bitten or sprayed with venom, it would become critical information for the hospital in its choice of serum.

If their young are threatened, you could be in a dangerous and tight spot. Snakes have been known to chase a car that has driven over a snake's batch of eggs.

Having said that, you are more likely to encounter snakes in their professional capacity in lawyers' offices than anywhere else.

29 November

A great fuss is made when a dignitary dies in Thailand. I heard today that a provincial judge died on Friday and there is to be a big turn out this afternoon at the City Hall. The place will be packed with other judges, lawyers, and court officials. Representatives from big business, the local authority, the police, and the military will be there.

I see now why things don't get done that quickly in this country. Functions like these take priority over daily routine. The great and the good will be attended by some of their staff. The higher the status of the official; the greater the number of their staff present. The normal white uniforms will not be worn but everyone will be in sober colours, black or grey with white shirts and blouses. It is by invitation only.

At the cremation service later in the week, roads will be blocked off and the police will be controlling traffic. The area around the crematorium will be at a standstill for one or two hours. The family will be outnumbered by friends, colleagues, officials, as well as members of the public who knew him.

30 November

No major incidents following the *Loi Kratong* festival. No problems with aircraft landing and taking off. The hot air lanterns were still, however, being let off along the flight paths. The airlines said they were going to publish their revised flight times on the internet and advise any cancellations so that people could refrain from sending up the *khom loi* when flights were scheduled, but nothing appeared on their website.

There were some incidents where tourists and locals were taken to hospital suffering from burns and other accidents associated with the firework displays. Police confiscated the more highly powered rockets and firecrackers that were being aimed at the crowd by over-enthusiastic youngsters. In the main, people enjoyed themselves, lots of *sanuk*.

1 December

Some commentators hold the view that the typical Thai is lazy. Although at first glance that may appear to be so, watch men and women working an eight hour shift in the hot sun on a construction site.

Observe how the rice farmers, bent double in the fields, move along the rows of planted rice skillfully plucking the plants and laying them in their baskets. They appear to be working slowly but they are pacing themselves. Toiling at speed may look impressive yet careful and methodical harvesting of the crop gets the job done more quickly in the long run.

They sing and laugh while they work, stopping only occasionally for a drink of cold water when they are thirsty. If, when they break for lunch, you have a chat with them and get a little closer to understanding how they treat the concept of work, you may see that essentially they regard work as something that has to be enjoyable and *sanuk*. A sensible life-work balance is important to all Thais. They will leave a job if they are not happy. The wages they are paid are not the main consideration. Working contentedly in a group is.

Their outlook is linked more to *mai pen rai* than laziness. They deliberately choose a lay-back lifestyle that is not too serious, calculating what is essential and what is not, what has to be done and what can be left undone. And, as we saw when *Goong* was confronted by police for not wearing a safety helmet, Thais truly value the freedom to do as they want (12 September).

In the 1970s, Lord Robens, while Chairman of the UK's National Coal Board, asked a miner why he frequently only worked four days a week when the normal working week was five days. "Because I can't make ends meet if I work only three days." The miner was thinking, as a Thai would, of his work-life balance; Robens had the worldview and work ethic that it was good for the economy and the coal industry for workers to attend every working day.

2 December

To celebrate the tenth anniversary of their opening, the car showroom held a *tamboon* today. Nine monks arrived at 10 o'clock and sat on the ornate chairs that the staff of the showroom had brought from their temple. Water was provided next to each seat for their refreshment.

The blessings lasted about half an hour with all the staff sitting cross-legged on the floor facing the monks. Sometimes just listening, sometimes with their hands in the *wai* position. Gifts of food, soft drinks, and toilet requisites were handed to each of the nine monks in the yellow buckets that are commonly used as containers. You will spot these yellow buckets filled with gifts on sale at most stores, large and small, in Thailand.

Male employees can hand the gift directly to the monk and then *wai*. Female staff put the bucket on a cloth which the monk then pulls towards him. By donating a gift it is considered that the giver receives merit. The ceremony ends with each staff member having a white cord, the *sai sin,* tied around the wrist by a monk. The monks are taken back to the *wat* in a fleet of showroom cars.

Government departments hold *tamboons* in a similar manner when there is an occasion to celebrate such as a new extention being built to a building or receiving a national award. You'll see lots of photos being taken at these *tamboons*.

3 December

All my neighbours have dogs. *Fon* has five. Generally, Thais won't neuter their pets. A government initiative, in collaboration with European veterinary surgeons, has not been as successful as was hoped. UK vets get disillusioned with the slow spaying and castrating speed of local vets. They begin to get bored and lose interest in helping in a voluntary capacity in a cultural climate that does not believe in sterilisation.

Dogs are principally kept to guard property. Usually chained during the day or kept in cages, they are released at night to roam freely in the compound as a deterrent against the *kamoey*, the petty thieves that one finds in every community. There is no redress on the owner if a dog bites or injures a thief or indeed anyone else on your own property.

If you are attacked on the road it may be difficult to prove who the dogs' owners are and more difficult still to get any compensation for hospital costs. Dogs running in packs may well be feral and rabid. They scrounge for food from neighbours and the monks at the temples. Ordinary folk may shoo them away but the monks will feed them. You'll see many dogs at the *wats*. They are discouraged from going inside temple buildings though they are free to go anywhere else in the temple precincts. Theoretically, Buddhists will not kill or harm any animal. That also explains the reluctance to sterilise.

Although most Thais won't harm dogs, there is a minority that will kill the animal if it is misbehaving or no longer wanted. I recall hearing gun shots on one occasion and, looking down the *soi,* saw a man dragging away a dog by its hind legs. Where he took it I do not know and the next morning everyone denied a dog had been killed.

4 December

Asked Geng if he had any plant pots but it was not a line he carried. His main business is the manufacture of garden ornaments and fountains. I asked if he knew where I could obtain some and after a few minutes he said his sister sold them as a side-line to her small food shop. It took even longer for Geng to tell me where the shop was. It's another Thai enigma. On the one hand they can be extremely helpful; on the other they may appear reluctant to part with any information. I think it can only be that they don't want to take responsibility if what they're saying turns out to be wrong. Or maybe he did not want to appear to be too pushy in suggesting I visit his sister's shop.

Similarly, asking the time of the cremation at *Dta* Sompet's funeral met with some hesitancy. That was because giving me the time straight away might be taken as making it obligatory for me to attend. They did not want to inconvenience me, their concept of *greng jai*. They told me eventually. I had enquired of the time as I had wanted to go. In the West that would be seen as normal practice. Here, the response is consistently more long-winded. Even after decades of observing cultural differences, one can still be astonished by their thinking and actions.

I found the shop for plant pots eventually. Thais don't give precise directions, they rely on stopping and asking the way of passers-by or making a few telephone calls. I only had to ask once, which is better than my average. As bad luck would have it, his sister didn't have any pots for sale either. I noticed she had three which were being used in a window display but she wouldn't let me buy those. After a bit of chatting and joking, I got her to change her mind. Persistent though not heavy persuasion works sometimes. Thais want to be helpful and avoid clashes and you can play to that characteristic. Try a bit of small talk, *pootwan*, and see for yourself.

https://www.youtube.com/watch?v=3kW7h-5lLC4

5 December

Today is King Bhumibol's birthday. (His Late Majesty passed away in 2016 though it is still celebrated.)

In the West there would be singing, dancing, and drinking at some national events. Any excuse for a party. What is striking in Thailand and what sets it apart from many other countries is the passionate and patriotic fervour that goes with it.

You would party in America to celebrate Independence Day; the monarch's jubilees are fun events in the UK. But you would not hear "God Bless America" and "God Save the Queen" at private parties.

Thailand is different. Workers on the construction site opposite are still partying. The sounds of *Sawng Phra Ja Rern, Sawng Phra Ja Rern* (Long Live Our King) is ringing out constantly from every house in the village. And it's well past midnight.

6 December

Eight year old Adisak was throwing a ball for one of the dogs to retrieve. They both seemed to be having fun and loving the game. It was a change to see them having a good time. Thais don't usually feel interacting with their dogs is important. They're kept for guarding the house rather than as pets. They aren't part of the family as they would be in the West. Thais would find it hilarious, perhaps unbelievable, if they were told some English families send them greetings cards and gifts at Christmas. "From my dog to your dog." I was pleased that Adisak was doing something that was keeping him out of mischief.

I doubt there's an adolescent alive who does not have some naughtiness in him but Adisak can be a little horror at times. His parents can't control him and he takes advantage of their lax discipline. I was to learn later that there was a little more to the cause of his mischief-making.

My dog started barking around the well in the garden. Adisak had disappeared. I went over to see what the commotion was. Had my puppy found a snake? No, he was distressed because his ball had been thrown in the well. Fortunately he had not jumped in to retrieve it. The well is deep and he would have drowned if we could not have got him out.

I asked Adisak if he had thrown the ball in the well but he said he had not. His face was expressionless and he walked off. Leading questions don't always get the truth or an explanation from a Thai, child or adult. Later I called him over and said, "You threw the ball in the well. The dog could have drowned. That's not good". He took the point. So perhaps a direct talking to will improve his behaviour in future. Given his home circumstances, that might be wishful thinking.

Thai men and boys can be very obstinate and aware that cultural norms favour male supremacy. It's as if they are given "get out of jail free" cards because family values encourage the idea that the male of the species can do no wrong. Even in divorce cases the justice system seems unsympathetic to the woman.

7 December

Sengdeuan and Lee came round two evenings ago. It's the first time Lee has been in the house, although his wife or one of their workers often brings round some fruit or vegetables. About once a week, as I drive or walk past, I drop off any surplus home grown vegetables from my garden. Giving is reciprocal in Thailand and it is common to exchange goods of roughly the same value and with the same frequency. It's an unwritten procedure which works well. Not giving a small gift at some later date would be unheard of. No one takes advantage of a person's generosity.

With Fon we tend to give each other plants or vegetables about once a month. That's just the way the unspoken "arrangement" has panned out. For other neighbours and friends, it may be more or less frequently. Every week or every three or four months. It's how it works in Thailand.

As Lee was with Sengdeuan it was evident that they wanted to discuss something. They wanted access through my garden into the land that they had allowed Lit to grow his bananas on. It can only be reached along a narrow path beside the *klong* owned by the local authority. They would not have been able to get a tractor along it. Lee said they wanted to knock down my wall, clear a three metre wide driveway to their land, do the work they needed to do, drive the tractor back, and rebuild the wall. They would also make the boundary wall between my land and theirs higher.

I had no objection at all. I saw their predicament. There are many strips of land with no legal access or right of way in Thailand. It can push land prices down and one relies on the friendliness of a good neighbour to get to your own property. Life can be made difficult and you may be forced to sell if a neighbour gets awkward and denies access.

Lee and I shared a bottle of wine together. It was not so much entertaining at home, that would be unusual in Thailand. It was ordinary hospitality and an opportunity for a chat.

8 December

Whenever I have asked a Thai why motor-cyclists (and sometimes cars) come out of *sois* without looking, I am never given a plausible reason. Even some seasoned *farang* expats resort to the old chestnut, "It's not just Thais, it happens all over the world." Yes, it does occur elsewhere, but these expats intentionally miss the fact that it happens more in Thailand than in the West. Why some *farangs* regard themselves as unpaid apologists for Thailand is something else that is difficult to understand. (There are also foreigners, of course, who perpetually criticise anything and everything Thai or associated with Thailand. These Thai "bashers" cannot seem to construct a balanced view of life here, they cannot see the good <u>and</u> the bad.)

Are the bikers adopting *a mai pen rai* attitude? Do they really believe it does not matter that they are putting their lives and the lives of others in jeopardy?

Is it related to the doctrine of predestination, whatever will be will be? That one has no control over one's destiny.

Is it because they are pretty certain that police officers called to the scene when there is an accident will usually find the other party at fault? Most officers will have first learned driving skills on a motor bike and are therefore sympathetic to, and possibly biased towards, bikers.

If motor cyclists are uninsured, and most are not, it may appear more pragmatic, and support the biker better, by getting the motorist or his insurer to pay.

Why do motor-cyclists come out of side-roads without looking? Is it one of the four reasons given above, a combination of them, or something else?

9 December

The postman delivered a letter to me today and I noticed it neither had a stamp on it nor my address. Handwritten in Thai, the envelope simply declared that there was a note inside that may be of interest to me.

The note, written in Thai and English, was a flyer for a property the owners wanted to sell. It gave details of the house and contact information. Knowing the area where the property was located I was surprised at the price being quoted. It was about double what a Thai would pay. Thais prefer to build their houses to their own specification instead of only redecorating or renovating. The value of the purchase to them is in the land and determined by location and not by any features in the house itself. If the house is old and they think someone may have died in it they will give it a wide berth. Thais fear ghosts.

The owner will sell the house at around the asking price only if he finds a foreign buyer. Probably he originally bought it or had it built at an inflated price and wants to recoup his cost. House values depreciate in Thailand; it is land that accounts for rises at a higher rate than inflation.

I buttonholed my postie later and he told me he'd been given a few envelopes to deliver to all the *farangs* on his round. He had been slipped a few hundred baht for the service. He is a fascinating guy and I get to hear a great deal of what is going in the neighbourhood when I chat with him.

10 December

A freemason may ask you if you are a cautious man if he wants to find out if you belong to a masonic order. He will conclude whether you are or not from your reply.

It would not be relevant in Thailand since all Thais are cautious by nature. They take nothing for granted. They'll check progress on a house build by visiting the site regularly, maybe more than once a day. They'll undoubtedly check that the materials are not being swapped for those that are cheaper or of inferior quality. They will ensure footings have been dug to the specified depth and not backfilled with earth instead of concrete. When the house is being painted they will watch carefully to see how many coats of paint are being applied. Even quality control engineers in the larger projects, especially if migrant workers are employed, will mark with a cross surfaces that have had one coat of paint to ensure another coat is given once the first has dried.

Banks, other than your own branch, will take details and possibly photocopies of I.D. cards and passports before allowing withdrawals. We Westerners tend to trust until we have a reason not to; Thais distrust until they have a reason to trust.

Inside rooms are generally locked in Thai homes when the owner is not present as it is common for maids, even if they have been with you for a long time, to steal. Low wages can result in petty thefts and is a contributory factor for the incidence of corruption amongst low paid Thais.

UK police for example are paid ten times the salary of a police officer in this country. It takes away the incentive to ask for bribes. On independence from Britain, Singapore tackled the corruption that was prevalent under colonial rule by increasing government salaries.

Thais smile all the time but that is not a sign of trust. They are slow at forming friendships and wary of getting involved with others until they are won over by your honesty and character. A well-off market trader in Bangkok who used *tuk tuks* extensively within the city once advised me to look carefully at a *tuk tuk* driver before agreeing to ride with him. As a Thai, he was being vigilant and could no doubt size someone up quickly by his outward behaviour and bearing. Not so easy for a *farang* to do the same. We may know the signs to look for if we were dealing with a Westerner; we would be clueless in trying to assess a Thai.

A well-known travel blogger in Bangkok suggested using only drivers wearing Buddhist images around his neck or adorning his *tuk tuk* or cab. I think that's too simplistic and unlikely to be advice of any value. It's common for Thais of any character to wear amulets and charms, there is not necessarily any religious or moral significance.

11 December

He was ousted from prime ministerial power in 2006, but Taksin is still a favourite for the media's attention. He regularly pops up in the Thai press, often on the front page, even though he has no political authority and no longer lives in Thailand.

His younger sister, Yingluck, has been PM since August 2011, and though not of the same party as her brother, her government follows many of the principles that Taksin's *Thai Rak Thai* established in the period 2001 – 2006.

The newspapers draw parallels and there are suggestions that his influence from afar may be far more than just brotherly chats.

Money under the table and business sweeteners to get contracts have always been features of Thai society. Tell me where in the world that does not occur. In Thailand, it is more open and transparent. Indeed, Taksin himself said you would never rid the country of corruption. His own downfall was based on fraud allegations.

Accepting a little sleaze fits well with the Thai view of freedom, doing what one wants within reason. It smoothes the path in many commercial transactions, and is really part of the price of doing business. Larger scale corruption and operations run by organised criminal gangs are the areas that need to be addressed. But it is a way of life in under-developed countries.

12 December

Almost all *farangs* are older than their Thai partners: an age difference of more than 25 years would not be uncommon. So a month rarely passes without an expat dying and his widow (less often it would be the widower if she predeceased him) organising the funeral. At the pre-cremation rites each evening you will often see more Thais than expats. Westerners tend to attend only the actual cremation. The Thai custom is to give merit and pay respect by visiting the temple, or the home if the body is there, on each of the evenings leading up to the day of the cremation.

Several monks conduct the rites with the mourners sitting cross-legged facing them. Food and refreshment are provided. Quiet chatter is not discouraged. Thais don't show their emotions by crying. Indeed, death is seen as a step towards re-birth and is not therefore a sad occasion. There is sorrow that someone has passed away at the same time as there is happiness that the deceased, with accumulated good karma, will return in another life as a more prosperous and higher ranking person.

The prayers by the monks, to which the mourners respond, are in expectation that the person's good deeds in this life will lead to a better next life. By attending, the mourners are transferring merit to the person who has died to further strengthen his karma. (The chapter "The End of a Life" in *Thailand Take Two* narrates in detail the death and funeral rites of *Dta* Sompet, an eighty-three year old Thai man. It illustrates the role of the family and community in the week long rites, and explains how Thais view death.)

Peter was an artist who had lived with various male partners and was murdered following a dispute with a lover over the tidiness of the house. A confirmed Buddhist, he was cremated after three days of religious rites. Only two or three *farangs* came to the pre-cremation services, there were about forty Thais who came each night. At the cremation, the split was 50% Thai, 50% expat. A few *farangs* took the microphone and made a short oration. Although that is not the Thai custom, a former Thai lover, whom he had dropped some years ago, travelled some distance to organise the funeral ceremonies. He made a very moving speech. *Namjai*, even though he had been jilted.

Tony lived on a *moobaan* and was clubbed to death by a burglar. There was talk, however, of its being a revenge killing but nothing was ever proved. His closest neighbours were too upset to go to the funeral.

Stuart died of cancer some months ago after a long illness. The funeral was conducted as a Christian rite with the service being held only on the day of cremation, as is the western custom. Many Thais came as well as his expat friends. His son lived in Australia so was unable to pay his last respects. As we saw on 27 July, his wife, *Noi,* had upset his friends in the final days of his illness by refusing to let them visit him. Stuart used to telephone them when she was out of the house. It must have distressed him immensely.

Bernard lived alone and was an atheist. A friend organised the funeral and contacted the British Embassy regarding the various formalities. The cremation was held at a *wat* but there were no monks present and there was no service. Some former colleagues of his, all Thai, whom he had worked with many years ago at Chiangmai University were present. A few friends said a few words before the committal. One was an American actor friend who rather overplayed his oration. The Thais who were there frowned at his attempts to steal the limelight. I was shocked but I'd heard similar over the top comments at funerals in England.

His only son had come over from the U.K. and arranged for some beer and snacks to be provided for the mourners when it was all over. Bernard's Thai friends made their excuses but did not want to join the others. One of them told me that they were uneasy that the funeral had not been conducted according to Thai traditions. Sad really, both Thais and *farangs* could benefit from understanding each other's culture and way of doing things.

Jack was the only friend that knew that Owen had died. He had never met his other friends. It was only after the burial that he gained access to his mobile phone contacts and rang me. He had gone to the hospital to visit Owen and been told he had been discharged three days ago as there was nothing more they could do for him. When he went to visit him, his wife said he was resting. Something in Wanpen's voice told him she was lying. He brushed passed her only to see a coffin laying in the back room. Jack told me he was speechless. The monks at the *wat* told him that he was to be buried the next day. So obviously they had known. It was only after the burial that he decided to ask Wanpen for his mobile phone.

Farang funerals are unlike those of Thais, who see it more as a celebration of life and not as a time of sadness. It's a social occasion where all relatives and friends meet up. Nuanjan was a Christian. Although her funeral was held in a church and the rites were not Buddhist, the atmosphere was not gloomy. It was very Thai. One difference was that the coffin was taken to the cemetery and lowered into the ground before the mourners arrived.

13 December

A video has gone viral on Youtube. There was an incident at *Gaw Larn,* an island off Pattaya, where a tourist was harassed by a sun lounge attendant for using her own towel and not hiring one of his loungers. He kicked sand on her towel and then she lost her cool and retaliated. (*Gaw Larn* is sometimes written as *Kaw Larn.*) The episode occurred in 2012 but has only now been considered for prosecution. The vendor will not face charges but the guy who took the video might – for bringing the Thai tourist industry into disrepute.

Those working in the areas around Phuket and Pattaya are notorious for trying to get as much money out of foreign tourists as possible. The worst scam is perpetrated by the Jet Ski operators who claim money for non-existent damage caused by the hirer. The military are concerned by that type of activity and are trying to control it. At the moment with some success but it may not last. Historically the police appeared to side with the operators.

14 December

Thais use the expression VIP a lot. Class and hierarchy are important. Today I was parking my car at a function held at government premises and saw two roped off sections for cars, one marked VIP and the other VVIP. I think that's taking class distinction too far.

The closing off of roads by the police when the elite are motoring along in a convoy is sometimes so overdone that there are no or few traffic police available for other duties. Traffic offense enforcement is low in Thailand at the best of times. This makes it worse in my view.

Where staff are delayed by these road blocks they often turn round and go home rather than proceed to their place of work.

15 December

"Buy two, get one free." Shopping promotions are popular in this country. As elsewhere, you need to check if the deal represents value for money.

Consumer regulations are neither strong nor effective. Unlike in the UK where there are rules about discounting from previously offered prices, Thai shops can push up a price and then in the next instant price it at a discount.

While special offers are attractive, loyalty cards are not much used. Promotional gifts for regular customers who spend a specified amount in a store are rewarded with discount vouchers which are rarely cashed. You see them being thrown away. Point of sale promotions seem to work; "no catch" vouchers" do not.

One bank offers a 5% discount on fuel purchases if you spend 15000 baht per month on the card. Thais take up such offers infrequently, preferring to buy little and often and usually for cash.

Different cultures; different attitudes.

16 December

Lee was supervising his workers this morning. They were putting up posts where I assumed he was going to make his perimeter wall. He was giving them step by step instructions to make sure they were level and at the correct depth. You could not watch construction workers and repeatedly tell them what to do in the West. It's accepted practice in Thailand unless you're a *farang*.

I wondered why he hadn't broken down my wall and brought his dumper truck in that way as we had agreed. It must have been hard work for the labourers to carry the heavy posts all the way from the factory to the new piece of land.

In the afternoon they started putting up plastic netting and fastened it to the posts. They were not after all going to build a wall. Lee now had to admit the change of plan but was uneasy telling me. He kept saying, "no money, no money." Sengdeuan said it was because I did not like walls! I had never said any such thing. It doesn't bother me. It's his land and his money.

It is an eastern concept not to be direct.

17 December

Noi wants nothing to do with Stuart's old friends now that he is dead. She snubbed them at the cremation, hangs up on them on the phone if they ring, and keeps them waiting at the gate when they pop round to see if she is okay.

Her family have moved into the house now. Stuart left no will though he was legally married to Noi, so she is entitled to his assets under Thai law as he has no close relatives.

Noi went to the Australian consulate to get help claiming his overseas assets. The officials correctly told her to get a Thai lawyer to assist. They have cancelled his passport and informed the relevant authorities in Australia so that his personal pension is stopped.

I think Stuart's friends might have helped if *Noi* had not been so mercenary and unfriendly: if only out of respect for Stuart.

18 December

There is a regional divide in Thailand not unlike the division between the richer and poorer States in America and the North - South divide in England. Watford Gap being the presumed boundary between the well-heeled élite and hoi palloi.

Those in the Thai provinces think Bangkokians are snobbish and patronising. Those in the regions consider themselves superior to hill tribe people. There is mutual loathing and mistrust.

Many well-off Thais have a Chinese background. One or both of their grandparents being ethnic Chinese who came to Thailand many years ago and became Thai citizens. Their families intermarrying with Thai stock. Thais with such traces are prevalent in the high positions of government and big business. Chia Tai Chor and Chia Siew Whooy emigrated from China in 1921 and set up a seed stall in a Bangkok market. Growth was fast and ruthless. The business they founded, CP, is Thailand's largest company with assets now well in excess of $50 billion.

I spoke with a Thai family who ran a successful business exporting canned tropical fruits to England and America. They had started from nothing and the company had grown at a steady pace due to their long and hard work. I asked the owner and his wife whether they considered themselves Thai or Chinese. What was remarkable was the long pause before they eventually answered. They clearly had the Chinese work ethic and ambition. *Mai pen rai* was not an important word in their vocabulary. They both had the rounded face of the Chinese, celebrated Chinese festivals, and attended functions where many Thais of Chinese descent were present.

Although their eventual answer was that they were Thai, I consider Chinese - Thai a more accurate description. By the same token, Thais with strong family backgrounds from Laos and Myanmar exhibit characteristics that more closely resemble their original native land than Thailand.

19 December

Writing about Thailand is not always that easy. Thais dislike any condemnation of their country if it comes from *farangs*. I try to give balanced reports on events and explain both sides of an argument or issue. I don't take sides. I observe and comment but I do not criticise. In the West, constructive and truthful criticism is seen as a positive contribution to debate; in Thailand it is not that readily accepted.

The coup in May is a good example of having to be careful how one reports issues or events. Condemnation of the coup and the regime change was made illegal. I presented the facts in what I believed was an honest manner. Technically the coup was against the constitution in the sense that it removed an elected government; though it was argued that it could be justified as its aim was to prevent violence from opposing political factions and to establish a more stable environment for future democratic elections.

Unlike the foreign media, I reported what the military government were actually doing: their moves against corruption; their removal of some senior government officials, and changes in the positions of army and police personnel.

There had been no violence and many Thais said they appreciated the changes the military were bringing about. It is probably true to say that they would have preferred more democratic means to achieve those changes and for action to be taken by elected governments. Neither of the mainstream parties had ever delivered that.

Some writers have made comments, often wild rumours and unsubstantiated gossip, about the monarchy. I do not do so for two reasons: I narrate only facts, it is against the lèse majesté law. In the West, we may want to ignore our country's legal speed limit on the roads even when we believe it is safe to do so. But it's illegal. The issue of lèse majesté carries the same logic. I have no sympathy for writers and bloggers cowardly writing from outside Thailand who flout LM.

Look at sites such as New Mandala and read the spin they put on Thai issues but also check other independent sources in order to form an opinion which is more accurately balanced.

Thais like to please. They'll tell you what they think you want to hear. In her doctoral thesis *Coming of Age in Samoa,* Margaret Mead relied heavily on her researchers to support her claim that Samoan teenagers had very puritanical attitudes to sex compared with their western counterparts. Years later, her results were entirely discredited. Samoan teens are as active sexually as any other normal teenager. Mead had been told what they realised would support her thesis.

Knowing that you are writing a book on Thai cultural differences and assuming, wrongly, that you want to write something startling or controversial, many Thais will circumvent the truth during interviews and research. I get round that by not asking leading questions and explaining I want accurate facts. I emphasise that they can be as frank as they like.

20 December

We are each justly proud of our own country. The Thais are no exception. We cheer when our country's team gets gold in the Olympics; something may stir inside us when our national anthem is played. But we tend not to be as nationalistic as the Thai. Most of us can take some harmless banter or a joke against our nationality; we can argue openly on the way our railways are run or how our banks seem to be laws unto themselves.

The Thais don't like talking about such matters. They are much more laid-back. *Mai pen rai* are the watchwords they live by.

If a *farang* makes any comment about Thais or Thainess, don't expect the same response. They are offended at any suggestion of disapproval by foreigners of their country. It's fine to be patriotic provided that it's not a step towards jingoism and xenophobia.

21 December

You marry the family not the woman in Thailand. Whether you are male or female, your partner will see his or her first duty to ensure financial stability for the blood family. Although, as husband, you are not of that same blood, you inherit the duties of providing for the wife's family. More than western countries, Thailand has this concept that being related by blood is more significant than being related by marriage. It is one of the cultural differences that we Westerners don't find that easy to understand.

You will effectively top up whatever your partner pays her parents or family each month to the amount that is needed. If a new motorbike is required or there are repairs to the house to be carried out, you are expected, as the richer *farang*, to provide. Thais have a firm belief that sons and daughters must repay their parents for the sacrifices they made in bringing them up. And it is well established in Thai culture that other members of the family are helped too. It is unquestioned. This is not a criticism, it is an observation of actual practice.

It does not matter if the marriage is legally registered or not. The family and community will regard the couple as married after the ceremonial wedding because it has been given public recognition in front of the "husband" and "wife's" family friends, and colleagues. The registration at the *amphur*, if it takes place at all, is usually with only the man and woman present.

Don't expect loans to family to be repaid. The word was used to soften the request for your help in paying off a mortgage or loan debt. Thais resort to loan sharks and take out payday loans which carry high rates of interest. When they find they are getting deeper and deeper into debt and can't make the monthly payments the obvious solution is the *farang* husband.

Families will help out in the West when a brother becomes unemployed but only as a last resort. Western men tend to be more self-reliant anyway and don't look for hand-outs from family.

In Thailand the family culture is so entrenched that the brother realises the family will always step in and it will not be his sole responsibility to resolve the issue. There is no stigma in his accepting family money or help. As your wife's husband, legally married or not, you are seen as part of the family when it comes to helping him out. However, as you are perceived to be the rich Westerner you'd be expected to pay for any service he may give you. Reciprocal giving has it limits.

Although he is supposed to assist when other family members are in need, it does not always happen. Sometimes he will, sometimes he will not feel such an obligation. Sons get to expect that support will always be forthcoming and take more of a *mai pen rai* attitude to financial difficulties they get into than their sisters. Sons are spoilt by their parents in Thailand. Daughters are treated differently and in general are more responsible.

The family forms the cultural fabric of Thailand. Western values are not the same. Our children are encouraged to become independent of family and are not in such regular contact; theirs have close bonds to their family.

22 December

Justifiably, Thais show off to indicate their social status. A minority of expats unconsciously do it, in my view, because they want to establish their superiority. A sort of colonial attitude. They don't understand or try to understand the different cultural norms that apply in Thailand and don't realise that in many things the Thai thinks differently from us.

One guy who has been banned on more Thai forums than I've had hot dinners puts his foot in it so often it embarrasses his Thai wife. Attending a Thai funeral, he felt the need to brag that he helped pull the coffin on its elaborate bier and how tiring it had been. So many people take up the ropes that it is in fact quite light work. Nevertheless, it is not an occasion to sing your own praises.

On internet forums they will embellish facts until they effectively become nothing more than tall stories without much foundation. They regurgitate the ideas and comments of other posters without apparently thinking through the logic of what they are saying. The best example is misinterpreting how Thais see *coups d'état*.

Certainly, Thais may prefer not to have coups and forced regime changes. They understand the ideals of democracy and the right to elect through the ballot box. However, they don't automatically assume every coup is bad and every democracy is good. They see how they work in western countries. Expats accept as true and self-evident that all coups are illegal and don't benefit the country. Being more pragmatic, Thais look at what advantages and benefits have been brought about by regime change and size up any net benefits.

23 December

With their caring nature, Thais won't put their dogs down by going to a vet for an injection to end their lives peacefully. Saw today a family leave two dogs at the local temple. The monks will look after them.

The predicament is that it just adds to the already high number of stray dogs you see wandering around the *sois*. Some become feral and dangerous, so it is best to keep away from them.

There are indeed some dog rescue centres in Thailand but they get their dogs mainly by collecting injured animals. Thais will never go to a centre to select a pet to take home. *Farangs* occasionally use them if they want to give a dog a good home.

24 December

One of the most graceful dances in the world is the traditional Thai dance, the *Ramwong*. The steps are light, fluid, and performed slowly. The dancers, more often than not attractive young girls in colourful national costumes, hold their bodies straight from the neck to the hip and use hand and finger gestures, facial expressions, and body movements to act out a folk story or to express an emotion.

The dances can be classical, regional, or folk. The performers do not touch one another as is common in most dances. Masks may be worn if miming a story.

Training starts at an early age, children aged around 7 or 8 years learn the movements firstly in school and then in specialised dancing groups. Suppleness is required and, for example, teachers make their pupils bend their finger backwards so that the correct finger movements can be accomplished.

Farangs by no means look graceful or at ease performing the *Ramwong*. As Thais appreciate your joining in, it does not matter in the least.

http://www.youtube.com/watch?v=ZpfCJsMsBOE

If control and clicking your mouse button does not work, copy and paste to your browser window.

25 December

Today is a normal working day in the Land of Smiles. It is not a public holiday, though the admin staff of hospitals owned by Christian foundations have the day off. Holiday or not, Thais don't pass over an opportunity to party and have fun when foreigners are enjoying themselves. *Sanuk* (fun) is part of their makeup. Giving and receiving gifts is par for the course all through the year in Thailand. Christmas Day just gives it added significance.

From November onwards the staff in the big stores will dress up in Santa outfits and there'll be plenty of carol singing and fairy lights around their Christmas trees. The Central World shopping mall in Bangkok draws crowds of *farangs* and Thais alike, whether for shopping or soaking up the festive atmosphere.

Expats will decorate their homes. Merry Christmas banners and flashing lights can be seen outside many houses, including those of Thais.

Midnight services are held in all the Christian churches. Restaurants run by expats serve traditional Christmas lunches. It's good business for them as they charge relatively high prices while not having to pay premium rates for working a holiday as they would in the West.

26 December

The earliest Thai literature was written or sponsored by the kings of the thirteenth and fourteenth centuries. King Ramkhamhaeng wrote in 1262 of the glories of Thailand (Siam as it then was) and of the achievements of his beneficent reign. The works that followed were mainly on religious themes and often written in verse.

The most famous and readable is probably *The Romance of Khun Chang, Khun Phuen*, which has been extremely well translated into English and French. The illustrated book, 1000 pages long, tells the story of two lovers from vastly different backgrounds. With its many insights into old Thai culture and power politics it is an absorbing read. The Romeo and Juliet story is written in beautiful prose in both the Thai and English versions.

While you will find few books in Thai homes and some students are not well read, I would disagree with the English ambassador to Thailand's view of the Thais. "They have no literature, no painting and only a very odd kind of music; their sculpture, ceramics, and dancing are borrowed from others, and their architecture is monotonous and interior decoration hideous. "

Sir Antony Rumbold was ambassador from 1965 to 1967. His father, a close friend of the Russian spy Donald Maclean, was rumoured to have been the fifth man in the spy ring uncovered by MI5.

27 December

The K-Pop craze in Thailand can be compared to Bieber fever in the West. Young Thais fantasising over their K-Pop idols, stars, and celebrities from Korean popular culture. Bands like TVXQ, a boy band, can top the charts for weeks.

The imported fetish for black hosiery worn by Thai teens, fashionable in Korea, was blamed for an increase in dengue fever by older and conservative Thais who believed mosquitoes attracted by the dark colour were spreading the disease! As well as such clothing, youngsters copy the short cropped Korean hairstyle, *Ting Gaoee* in Thai, and like to whiten their skin to more resemble Korean girls.

Fans pay over 5,000 baht a ticket to listen to concerts by touring Korean groups. Fan clubs on Twitter attract over 35,000 followers. Korean soaps are avidly watched. Young, and indeed more mature Thais, learn Korean so that they can understand more fully the story line, which is usually more realistic than their Thai equivalents. The films are anyway subtitled in Thai.

28 December

Was visiting a friend who had an apartment at Wat Dhammakaya and had parked my car in the crowded car park. I had touched the wing mirror of a badly parked truck but when I checked there was no damage to either vehicle. Not a solitary mark.

Spent an hour or so chatting with Robert and then returned to the car park to find a group surrounding my car and claiming I had damaged the truck. The "damage" was on the furthest side of the vehicle. They had obviously seen me checking earlier to see if I had caused any damage to his vehicle and saw an opportunity to make a claim.

I pointed out that there was no damage to my vehicle and that his alleged damage was not in a place where my car could have even touched his. They were having none of that logic. I called my insurance company and the agent arrived in about twenty minutes. Responses are fast in Thailand. He saw my point of view but did not seem too keen to argue my case. I had pointed out to him that there was rust on the other guy's truck. Clearly it was old damage.

I saw him examine the rust closely. I also saw him discreetly put the 200 baht he was offered in his pocket.

I got in my car and drove off.

This kind of opportunism is not unique to Thailand of course.

29 December

The English language is rich in vocabulary. Thai has fewer words. You understand the precise meaning from the context. *Sawatdee kap*, for example, can mean hello or goodbye. When you meet someone it means hello; when you leave, it means goodbye.

I wanted an electrical plug at the warehouse and was shown a socket. I did not know the Thai for "plug" and for the life of me I could not explain what I wanted. Pushing three fingers into an imaginary hole to mimic a plug going into a socket was obviously amusing to the salesgirl but it didn't get me very far. In another aisle, I saw what I wanted and called her over. Seemed odd that plugs and sockets were not displayed in the same place.

"This is what I want. I'll take two. What are they called in Thai?"

"Plug." We call them both "plug."

There may be a specific word for socket but it is never used. Most Thais say plug. I also needed some half-inch flexible hose to join some rigid tubes. I knew I was going to have trouble describing that to a sales assistant. Gesturing with my hands again, I eventually got what I had visited the shop for.

"What are they called in Thai?"

"I don't know. I don't think there's a special word for it."

She came back with my change and said the owner had told her the word was *tek*.

An interesting afternoon. It reminded me a little of the Ronnie Barker *Four Candles* sketch where there was amusing confusion in the shop with the words four candles being mistaken for fork handles.

https://www.youtube.com/watch?v=pV1IP4N9ajg

30 December

Up to date statistics on crime rates in Thailand can be obtained from a number of sources on the internet. Although, since the military government came to power, the responsibility for reporting crime figures lies with the Royal Thai Police. It is prudent to check independent international sources as much as possible.

Poor law enforcement, weak gun control, corruption, and inadequate police detection all contribute to what is seen by outsiders as a tolerant attitude to crime.

Particularly in rural areas there are few if any police patrols at night and responses to a call for assistance may be slow or delayed till daylight hours. As in some western countries the emphasis can be more on collecting fines for minor traffic offences in order to improve revenue targets than in strong policing and implementation of regulations. Police sleaze may never go away but the military appear to be attempting to change the accepted culture of accepting cash bribes instead of prosecuting. Singapore's experience was that corruption and bribery were minimised when salary levels were improved and a zero tolerance policy for many offences adopted.

Easy pickings from foreign tourists who are perceived to be much wealthier than the locals, and the blind eyes turned towards prostitution and financial scams also encourage criminal activity. There are cases of tourists being drugged in the girly bars and robbed and murdered.

It is well known that at the Full Moon parties, where the only Thais present are the staff of the bars and restaurants, drugs are openly sold. Foreign embassies advise that there have been cases of rape at these events and that police surveillance is inadequate. The authorities are aware of the dangers but are not strong enough to control the vested interests that run the businesses in these tourist resorts.

The *mai pen rai* attitude of the Thai does not contribute to putting laws and regulations into practice. There is a cultural dislike of causing conflict. Best to let things be if at all possible; problems will go away.

31 December

Countdown celebrations are taking place all over Thailand tonight. Crowds have gathered at the Centre World mall in Bangkok to begin the festivities. Lots of music and booze while the large clock counts down the minutes and seconds to midnight. Everyone is in happy mood.

Earlier in the evening shoppers hunted for bargains in the stores. Sales and special discounted offers take place before the New Year in Thailand. Westerners abroad have to wait in line for the shops to open on the first day of January. Banks and stores will give out calendars or free gifts to loyal customers.

My local hardware shop gives me a T-shirt every New Year's Eve. It has the shop's telephone number on the back but it's great for wearing in the garden when weeding or planting.

Gaw (Kaw) Pangang traditionally hosts a full moon party on New Year's Eve. We had a glimpse of the young enjoying themselves on this island on the southern tip of Thailand on 17 November. Tonight it draws the largest crowds of the year. As you can see, the only Thais are those working in the bars and restaurants.

www.youtube.com/watch?v=o4H17SLp1io

26 March: 200,000 baht raised so far
27 March: A party in Sydney
28 March: It's private
29 March: Salute the uniform not the man
30 March: Youthful independence
31 March: Khun Yai's house

 1 April: Rules are there to be broken
 2 April: Don't shake hands
 3 April: Repeat after teacher
 4 April: Two at a time
 5 April: Dad's white lie
 6 April: Holiday dates in Thailand
 7 April: Catching Thai insects; Faa and Fon
 8 April: Faa gives me some fried *maleng*
 9 April: Having it both ways
10 April: A fatal bike accident
11 April: *Poot len, poot jing.* Be careful
12 April: The very rich, the very poor
13 April: The Songkran Water Festival
14 April: No need for central heating
15 April: The coach to Chiangrai
16 April: Pistols at dawn
17 April: Royal titles
18 April: State control of key industries
19 April: 100 days after the murder
20 April: Always carry an ID card
21 April: Sex changes and lady-boys
22 April: Black, you're in; red, you're out
23 April: He's left the country
24 April: Tipping in Thailand
25 April: It's not a smiling matter
26 April: Weelai as an agony aunt
27 April: I'm going to have to give you a ticket
28 April: Hard rice
29 April: Will they move the telephone box
30 April: Sitting next to Nelly

 1 May: Government officers work hard
 2 May: Eating with the servants
 3 May: Khun Lit is dead
 4 May: Family first, friends first; Goong
 5 May: Divorce in Thailand
 6 May: Earthquakes

19 June: Thai banks
20 June: Put it in an envelope
21 June: Not keeping appointments
22 June: Princess Diana's umbrella
23 June: Tong's appraisal interview
24 June: Outside dunnies, squat toilets
25 June: The Thai mafia
26 June: An expensive watch
27 June: General Prayuth's broadcasts
28 June: Weerot experiments with drugs
29 June: Lots of cars, lots of music
30 June: Sawat becomes a monk

 1 July: Thai monks and orange buckets
 2 July: Surachai won't buy his wife kitchen gadgets
 3 July: Red balloons
 4 July: Two nations; one friendship
 5 July: Carrying buckets of cement
 6 July: Back to good old Blighty
 7 July: Rained off
 8 July: Fifteen minutes late
 9 July: Two totally different foreigners
10 July: Nobody knows
11 July: All change, all change
12 July: 300 baht a day
13 July: The *wat* versus the village
14 July: Discussing the coup
15 July: Sorry, you'll have to sing the national song
16 July: The chain gang
17 July: Freedom
18 July: One hell of a racket this morning
19 July: Then the cavalry arrived
20 July: Lee and Thai jealousy
21 July: A red light on an elephant's tail
22 July: French expats
23 July: No telephone
24 July: People dying too often?
25 July: Education league tables
26 July: Cakes in the office
27 July: Leaving the scene of an accident
28 July: Keep fit
29 July: The handsome white uniforms
30 July: High speed train links
31 July: Her very short trousers, Siriporn

Matt Owens Rees

About the Author

Are you sometimes surprised when visiting a foreign country? Do you like discovering a side of the people's lives that tourists rarely see?

Matt Owens Rees has written extensively on Thais and Thailand.

Thailand Take Two describes the main characteristics and differences between Thais and Westerners. It covers aspects of Thai life such as the class structure, the laid-back lifestyle, and the attitude towards saving face or self-respect. While it deals with each of the ten main topics in chapter order, it gradually introduces readers to many ordinary Thais who tell their stories in their own words.

A Thailand Diary is a lighter read with more 365 diary entries. You can take a virtual look inside the everyday lives and experiences of the Thai people, and how they and foreigners interact in this amazing country. For perspective and to show that nothing is ever only black or white, comparisons are shown with western scenarios in order to illustrate some of the cultural differences. Expats in Thailand are compared to expats in other countries: surprisingly, you will see that those living here are unlike those who have made their homes in other parts of the world. A number of comparisons are made with France and South Korea in order to highlight the cultural differences from Thailand that are discussed.

A Thailand Diary and its sister volume *Thailand Take Two*, explain these cultural differences by "telling it as it really is." A no holds barred set of accounts of Thai life and customs often told through the words and actions of the ordinary Thais whom you will meet in the diary's pages.

I hope you enjoy flicking through the pages of *A Thailand Diary* at random and meeting your new Thai friends in its pages. Remember that it's a diary. As in all diaries, some days are more eventful than others. Sometimes an entry may shock you. Sometimes it may be flippant and short. Sometimes more serious and detailed. It may introduce you to a Thai character or it may be an observation on life in Thailand. It will always be a true account of what happened. Only names have been changed.

Escape to Thailand is an account, written my Matt, of an expat friend's experiences on moving to Thailand permanently. Many twists and turns during Derek's time here until his untimely death ten years later.

You may also enjoy *"The Death of a Thai Godfather."* Written as a novel, you may see parallels with actual current Thai events and similarities with some of the cultural and lifestyle concepts you have noted in my other volumes.

Matt Owens Rees was asked to write a short volume of 7000 words on Ajarn Ubolwan's doctoral thesis: *The Way of Meekness – Being Christian and Thai in the Thai Way*. Ubolwan is a distinguished Thai academic and her dissertation is worthy of a read in its own right. University submissions can be heavy reading but Ubolwan highlighted characteristics of the Thai people that are quite similar to those we see in *Thailand Take Two* and *A Thailand Diary*. It therefore made sense to draw attention to those similarities.

Through field research and discussions with Thais, either in normal conversation or in the lecture theatre, Matt Owens Rees presents a rich picture of the real Thailand: warts and all. Despite not being similar in style, his books reflect on some of the observations in "Mai Pen Rai Means Never Mind." In his opinion, the best book written on Thais and Thailand. Penned by Carol Hollinger in 1965, its insights are still very revealing and up to date. Sadly, Hollinger passed away at 45 years old before she could see her bestselling book in print. *Thailand Take Two* and *A Thailand Diary* are dedicated to her.

A typical Thai comment when referring to foreigners in this country is that they don't understand Thai traditions. These books will help explain the reasons behind the cultural differences and be a useful guide to enjoying new experiences and appreciating a lifestyle so different from that of the West.

Glossary of Thai Words

There is no single official transliteration system in Thailand for giving a Thai word, written in Thai script, its Romanised English spelling. You will meet several different forms.

Amatyathipatai (amart); an élite upper-class regime

Amphur; local government office

Angyee; a Thai criminal group

Ajarn; university lecturer

Arai na; what do you want?

Aroi dee; tasty, delicious

Avuso; sinecure, jobs for the boys

Bat prachachorn; Thai ID card

Bai see moong; 4 pm in the afternoon

Bhikkhuni; a female monk, though without full rights

Bhusa yong; the tape between the monks' table and the coffin

Bpratet tai; Thailand

Bunnag; a 19th century noble class of people

Chang; builder (also the word for elephant)

Chao lay; sea gypsy

Chook dee; good luck

Dtrong pai; straight on

Farang; white foreigner

Farangset; French

Farang kit mark mark; the farang thinks too much

Garuna; formal word for "please," in announcements

Geng; clever, skillful; also a popular nickname

Gnap sop; funeral ceremonies

Goong; shrimp

Greng jai; consideration for other people

Jai rawn; hot tempered

Jai yen; cool-hearted, calm

Kana rasadorn; a group of military officers

Kao niao; sticky rice

Kap, krap, ka; a polite particle at the end of sentences

Kawpkhun krap; thank you (male speaker)

Kawpkhun ka; thank you (female speaker)

Kawp krua gawn; peuan gawn; family first, friends first

Kee niao; mean, "sticky shit" (NOT kao niao, sticky rice)

Khaek; Muslim, (also the word for guest)

Khom loi; hot air balloon released during Loi Kratong

Khun; Mr., Mrs., Miss

Khunnang; system of kickbacks, bribes

Kin meuang; the state's percentage cut of a transaction

Kit mark mark; thinks too much, serious

Klong; a canal

Kon asia; an Asian person

Kon lao; person from Laos

Kon mee itthipon; mafia godfather

Kon negro; a Negro

Kon tangchat; foreigner

Kong seuh pa; wild tiger corps

Krapom; yes, agreed (only used by male speakers)

Kratong; hand-sized raft floated during Loi Kratong

Kroo; teacher

Lamyai; longan tree

Lanna; a northern Thai region (a million rice fields)

Lek; small, tiny

Liao kwa; turn right

Longkong; longkong tree

Lung; uncle

Mae ji; A Thai nun (but not a member of the Sangha)

Mae sue; a go-between in marriage negotiations

Mai ao krap; do not want, i.e. "no thank you"

Mai pen rai; a laid-back attitude, it doesn't matter

Mai mee panha; no problem

Maleng; an edible insect

Mamasan; brothel madam

Maw; doctor

Mia chao; rented wife

Mia glang tasee; slave wife

Mia luang; principal (legal) wife

Mia noi; minor wife

Moo; pig

Moobaan; housing estate

Mun; it (derogatory)

Nai luang; the respectful term for H.M.King Bhumibol

Nam; water

Nam jai; giving and sharing

Nam mon; holy water sprinkled by monk

Nawng; a younger person

Oun; fat

Pa; aunt

Pai nai krap; where are you going?

Paradorn; fraternity

Parsa racharap; royal language

Pee; an older person

Phak puak; social circle of friends

Phra hat; hand (royal language)

Phra phak; face (royal language)

Pitak Siam; a political faction in 2012

Ponsawadarn; history, story of the kings

Poo dee angkrit; polite and reserved person

Poo mee itthipon; mafia godfather

Poo peepaksa; respectful term for a judge

Poot mark mark; you talk too much

Pootwan; sweet talk

Prai; serfs, plebs; contrast with the amart or élite

Prungnee; tomorrow

Poonoi; person of low status

Pooyai; person of high status, a superior

Pooyaibaan; village headman

Rot dai mai krap? Can you give me a small discount?

Ruam took ruam sook; sharing the good and the bad times

Sai sin; white cord put round your wrist by a monk

Sakdina; early system of tax collection

Sala; temple meeting hall, also an open pavilion in a garden

Sam nuk bun kun; reciprocal giving

Samsara; the Buddhist cycle of cause and effect

Sangha; the Buddhist church

Sang katan; ceremony of merit in front of a monk

San phra bhumi; spirit house

Sanuk; fun

Satang; a low value Thai coin

Satang rawn; corrupt or hot money

Sat nam; water ceremony at a funeral

Sawatdee krap; sawatdee ka; the greeting for hello and goodbye!

Sawng phra ja rern; long live the king

Sawngtaew; two-bench open taxi

See moong chao; 10 am in the morning

See tum; 10 pm in the evening

Sin nam jai; a goodwill gift, a type of bribe

Sin sot; wedding dowry

Soi; lane, small road

Somrak; proper love

Sutras; holy scriptures

Tabian baan; house registration document

Talapatr; traditional fan held by a monk

Talay; sea

Tambon; district

Tamboon; merit

Tambonbaan; house warming

Tamboon roi wan; funeral rite 100 days after death

Tee see; 4 am in the morning

Tuk jai, mai tuk tong; all heart, not all correct

Tura mai chai; it's not my concern

Upakka; being calm in difficult situations

Wai; a Thai form of greeting, hands in a prayer-like position

Wan wai kroo; teachers' day

Wanna; boss

Wat; temple

Extracts from Other Works by Matt Owens Rees

Without spoiling the developing plot, here are some extracts from *The Death of a Thai Godfather.*

"It sounded like a shrill whistle. Something flew past Anilek's right ear. A moment later, another high-pitched sound. He felt something pierce his neck. The crowd screamed as two motor cyclists raced away on their powerful machines, throwing their guns away as they disappeared into the distance.

"This was a hit. Anilek collapsed. Was he dead?"

"When he took his wife away from labouring in the fields he was going contrary to the traditions of generations of his family. They had felt it a duty to toil for others. It was not their position in society to have wealth and privilege. Granddad believed that was not an unalterable status. He did not want to take away what the elite had but he did want the opportunity to create a business for himself that would give his family a good livelihood and some security for the future."

"(Tawin) feels strongly that people get the wrong impression of Thai "mafia" families. We are no different from other businesses that work hard and grow in order to secure a family's future. As I said, we are not all violent gangsters."

"He is right to dislike the murdering side of the Sicilian type mafias of old. They were vengeful bloodthirsty types who wanted more and more wealth, more and more power. Family honour for them could never be compromised. Insults meant public retribution by the most horrific methods possible. While their attention to business was paramount, the importance of maintaining family power, prestige, and face was uppermost in their minds. Our family, by contrast, makes its decisions solely on business criteria. Our decisions are based on what is best for the life that we have chosen to lead."

"We run our businesses in a fair way, Lek. We have to make tough decisions when people betray us but we are not corrupt in our activities. Greed is the big problem. And, irrespective of what many may say, it is not unique to Thailand and is nothing to do with mafias. Those we trade with do not have complaints about how we interact with them. Those we employ earn good wages and have job security. Our companies are operated with ethical and honest principles."

"That is entirely reasonable and a common sense way of working in my view, said Tawin. It is tragic that mafias have this reputation for rigid, secret, and destructive chains of command. The fact is that our system functions efficiently if done with honesty and respect.

"There is no business reason for taking revenge on innocent women and children. That is not the true mafia philosophy. That is not my philosophy.""

Escape to Thailand.

Names have been changed but *Escape to Thailand* is a true biographical account, written by Matt, of one of his expat friends. It shows his experiences, frustrations, and hopes on moving permanently to Thailand. It is written from Derek's perspective. Some expats may well relate similar experiences; others will have widely different observations on their life here.

Following a bitter divorce and a forced early retirement from his job in a bank, Derek struggles with making the final decision to leave England for good and settle for the rest of his life in Thailand. We begin to understand the turmoil going on in his head when he realises what he is leaving behind in the land of his birth. We see from his questioning that he is still unsure whether he is doing the right thing or not.

He explains how he felt about some of the cultural differences that awaited him and how he coped with them. He compares them with the very different experiences that some of his expat friends encountered. Culture shock is not the same for everyone. We see him getting to grips with his new life but is he really settled here? Are there going to be some unpleasant surprises in store for him? Who is wearing the trousers? He or the Thai lady he was meeting.

Was Derek seeing only the acceptable parts of Thai life? *Escape to Thailand* leaves the reader to consider and try to understand the way events were unfolding. The problems of Thai and western relationships, even if they seem to be surmountable in the short term, are brought out in this true account of his early days in Thailand.

With many glimpses into the lives of ordinary Thais, the biography becomes a "fly on the wall" experience for the reader. Seeing what the average tourist or visitor rarely sees.

Readers may think what they would have done in his place, how they would have coped with his doubts and frustrations. Whether they would have fallen for the charms of his new wife, Toy. Whether they were both madly in love or whether he had burnt his bridges and was making the best of his new life in Thailand. *Escape to Thailand* is by no means judgmental.

His life style is very different from what he had in England. He spends a great deal of time on the internet and at home alone. He likes making visits to schools to teach English and he certainly seems to enjoy doing so. The kids, I am sure, love him to bits.

Some extracts.

"An inner voice was telling me. "Get off this plane now." But it was too late. Thai Airways Flight TG 911 was preparing for take-off. Rather an unfortunate flight number given the events in America in 2001. The 747 jumbo let loose the power of its four engines with a roar. With the brakes released, all 340 or so passengers, including me, were forced back into their seats as we gathered speed down runway 2 at London's Heathrow Airport and started the ascent into the mid-morning sky."

"To be honest, it is a bit of a fight to get Toy to realise we can't eat out very night. I am not a "cheap Charlie" as she calls some *farangs*, but I don't have endless resources. We get to see Kanya a lot more than we used to. She's a bright and lively young lady and she's good company. But you can have too much of a good thing and as I have said, I don't have a limitless source of cash from my atm. We'll have to establish some ground rules on how often we meet as a threesome. I hope Toy will be my wife pretty soon and as much as I love Kwang and will do anything for her, I see Toy and myself as a couple who can be alone together most of the time. Thais are so family oriented that they can't seem to switch them off for even one minute. A clash of cultures, I suppose. We'd expect to see family regularly in the West, but not as often as the Thais do."

www.ingramcontent.com/pod-product-compliance
Lightning Source LLC
Chambersburg PA
CBHW050803260726
48660CB00004B/1223